PROPHET OF THE SANDLOTS

"...a vivid contribution to the literature of baseball...."
—*People*

"Winegardner...recounts his travels with a warmth for the old scout that is both touching and revealing." —*The New Yorker*

"A real jewel for baseball purists...a knowledgeable, loving, fascinating portrait." —*San Diego Tribune*

"Winegardner has produced a nonfiction novel, a book as warm and caring as Tony Lucadello himself."
—*Cleveland Plain Dealer*

"...a fascinating book..." —*Philadelphia Daily News*

"...a warmhearted, life-affirming story..." —*Houston Chronicle*

"...a fond monument to an intuitive solo practitioner of a trade that's fast becoming corporatized..." —*Wall Street Journal*

"Winegardner has penned a near-perfect portrait of a man whose lifelong dedication to baseball deserved no less a tribute...a grand slam." —Jim Brosnan,
author of *The Long Season*

BY THE SAME AUTHOR

Elvis Presley Boulevard:
From Sea to Shining Sea, Almost

PROPHET

of the

SANDLOTS

Journeys with a Major League Scout

Mark Winegardner

Introduction by Daniel Okrent

Prentice Hall Press

NEW YORK   LONDON   TORONTO   SYDNEY   TOKYO   SINGAPORE

◇S⟩ P E C T A T O R

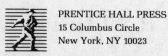 PRENTICE HALL PRESS
15 Columbus Circle
New York, NY 10023

Copyright © 1990 by Mark Winegardner

This edition reprinted by arrangement with The Atlantic Monthly Press

PRENTICE HALL PRESS and colophons are registered trademarks
of Simon & Schuster Inc.

Library of Congress Cataloging-in-Publication Data

Winegardner, Mark, 1961–
    Prophet of the sandlots : journeys with a major league scout /
Mark Winegardner.
        p.   cm.
    Reprint. Originally published: New York : Atlantic Monthly Press,
1990.
    ISBN 0-13-726373-2
    1. Lucadello, Tony, 1913–1989.   2. Baseball—United States—
Scouts—Biography.   I. Title.
GV865.L79W56   1991
796.357′092—dc20
[B]   90-23602
                                                              CIP

Designed by Laura Hough
Manufactured in the United States of America

10   9   8   7   6   5   4   3   2   1

First Prentice Hall Press Edition

For Robert Louis Reschar
and for Laura and Samuel,
with the love, memories and dreams
of ball games past, present and future.

Acknowledgments

Thanks to Clair Winebar, with whom I traded my first baseball cards; to Diane Cabe and Jon Ellestad, whose support and friendship allowed me to keep my day job and still get this book written; to Diana Finch, Gary Fisketjon and Anne Rumsey, who held my hand when it needed holding and who made this a better book; to Virginia Lucadello, the strongest woman I've ever met; and, especially, to Tony Lucadello, who trusted me, befriended me and taught me to see baseball with new eyes and to love it as much as I did when I was eleven years old.

Contents

CONTENTS

CONTENTS

Introduction

Anyone who has spent time writing about baseball knows that scouts are the most appealing figures in the game. They are, by and large, unknown to the point of anonymity, which makes them deliciously accessible to reporters burdened daily by having to interview overexposed, know-nothing, twenty-five-year-old zillionaire athletes; they travel in circles enlivened by endless talk behind countless backstops, endless talk at countless diners and bars; and they have a story—a beginning-middle-and-end story—for every prospect they've ever seen. A good scout's aptitude for ball talk is a more valuable tool than his radar gun or his stopwatch; he takes it with him to dinner, he takes it to bed, it arises with him every morning.

Consequently, the names and numbers of scouts line every baseball writer's Rolodex. Writers turn to scouts when they can't get a straight answer about a team's plans from the media-wary general manager; they hit up a network of scouts for every Sunday notes column, thereby finding trade rumors that are equal parts thrilling and unlikely; they turn to scouts when their own judgments fail them and they want to offer their readers an opinion of a particular ballplayer's skills. It's not true for every baseball beat man, but as often as not when you read that Slugger Smith can't hit the outside curve, it's a scout's matter-of-fact appraisal that informs the writer's assertion. Matter-of-fact? Try this one, a written report I once saw on Ed Kranepool when he was playing out the string with the Mets: "No range, no glove, dead body, can't hit anyone. If this guy had any class at all, he would have retired three years ago."

Best of all, scouts speak their own language—or, rather, their own school of languages, each scout having a way of phrasing as distinctive as the oddball clothes so many seem to wear. This diction ranges from the breathtakingly concise to the overwhelmingly baroque. In the first category, I once met a legendary scout whose vocabulary apparently consisted of only two phrases: "Prospect," and "No prospect." He was as terse, and as predictable, as a little boy looking at his friend's baseball cards and pronouncing, "Got 'im, got 'im, don't got 'im, got 'im, don't got 'im." Ask this man about the weather, and he would likely squint out the window and say, "No prospect." He was usually right, too, about the talent as well as the climate.

Most scouts, though, talk the way rivers run, constant ripples of words adding up into mighty torrents. The older the scout, the richer the language—the result not only of the decades spent in ballparks engaged in ball talk but also of reaching maturity before the age of television and its homogenizing effects on our collective speech. Southern scouts of this era are rich in impossible simile, westerners in laconic irony, ethnic midwesterners in the arrestingly peculiar diction of a first-generation English speaker.

Inevitably, though, writers turn to scouts not just for their knowledge and their language but for their nature: No one loves baseball more, and no one knows baseball better. In the grotesquely inappropriate words of Cincinnati Reds owner Marge Schott, "They just sit around and watch baseball games all day." Schott's words were inappropriate because she meant to be dismissive, but you could suffuse the same words with praise: Only a scout loves baseball sufficiently to watch hundreds upon hundreds of games a year, sometimes three or four in a day. These are men who labor long hours for meager dollars because of their ardent passion for the game, who burn, bleed, and persist in their tiring work simply to *share*: "I found this kid," the scout writes to his front office, sitting on the edge of his bed in a tiny, threadbare motel room in East Nowhere, "tall and strong, runs like the wind, a plus arm, good parents, good student, takes coaching." And then he turns the kid's fate over to someone else, gets in his car, and goes looking for the next one.

No surprise, then, that scouts have, more and more, become the subjects for writers who work in longer forms than the daily newspaper story. I don't think the great Roger Angell ever wrote a more memorable piece than his profile of the Milwaukee scout Ray Scarborough. And I think very few people have ever written a baseball book that approaches the revelation of the game's essences as great as the one in your hands.

I remember when the book was first announced by its hardcover publisher. I had never heard of its author, a young man named Mark Winegardner. The idea—a year on the road with a scout, moving from high school field to sandlot to college stadium, looking for professional prospects—seemed an obvious, even tired one. And I'll admit to the suspicion I felt when I learned the subject of the book was Tony Lucadello. Lucadello, a much beloved figure, a full-time scout for nearly fifty years, had killed himself on a high school diamond not long before, and it seemed almost too neat, too tidy, that a writer had happened to be following him in the last year of his life. It was a book I would get to later, when I had some time, but that I'd nonetheless get to with a little bit of wariness.

How unfair I was! Winegardner's heart was in the right place, his prose was as simple (and nearly as compelling) as the modest little man whose life he had chosen to chronicle and the fact that I knew the end of the story—Lucadello's death—

somehow made the experience of reading the book all that much more moving. "What can you say about a girl who died?," Erich Segal wrote in the first line of his hugely successful schlocky weeper, *Love Story*, nearly twenty years ago: ending in hand from the outset, you could hardly *not* read what followed. And what you read, you read with a foreknowledge that made every line sharper, every accretion of fact more telling.

Imagine, how, the technique at work in a real book, by a real writer, about a subject of inherent interest and emotional heft. (Actually, it isn't Winegardner's technique at all—I've imposed it on him. He's too careful, and too honest, to reveal his ending on page one. I, on the other hand, leap over the boundary of care, assuring you as I jump that the book is enhanced by knowing where it will lead.) If I were sitting near you as you read this introduction, I wouldn't let you get up until you had begun the book itself, knowing that once you've begun it you cannot fail to complete it.

But as I'm *not* sitting next to you, the best that I can do is shut up and get out of the way. In Tony Lucadello (who, incidentally, carried neither radar gun nor stopwatch), you have the perfect model for all that is noble, appealing, and unforgettable about baseball scouts; in Mark Winegardner, open and ingenuous, you've got an ideal writer. His only apparent uncertainty comes from not knowing which he loves more, baseball or Tony. As you'll see, there's really no difference between the two.

—Daniel OKrent

"A prophet is not without honor,
save in his own country."
—MATTHEW 13:57

1

Home Field Advantage

A good fifty years ago, the St. Louis Cardinals had a Class D minor league baseball team in Fostoria, Ohio, and the short-stop on that team was a five-foot-five kid from the South Side of Chicago named Tony Lucadello. Tony's parents, first-generation Italian immigrants, had moved from Texas, where Tony was born, to Chicago so Tony's dad could work in the northern Illinois coal mines. As a teenager, during Prohibition, Tony got his first job—delivering sealed cases of what he was told was olive oil. His next job was baseball.

Baseball had an intricate minor league system in those days: AAA, AA, A, B, C and D. Big, rich organizations like the Cardinals and the Brooklyn Dodgers had as many as thirty teams. Back before television or peewee soccer or even Little League, kids all over America threw baseballs against garages and barns and stoops from dawn until a pickup game started in a nearby vacant lot or someone bodily restrained them from making any more dents in the siding. Back then, baseball talent was plentiful enough to stock professional teams in every town large enough to appear on the Rand-McNally map. And in 1934, thirteen years before Jackie Robinson broke the color barrier, every big city still fielded two teams of major league ball players, one black and one white.

Tony Lucadello was a dirty-uniformed, clean-living little guy who never drank or smoked or swore, who always knew how many outs there were, who never threw to the wrong base, who always was the first to the ballpark and the last to leave, who never made a one-handed catch unless he absolutely had to. Not a lot of talent, really, and a build more like a jockey's than a ball player's. Still, with his attitude and the fundamentals, who knows? Branch Rickey, architect of those dominant St. Louis Cardinals teams of the 1930s, who himself didn't drink or swear or even attend the ballpark on Sundays, would surely have liked to see Tony join his hard-drinking, foul-mouthed big league club.

But this was Class D ball, the lowest rung of the minors, twenty-seven shortstops away from Leo Durocher, the 1930s St. Louis Cardinals starter who would go on to manage the Dodgers, Giants, and Cubs—and coin the phrase "Nice guys finish last." After two so-so years, Tony Lucadello's big-league dreams fell victim to a shoulder injury. Tony figured his last hurrah in baseball was getting the St. Louis Browns to sign his more talented younger brother, for which Tony received a two-hundred-dollar commission. Johnny Lucadello inched his way up through the Browns organization, and eventually played six seasons in the majors, even with four seasons lost to World War II. Tony, meanwhile, settled into Depression-era Fostoria, Ohio, happy to find a job with the Fostoria Screw Company.

A half century later, Tony still lives in Fostoria, in a little white house with an aluminum carport, two blocks from the reservoir. He married a hometown girl, and one daughter, Toni, teaches at a Fostoria elementary school. Fostoria hovers at its 1930s population of about fifteen thousand, and people continue to drive an hour to Toledo for Christmas shopping.

The constant for Tony has been baseball. He has never relinquished what he knew then, and he's learned volumes more, driving leased cars 2.3 million miles down the back roads of nine states and three Canadian provinces, roads which led him to hundreds of thousands of ball players, including a thirteen-year-old boy named Matt Stone, another shortstop, who, on a tart October Sunday, was in his Wayne, Ohio, backyard, firing baseball after baseball at a specially built white cinder-block wall as tall as himself and as wide as a small shed.

The balls came back, taking erratic hops off the tufty grass, but Matt eased each one into his glove, a tiny, anachronistic fielder's mitt that wouldn't have looked odd on one of the 1934 Fostoria Redbirds. He fielded, planted, and threw in one fluid motion, then positioned himself in front of the next ball. The throws became harder and harder, making dull thwacks that echoed from the other small ranch-styles in the neighborhood. None of the neighbors peeked out from behind their curtains, and none came over to tell the boy to stop throwing. By now they must be used to the noise, since Matt Stone had, over the past three years, thrown more than 150,000 balls off that wall.

Tony, off to the side, near the tire swing, studied Matt's throws. "That's it, boy," he said. "Soft hands." He nodded. Matt Stone is an amazing ball player. If I squinted enough to blur the image of a shy and unformed adolescent, I'd have taken him for a star college infielder.

"Now make sure you're squeezing the ball in the mitt," Tony said, "and throwing across the seams." Tony wore a narrow-brimmed wool houndstooth hat, part of what—in 1987—is a pretty huge collection of men's dress hats. As always, he sported a jacket and tie, either decades old or purchased from a rural menswear store that's no slave to Manhattan fashion. Yet the tie's busy, mottled stripes and the jacket's indeterminate fabric lent Tony a particularly midwestern humility that made him seem like Everygrandpa—especially if your grandpa, like both of mine, was a salesman. Though Tony is probably the most successful major league baseball scout who ever lived, to look at Tony Lucadello is to wonder if maybe he left his sample case in the trunk of the car.

A ball glanced off Matt's little mitt. "That's okay, son," Tony said. "It took a bad hop. The important thing is, you were positioned correctly. Remember that."

Matt nodded, a little winded, but he kept throwing, another fifty balls, and he fielded them all with clean effortlessness. The wall—in the heart of Detroit Tigers country—bears the emblem of the Philadelphia Phillies, Tony's employers. Maroon letters above the emblem proclaim the Tony Lucadello Wall. The Stones named the wall—which without the lettering might be mistaken for an unfinished barbecue pit—after the man who suggested four years ago that Matt's father build it.

"Now do some hitting," Tony said. "Start out easy."

Matt's father handed Tony a Hefty bag filled with plastic golf balls. The seventy-five-year-old scout knelt across from the boy on an imaginary home plate, tossing the plastic balls into every corner of the strike zone. "Good," he said. "Don't overswing, now."

As he has done almost two hundred thousand times before, Matt cocked his bat and swung, cocked his bat and swung. His swing was, if possible, more fluid than his fielding. He connected on every one of the three dozen balls Tony offered up, stroking line drives to all fields, hitting them ever longer. The balls are designed so weekend golfers can practice swinging in the backyard without driving balls into the neighbors' rosebushes, but Matt began to slash balls over the garage and into the street.

When the bag was empty, Matt, his mother and father, his two sisters, Tony and I picked the balls off the lawn. "It's got to be a weird feeling to be just thirteen," I said to Matt, "and

4

have the guy who signed Mike Schmidt and Fergie Jenkins interested in you."

"Yeah, I guess," Matt said. He shrugged, uncomfortable with this peculiar writer guy all the way from Washington, D.C., coming to his house and asking him stuff. But he turned and smiled. "It's great," he concluded. "I probably would have given up if it wasn't for Tony."

Four years before, Matt got cut from Little League. He came home in tears, but his dad didn't know enough about baseball to know what to suggest. Even if he had, Gene Stone worked second shift, and he couldn't play catch with his son after school. For weeks, Matt cried himself to sleep.

Gene's nephew Todd Adkins had been a good ball player, good enough that he'd been signed to a professional contract by this little old man from Fostoria named Tony Lucadello. At a Saturday American Legion Tournament, Gene told the scout about Matt's problem and asked if he could be helped.

"Build a wall in your backyard," Tony said. "Five feet high, four feet wide, angled at the base, and then give him one baseball and have him throw it up against that wall. Body control is the key to it all—learning to position your feet—but the wall teaches that."

Tony went on to explain the plastic golf ball drill too.

Gene Stone thanked him.

"You won't build the wall, Gene," Tony told him. He'd told other fathers the same thing, received the same interested nod, yet no father had ever built a wall. "Maybe you'll put up a basketball hoop. Maybe Matt will develop basketball talent."

Gene Stone built the wall, despite the quizzical stares of the neighbors, which are what you get when you build a detached cement wall in a small-town-Ohio backyard.

Two weeks later, Matt noticed he was improving. Next summer he was the starting shortstop on his Little League all-star team. A year later, Tony took him along for show-and-tell at a University of Michigan baseball camp, and Wolverine coach Bud Middaugh said Matt's fundamentals were better than any of the Michigan varsity's. Today Matt is, in Tony's words, "the best prospect in my territory. No question. All he needs to do is grow."

Tony thinks Matt Stone is living proof of what can be done—what *must* be done—to ensure baseball's future.

"That's why I agreed to do this book," Tony said, as we drove back to Fostoria, past cornfields in midharvest. "I had doubts, to be honest with you. Why would anyone want to read about me? I'm not famous. I don't want the attention. I'm just a old man who loves the game of baseball. I've given my life to it. And you—maybe you can help me spread the word. Maybe you can help me save the game of baseball."

Matt Stone was the first prospect Tony Lucadello showed me. Most full-time pro scouts see only college players. Many see kids from city high schools, but usually only on the recommendation of one of the part-time scouts, or bird dogs, who work for them. Matt Stone was an eighth-grader.

The next prospect lived right in Fostoria. Jason Myers, a blond fifteen-year-old, about six feet tall, had a kid's face and a cracking voice. And he had a wall in his backyard—white, with a Phillies logo painted just above the strike zone, like Matt's.

Tony watched Jason throw about fifty balls off the wall. Tony has a scout pose: hands thrust deep into overcoat pockets, hat brim tilting forward, head nodding, face impassive. That blank poker face is a master scout's stock-in-trade, developed over the years to prevent lesser scouts from learning what ball players Tony likes and then going after them. Tony has had so many prospects stolen out from under him that he has not only perfected the poker face but also scouted in secret, concealed in his car or behind telephone poles or on rooftops or even—at the age of sixty-eight—from the top of a loblolly pine.

"How'm I doing?" Jason said, looking for validation in the scout's blank face.

"Fine, that's fine," Tony said. "Increase your speed gradually. Don't try to impress me or this young man [meaning me]. You don't want to get hurt, do you?"

Jason is older, bigger, and stronger than Matt Stone, but half as polished. The wall had been up only two months. But where Matt Stone was wiry, automatic and self-deprecating, Jason Myers is balletic, deliberate and intense. He thinks every motion through, from placing his long, thin fingers across the seams, to bringing his arm over the top, to positioning his feet for the ground balls. Jason seethes for success. At school, he tells his friends that one day he'll pitch in the majors. He guarantees it. They sneer, as good adolescents are wont to do. And then Jason comes home to his wall and throws. When friends come over, Jason tries to get them to throw with him. They do, but they wonder why that's all he ever wants to do, and some of them get sick of it and don't come over as often as they might. He's left with his mom to toss the plastic golf balls, and she doesn't put them near the plate consistently enough for Jason, who has the longest, fastest swing you're likely to see in a kid who can't yet drive a car.

Tony knelt to toss the balls to Jason, scattering them to every corner of the strike zone as Jason lashed line drives. Barbara Myers looked on with me, smiling, not yet taking for granted the presence of a major league scout in her yard. Barbara Myers seemed like the kind of midwestern mom who will drive her kids to predawn practices, who will send away for sports equipment not available in small-town hardware stores, who will watch every practice without ever yelling at a coach. My sister and I swam in high school; yet Bryan, Ohio, had no indoor swimming pool. My mother, who resembles Barbara Myers enough to be her sister, never complained about taking off from work to drive us to practices in Toledo, an hour away, or about spending her weekends in muggy Dayton natatoriums. When Tony suggested the wall to Barbara Myers, the wall went up the very next week, no questions asked.

In August, I saw a newspaper article about Tony. On a whim, really, I decided to write a book about him. I just called up and asked him if it was okay. He didn't say no, but he didn't say yes. He talked to me for about an hour, telling stories about baseball, finishing most of them with "Now, would that be of value to you? Would that be the kind of thing you'd want to put in a book?" He agreed to let me tag along on a scouting trip in October, but he still wasn't sure he wanted to go through with the book. I think he had the idea that I was going to take up a lot of his time, conducting endless interviews and involving him in every torturous draft. A reporter from a Findlay, Ohio, newspaper had already tried to write a book about Tony, which every publisher in America had rejected. I think Tony had taken that hard, as if these strangers in New York City were rejecting his life itself.

He tried to say no, but when he found out I'd grown up so close to him and that my parents still live near there, he decided to help a young man from northwestern Ohio along with his little career.

But when I reached Fostoria, even that first trip was in jeopardy. Tony's wife, Virginia, had fallen down the basement stairs that morning, and although nothing seemed to be broken, the doctor had ordered her to stay in bed until he could study the X rays thoroughly. Tony wasn't sure he'd be able to leave her alone for a week, and I was certain this trip was doomed.

"Why don't we go down in the basement?" Tony said. "We can talk down there. Your visit won't have to be a total waste that way. We'll have to see what happens."

Tony opened the refrigerator and offered me anything I saw, then led me downstairs. "Now you watch your step. This is where she fell, right here. And you watch your head, too. I can't have company coming here and banging their head. A tall man like you couldn't live in a house like this. This is a short man's house."

I dodged a series of vents, pipes, and door frames, winding through a laundry room and an unfinished storage nook and into Tony's office: an eight-by-ten room big enough for a daybed, a small desk, a table, a filing cabinet, and two chairs. Photographs and papers and bats and plaques and trophies covered the room's every inch. One plaque, from Phillies executives Ruly Carpenter, Paul Owens and Dallas Green, proclaims Tony "by far the finest baseball scout in the game," echoing the many baseball insiders lobbying to allow scouts—and Tony in particular—to be voted into the Baseball Hall of Fame. The office is Tony's personal hall of fame, yet not dusty or pretentious enough to be called that. Tony Lucadello's basement room, lined with aging, autographed glossies, felt more like the back office in a revered delicatessen, a place where bank deposits are calculated, where business is conducted.

On the gray-paneled walls hung framed photos of most of the forty-nine major leaguers Tony signed. No one knows what the record is, but forty-nine is a safe bet. In 1980 the Philadelphia Phillies tabulated the numbers for all their scouts, and Tony had more than everyone else combined. An amazed publicity department called around to other teams and found that even the best veteran scouts had about half that many.

Because scouts aren't famous and because no one keeps records on scouts, baseball writers seem loath to admit scouts to the Hall of Fame. But forty-nine major leaguers are hard to refute; in a profession rich with yarn spinners and braggarts, no man has ever claimed more. "Pick any one of those players," Tony said, "and I'll tell you a story. There's a story that goes with every player I ever signed."

"Okay," I said, taking out a notepad. "Give me a sec to absorb all this."

"Take your time. Look around. Ask me anything."

About half the photos had snapshots tucked into the corners of the frames, and Tony told me they were mostly of wives and children. "When I sign a ballplayer, I've had him in my files for years. I get to know the young man's family, especially the mothers. The mothers want to know what kind of life their sons are going to have. After I sign a player, I try to keep in touch. I don't want to bother anyone, of course. Many of these people like to keep to themselves, and I have to respect that. But I'll hear from them time and again. They write me. They like me, you see, because I took the time to get to know their whole family. That's one of the ways I'm different. I'm different from other scouts. Not to put anyone down: they're fine, fine men. They're my friends. They have their ways of doing things, and I have mine, that's all. I'm *different*. If you want to write a book about scouting, I think you should talk to them, too. I'll introduce you. They'll all tell you: I'm *different*."

Tony's most famous signee is Mike Schmidt, the best third baseman of all time. He thinks two others have a chance at the Hall of Fame: Cubs and Rangers pitcher Ferguson Jenkins, who won 284 games and is a sure thing, and Expos and Dodgers reliever Mike Marshall, who won the Cy Young Award in 1974 but whose enshrinement is less likely. Tony won't claim Ernie Banks—although he was the one who recommended that the Cubs sign their all-time best player—because Banks was already playing professionally, albeit for the Negro Leagues' Kansas City Monarchs. Banks, however, claims Tony.

Tony has signed a number of other good players, including Alex Johnson, Larry Hisle, Toby Harrah, Don Elston, Grant Jackson. But on the walls of Tony Lucadello's office, obscure players rubbed shoulders with the stars. Scattered throughout the gallery are photos of a number of front-office people—Tony's bosses over the years. Dallas Green, who managed the Phillies to the 1980 World Series championship and is Tony's best friend in the game, merited two photos: one above the daybed and one above the Kleenex box on the filing cabinet. Cubs owner P. K. Wrigley, who hired Tony to his first scouting job in 1942, hung over the pillow.

On the wooden desk was a coffee cup in the shape of a baseball, a transistor radio, a weathered desk blotter, a pocket dictionary and *The Directory of College Athletics*. Above the humble, funky four-drawer desk hung three featured photos. One is of Grant Jackson, the only Fostoria kid ever to make the majors. Another is of Tony and Mike Schmidt at the reception held to honor Schmidt's five hundredth homer: Schmidt wears a four-hundred-dollar sweater while shaking the hand of the scout who signed him, who wears an impish smile and a sensible suit. The third is a faded, blurry snapshot of St. Louis Browns second baseman Johnny Lucadello.

"There's a story to all these players," Tony said.

"Okay," I said. I looked at the nearest photo. "Tell me about Toby Harrah."

Tony's eyes twinkled. "Oh, boy. Now *that's* a story," he said, sitting down behind the desk and motioning me to sit in the room's other chair.

In the little town of LaRue, Ohio, a five-six, 160-pound kid named Toby Harrah played shortstop behind a left-handed pitcher, one of the best prospects in the Midwest. While other scouts drooled over the big lefty, Tony Lucadello saw something in the shortstop, and he took Toby aside and asked if he was interested in being a big-league ballplayer.

"No," Toby said. "I'm going to Ohio Northern. I'm going to play football and basketball and baseball. I'm going to be a three-letter man."

"That's how he was," Tony said. "Cocky as all getout."

Sorry he wasn't able to sign a prospect from under the nose of every scout in the area, Tony at least had the consolation of having the kid stay within his territory. The scout placed Toby Harrah in his "follow" file. By that September, an injury ended the big lefty's baseball career, and the Detroit Tigers, who had drafted him in the second round, chalked one up to fate. Meanwhile, Tony Lucadello placed a phone call to LaRue, Ohio.

"Mrs. Harrah, can you tell me how Toby's gettin' along in school?"

"Oh, he's not in college."

"He's not? He told me he was going."

"Aw, you know how he is. He's working in a factory over at Marion. He unloads trucks."

"Workin' pretty steady, is he?"

"Yeah, he works four, five hours a day, pretty steady."

Tony called back when Toby got home. "I thought you were going to college."

"Nah. I went down there. It wasn't for me."

Tony arranged a workout with Toby Harrah, who showed up at the Findlay High School field with a pal from the loading dock. "Toby impressed me then, even more so," Tony told me. "Unloading trucks made him bigger." But Toby said he wouldn't sign unless an offer was extended to his buddy, who couldn't have cracked the lineup of a B-division church softball team.

"I want to sign a young shortstop here by the name of Toby Harrah," Tony said when he called the Phillies office. "But he won't sign unless I sign his buddy."

"Can his buddy play?"

"He can't play at all. He never even played high school ball. But if it's okay with you, I'm going to sign them both."

"What!"

"I was going to give Toby a thousand dollars. But I'll give five hundred to his buddy and five hundred to him. Then let 'em go to spring training together, take the buddy aside, put a catcher's mask and a belly protector and shin guards on him, put two guys out in front of him and stick him out in center field. Otherwise he'll get killed. Keep him down there ten days and release him."

"Are you serious?"

"Of course I'm serious."

"Go ahead."

From Florida, Phillies coaches called Tony to ask why he'd signed a kid who couldn't play as well as their wives. Their low opinion of the stunt may have spilled over onto Toby Harrah, who was lightly regarded by many in the Phillies organization. After the Washington Senators picked him up in the free-agent draft, Harrah went on to play in the major leagues for sixteen years, perhaps the best-hitting shortstop of his era.

"Now isn't that a story?"

"Yep," I said.

"You can't be around baseball as long as I have without having stories. Is that the kind of thing you'd want to put in a book? Stories?"

"Maybe."

Tony nodded, stroking his face and sizing me up. "Well, I'm no book writer. You'll have to tell me what you want." He paused. I was still scribbling notes about Toby Harrah, and Tony reached into a desk drawer and pulled out a swollen file full of yellowing papers and correspondence. "This," he said, tapping the file as if it were a map to the Lost Dutchman Mine, "this is something that ought to go in a book."

Oh no, I thought. Any writer can tell you that "something that ought to go in a book" tends to preface the dullest ideas. Fear of this phrase is what makes writers at parties pretend to be insurance salesmen, a tactic which renders any interlocutor mute.

"I must have written this about 1945, when I was just a

young scout," Tony said, gingerly leafing through the file. "About two years ago, my wife said that there was this messy, rusty steel trunk out in the garage that had been there for years, and she told me I ought to throw it out. Junk. I went out and looked at it, and I could see I couldn't open it, so the neighbor—he's pretty handy and he's got tools—and he came over and he opened it up. And in that trunk I found material that I had written many, many years ago. I don't remember writing it. I'd even forgot about all the ideas here, but I read through it and I knew this was something."

The idea had come to Tony as he traveled through Kentucky and Indiana, where every house has a basketball hoop nailed to the barn or garage. "There's no shortage of basketball talent in this country, none whatsoever. Kids are out practicing every day, all year 'round, and they're having *fun* doing it." He remembered his own youth, throwing thousands of balls off the front steps of his parents' house, and that's when he came up with the idea for the walls. But not until forty-two years later, as Tony read through his own notes, did the idea intensify into a vision, a dream. What Tony Lucadello saw then were millions of walls. In every American backyard, there would be a four-foot wall. At every American high school, there would be a twenty-foot wall. At any given moment, there would be as many American boys throwing against those walls as shooting at those basketball hoops. These American boys would become American men with all the right baseball tools, and American universities would repay the hundred dollars these boys' families had spent on building a wall with fifty-thousand-dollar college scholarships. Many of the young men would star on their college teams, graduate from college and enter pro ball, resplendent with the sound fundamentals Tony almost never sees in today's baseball players, and the American game of baseball would be stronger than ever, its future assured.

"You probably don't believe me," Tony said. "No one

does. It's so simple, no one believes it. But you saw Matt Stone. His father built the first wall, and that boy is living proof."

A few months before Tony found those papers, an unemployed man named Bruce Edwards had approached him and asked to be a commission scout. Tony, soft on situations where baseball and philanthropy cross, helped him out. But commission scouts can't hope to make more than a couple of hundred bucks a year, and Tony figured his new friend might be able to make something of all these old papers. For two years, Tony and Bruce met, discussing these old notes, typing them up and compiling them into a manual they called *The Lucadello Plan*. During this time, Matt Stone was in his backyard throwing thousands of balls against the Tony Lucadello Wall and developing into the best prospect in Tony's territory. Bruce and Tony made Matt's story central to the manual. Tony told Bruce he could keep all the proceeds, but they didn't have any luck finding a publisher, so Edwards paid to have it printed locally.

Tony gave me a copy. *The Lucadello Plan* gives clear instructions about how to build the walls and how to practice with them. Six rules allow each kid to teach himself how to improve his game:

1. Learn to position your feet for ground balls.
2. Keep your head and glove down.
3. Grip the ball across the seams.
4. Throw with a strong, over-the-top delivery.
5. Take 100 grounders off the wall every day.
6. Play with enthusiasm.

The manual reminded me of a "text book" assigned by a journalism prof of mine: a photocopied, plastic-bound manuscript which he himself had written, with grainy photographs, handwritten footnotes and a few missing and miscollated pages. *The Lucadello Plan,* slightly slicker and more carefully edited, has the same midwestern roll-up-your-sleeves functionality and charm.

"Every high school coach—or any coach, or any father—should have a manual. I'm not saying that because I want to sell the manual, but the manual should be sold, because it gets to the foundation of our problem: getting the six-, seven-, eight-, nine-, ten-, eleven-, twelve-, thirteen-year-old kids to *practice* again. They'd be able to swing the bat fifty times and field a hundred and fifty ground balls in just one hour. Each of them would be taking ground balls every ten seconds. A boy would improve his talents so much, *so quickly,* that he won't want to do anything but play baseball."

Fostoria, Ohio, has two motels, and Tony made a reservation at one of them, the L & K, while I waited in the living room and chatted with Virginia Lucadello. While Tony and I had been down in the basement, she had made arrangements for her sister to come over and help out with things. "I don't want Tony to have to cancel his trip on my account," she said. "Baseball is Tony's life, you know, what keeps him active. He doesn't have any hobbies, and he isn't handy. I want him to take his trip." On TV the Toronto Blue Jays and the Detroit Tigers were playing for the 1987 American League East division championship. "Hasn't this been a wonderful pennant race?"

I nodded. "I think the Blue Jays are going to win."

"Oh, I don't know," she said. "I'm pulling for the Tigers. I really think they're on a roll." She let the reading glasses she wore on a chain around her neck dangle as she talked to me. All around her, on two end tables and on the arms of her chair, lay an eclectic scattering of books and magazines: *Good Housekeeping,* Norman Mailer, crossword puzzles, *Sonnets from the Portuguese,* Ernest Hemingway, *Reader's Digest, Mac-*

beth, *King Lear*, the Phillies 1987 media guide, *The Poems of Longfellow, Haiku Harvest*, and an Ohio roadmap. Even without these, she would have looked like the eyeglasses-on-a-leash county librarian, one who would have allowed sixth-graders who loved books to sneak into the adult wing of the library, who would have recommended Jack London and Thomas Wolfe and Pearl S. Buck and John Steinbeck. She had a heating pad wedged into the small of her back, but she was cheerful about her fall. "It's the craziest darn thing," she said. "As many times as I've been up and down those stairs. Mercy. Well, nothing's broken. I just bruised my back. And my pride." She laughed. The Tigers scored first. "I do think they might win this."

"Maybe so," I said.

"Ready?" Tony said. "I got you a reservation. I hope it's a nice room."

"I'm sure it'll be fine."

We would be leaving early in the morning, Tony told me, so I said good-bye to Virginia Lucadello. I wanted to drop to my knees to thank her. I wondered if her insistence that Tony take this trip was swayed by my presence, and I wanted to let her know I admired her selflessness. But people from northwestern Ohio don't practice such showy displays of emotion, for which other people from northwestern Ohio are more or less grateful, so I just said it was nice meeting her, and I hoped the Tigers would pull it out, and she adjusted her heating pad, smiled and said she enjoyed meeting me, too, and hoped Tony and I would have a nice trip.

"I want to check on something," Tony said, on our way to the motel. "This will only be a little out of our way." He drove a leased white 1985 Chevrolet Caprice with burgundy interior: Phillies colors. In the middle of the front seat was a box which once contained official Rawlings baseballs and now served as

Tony's filing cabinet, filled with letters to prospects, memos to himself, and notepads on which to calculate his mileage. On the dashboard was an old vinyl eyeglasses case stuffed with pencils and ballpoint pens. On the backseat were some spare hats.

We passed Grant Jackson's mother's house and Jackson Park, a small lot with a rusty swing set, named after Fostoria's most famous athlete. It's a poor, mostly black neighborhood of small wooden houses and cluttered, neglected yards. In small-town Ohio, that's what constitutes a "bad" neighborhood: a few black people and some weedy lawns.

"I'm looking for a wall," Tony said. "It's this house here. I don't want to stop and let this young man think I'm checking up on him, but I heard he built a wall. Aaron Hampton's his name. Good young ball player. Runs like a deer. A little raw, though. I told him to build a wall. Help me look for it, will you?"

Tony passed the house and pulled into a driveway half a block down the street. "I didn't see anything," I said.

He turned around and drove down an alley behind the Hampton's house.

"There it is!" I said.

"Where?"

"Right behind the house there." This wall wasn't as permanent as the other two I'd seen that day. Actually this was just a stack of cinderblocks, unmortared and unpainted. But the grass in front of it was brown and trampled.

"I knew he'd do it," Tony said, beaming. "His parents think he'll be a football player, but I had a feeling he'd build a wall." Tony slapped me on the thigh. "This young man'll be a good one."

The L & K Motel sits on the southwest corner of Fostoria, right at the corporation limit, flanked by the town's lone golf course on one side and fallow fields on all the others. A few foursomes were out on the course. This was October in the snowbelt, and even though the oaks and hickories were only this week ablaze with color, the first snows would be here soon enough to make this one of the last rounds of the season.

"Used to play a little golf myself," Tony said. "I figured I could use another interest." Like most everyone I grew up with, Tony pronounced the word "innerst." "I enjoyed it all right, but I never got that caught up in it."

We pulled into the L & K parking lot, and Tony waited while I checked in. As we walked to my room, he pointed to the barren field across the road. "There used to be a baseball stadium over there."

"The Fostoria Redbirds, right?"

"Yes."

I unlocked the door and set down my suitcase. Tony pulled up a chair at the room's little round table by the window. "You know, that field is the site of the best catch ever made in the history of the game of baseball."

"Oh yeah?"

Tony nodded, working a toothpick around in his mouth. "And I made it."

"The best ever?" I sat in the other chair and propped my feet up on the bed.

"I'll tell you, and you see if you don't believe it. It was 1936, my first year in professional ball, and the Fostoria Redbirds, we were in second place and playing the first-place team here, on our home field. The boards on the ball diamond's outfield fence were put in the wrong way, so that there were these two-by-fours nailed to the inside of the fence rather than on the outside. All the advertising was on the outside of the fence. It was a mistake, but they decided not to correct it until the season was over.

"Before the game started, the manager, George Silvey, asked me if I would play center field for a couple of games so they could play a shortstop the office had sent in there for ten days. The center fielder wasn't hitting and I was, and I said okay, I can play center. So I went out there, and every inning I'd go out to those two-by-fours and practice stepping on the bottom one, which was about two feet off the ground, and hoisting myself up about two feet over the fence.

"So we're going into the top half of the ninth inning, and it was getting dark, too dark to play, really, but the umpire wouldn't call the game. We were winning by a score of 4 to 3. They had the bases loaded, and their leading hitter, an Eyetalian fellow who led the league that year with forty-seven home runs, was at the plate. He hit a line drive right at me, like a golf ball. I dashed to the fence, put my right foot on that two-by-four, and hoisted myself up to try to catch the ball. The ball kept climbing, climbing, climbing. I could see that I wasn't going to catch the ball, that it was going to be about five foot over my head. But up and behold, just as I lingered there reaching up with my arm, a pigeon came by, and the ball hit the pigeon, and the pigeon came straight down, about a foot over the fence, and I reached over and caught the pigeon backhand.

"As I caught the pigeon, I flashed it at the umpire, who was running out to the outfield to see what happened out there, and he signaled that the batter was out. Then I jumped to the ground, and stumbled, on purpose, so that I could take that pigeon and hide it in my back pocket. And then I saw our manager, George Silvey, running out towards the outfield, too. When a game was over, George Silvey wanted that baseball; he said too many ball players kept the ball, hid it in the glove or in the shoes or wherever. When I saw him coming towards me, I figured he was going to nail me just about where that umpire was, and then the umpire was going to see what I caught. I start running away from him, dashed out toward right field, but George could run and he cut me off, nailed me to the ground, and he's screaming, 'Where's that ball?' I said, 'It's in my back pocket,' and he reaches back, pulls out this pigeon, and he says, 'What's this?' I says, 'That's what I caught, you dummy. That's what won the ball game for you. I made the greatest catch ever made in this game, I won the ball game, and here you're screaming about the ball.' And he still wants to know where the ball is. 'Where do you think it is?' I says. 'It's over the fence.'

"So we wait until the ump went home, and then he made all us players jump the fence and walk on our hands and knees out there in the weeds until somebody stepped on it. All the ball players went into the clubhouse, except me and George, who went and got us a spade. We waited until everybody left and then dug a hole under home plate and buried that poor pigeon."

Together Tony and I roared in laughter, and I wouldn't have asked him if that had really happened even if it meant a zero balance on my Visa bill.

"That happened right across the street there," Tony said. "Fifty-one years ago. About eight years after I made that catch, they tore the stadium down, during the war I think it was."

I flipped on the TV and we watched the end of the Tigers–Blue Jays game, chatting about baseball and baseball players, those Tony likes and the many he does not. While today's players are better athletes, he said, about three-fourths lack the skills to be first-division major league ball players. As if on cue, Blue Jays shortstop Manny Lee let a sharply hit ground ball go through his legs, and as Virginia Lucadello had predicted, the Tigers won their division. "That's what I mean, right there," Tony said in disgust. "Anyone can make an error, but letting a ball go right between your legs?"

Tony Lucadello got up to leave. "Well, I'll see you tomorrow morning. I want to get an early start, so be ready by eight, okay?"

"Okay."

He put on his hat and overcoat, shuffled out to the leased

Phillies Chevy, and drove off. The sun was setting into the golf course. I turned off the postgame wrap-up, put on my coat and a Cincinnati Reds cap, grabbed my glove and a worn baseball, and walked across the road into the field where the Fostoria Redbirds had played. I stood about where I thought the pigeon's bones must be, and I threw myself pop-up after pop-up. A few times, I tripped and fell over dirt clods, but I kept at it until the sun went down and the temperature dropped about ten degrees and I could imagine professional baseball in Fostoria, Ohio.

2

The Real Miami

"Everyone asks me, 'How long are you going to keep scouting, for heaven's sakes?' " We were in Tony's white Chevy, meandering down county roads, around tractors, combines and farm wagons, across one-lane bridges, over the flat black earth of northern Ohio on the kind of sunny fall day that makes you want to pick a bushel of apples or find a date to the homecoming dance. I leafed through the Sunday *Toledo Blade*. Tony drove, past Bloomdale, Eagleville, Bairdstown, North Baltimore, Van Buren, across the lower branch of the Portage River. "I say, well—and you can do this, too—why don't you judge me on the most important thing about scouting? If you want to learn about *me*, about how long a seventy-five-year-old man is going to scout, then this is what to judge me on."

His tone was serious, a history professor lecturing on his pet battle, but he had a trace of a grin. You had to look hard, but it was there. Corner of the mouth. Right corner. I still had some remnant of student in me, and I cautiously raised my hand to ask the pregnant question. "Um, well, so what is it? The most important thing about scouting?"

Tony nodded, the pleased mentor. "The most important

23

thing about scouting? Well, I'm going to scout as long as I can drive this car. Now, you're riding with me. Grade me on that, and then you'll know how long I'll scout. If I can't drive this car safely, effectively, then I shouldn't scout. My time is up. And that's the most important thing, not how I find talent but how I drive this car: can I get there and see that talent?"

As he told me this, Tony slowed down to about thirty-five, behind a battered Ford pickup that was missing its tailgate and filled with rolls of fencing. He could have passed the truck—no one was coming—but he was caught up in his story, and he didn't. The truck pulled into a field, and Tony sped up. I thought, Big deal, everyone's done that. My dad does it all the time, and he's only fifty. Slowing down instead of passing is certainly not unsafe driving, and I didn't feel like I was in danger, but I did feel guilty and oddly responsible, as if any criticism of his driving, even unspoken, trifling criticism, might deprive baseball of Tony Lucadello. "I think, from what I've seen so far, you'll be at it for a while yet."

Tony waved me off. "Don't grade me so quick. Just watch and see what you think."

"Okay."

We got on I-75, in the right lane.

"That's my home in a lot of ways, the back roads there. Not just around here, around my home town, but all the back roads all over my territory. Of course my territory's smaller now. When I first started out, with the Chicago Cubs, my territory was nine states, can you believe that? Iowa, Wisconsin, Illinois, Indiana, Kentucky, West Virginia, Michigan, Minnesota, and Ohio. Plus, parts of Canada. I put somewhere around seventy thousand miles a year on my cars. When I came to the Phillies, one condition was that I'd get a smaller territory, just five states and Ontario. I got rid of Illinois fifteen years later, and for the next twenty-one years, I had four states. Now, just this year, I cut back to only Ohio, Indiana, and Michigan. The coaches down in Kentucky, they ask after me, and I miss them, hated to give it up, but I'm getting to be an old man now, and I have to think about that."

"What is it about the back roads?"

"Well, of course, when I started out, they didn't even have the interstates like this. And they help. They save time. But it doesn't take much to scout cities. Everyone knows who the good ball players are. They're written up in the city newspapers, for heaven's sake. They're recruited by all the colleges, everyone knows them. I scout them, too, but where I really shine are the players out in the country, the kids in the small towns. That's my bread and butter, where I've had most of my success, where my skills come into play. You see, I stay ahead of the other guys, the other scouts. I would say that probably 75 percent of the players I've signed are players other scouts said, 'Gosh, Tony, what'd you see in him?' But I stay ahead of the other scouts, because I have to—especially these days, with the *draft.*"

Tony claimed he'd never said a swear word, but if he ever slipped, he must have used the same inflection as when he says "draft." Before 1965, when major league baseball instituted the amateur draft, if Tony found a player he liked, he could offer him a contract on the spot. Often, the first scout to find a player would be the one to sign him, and in Tony's territory Tony Lucadello was the first scout more often than not. His only real obstacle was getting the Cubs or the Phillies to pay enough to make a player sign or to beat a competing team's offer. Since 1965, though, the only way Tony can sign a player he likes is by convincing the Phillies to draft that player. Sometimes he doesn't even have a chance; for the past fifteen years—since Mike Schmidt made the majors, actually—the Phillies have been a top team, which gives them rotten draft choices. In 1987, Tony's top prospect was Cincinnati's Ken Griffey, Jr. But the perennially hapless Seattle Mariners made Griffey the first choice in the entire draft, twenty picks ahead of the Phillies.

"Mr. Ruly Carpenter, you know who he is, he used to own the Phillies," Tony said. "Mr. Carpenter says to me, 'Tony, the draft's killing you.' He says if it hadn't been for the draft, I'd have a hundred major league ballplayers, not just forty-nine."

"What do you think?" I said.

Tony stuck out his lower lip and mulled that over. "Could be. I'd have more than I have now. You can't tell, really. Maybe more like two hundred."

We passed the Neil Armstrong Air and Space Museum at I-75 exit 113, in Wapokoneta, Ohio. "Have you ever been there?" Tony said. "I always meant to stop. I've been by it so often."

"When I was in junior high, my class took a field trip there. All I really remember is that it had this big planetarium, and it was dark, and I tried to get a seat there next to this girl Pam, who I had a crush on."

Tony smiled. "Can you imagine walking on the moon?" He shook his head, swerving the car into the left lane to pass a school bus. "I would have liked to do that. Do you remember when that happened, a young man like you?"

"Absolutely." I was seven years old, and my family was driving down the Indiana Turnpike, coming back from a visit with my grandparents in Jacksonville, Illinois. Mom had the radio on and my little sister and I hung over the front seat of our yellow Electra, straining to hear and to get a blast from the air conditioner. The speed limit was seventy then, but Dad drove almost ninety, frantic to get home to Bryan, Ohio, before man set foot on the moon. We hardly spoke—not even my sister, whose attention span remained short until early adulthood—but when we did, we whispered. We got off the Ohio Turnpike at exit 2 and headed south on Ohio 15. Dad made the tires squeal on the off ramp, and no one complained. When we got home, Dad parked the car in the driveway, unwilling to waste the few seconds it would have taken to pull into the garage. We ran inside, flipped on the old RCA console TV and sat cross-legged in a twitchy semicircle on the beige shag living-room carpet. Slow to warm up, the television finally flickered to life at almost the exact moment Neil Armstrong opened the hatch of the lunar landing module.

"How about you?" I asked Tony.

"I was in Bloomington, Indiana, at a ballgame."

Another difficulty in modern scouting, Tony explained, is the evaluation of what scouts call "signability," a quality as important as bat speed, movement on a curveball, or ability to turn a double play. Scouts must find out if a player, once drafted, will sign, and for how much. Teams can only draft players after their senior year of high school, after their junior or senior year of college, or after their twenty-first birthday. Scouts must be able to tell their teams how committed a high school senior is to attending college, or whether a college junior intends to finish before signing. Players out of high school but not yet in their senior year of college have the most bargaining power, since if they forgo turning pro, they will have another chance next year. College seniors or dropouts have no bargaining power and, except for the obvious blue-chipper, will usually be drafted low and signed cheaply.

Tony wasn't enamored of the system, but he'd succeeded within it, urging his team to risk low drafts on college-bound kids and then landing them by offering a big signing bonus and getting a handshake agreement from the kid that he'll finish his education. Another of Tony's favored tactics was finding out about twenty-one-year-old sophomores or, as he did with Toby Harrah, college dropouts who can be signed as free agents without using the draft at all: a whiff of the sweet smell of the old days. "I've had more success with free agents than anybody," Tony said. "I have players with the club now, players I signed for five thousand dollars, doing better than high drafts who got over fifty thousand. Just this week I got a telephone call from Mr. Giles. Bill Giles—do you know Mr. Giles?"

William Giles owns the Phillies. Tony asked the question as if he thought I might have played some tennis with Giles. I was about fifty years younger than Tony, and the only really famous person I've met is Norman Mailer, who told me to call him "Fuckface." There is no one listed in my address book whose name you would recognize. Still, Tony knew I'd written a book and been to New York City, two things he'd never done, and he often asked if I knew reporters, ballplayers, and league presidents, always with a tone of sincere curiosity. If I'd lied and said, 'Yes, Donald Trump lets me use his private plane every other Wednesday,' Tony would have nodded and believed me. For all the traveling Tony had done, he'd left the Midwest only when ordered to Philadelphia for a meeting. "I know who Bill Giles is," I said. "I don't know him personally."

"Mr. Giles said to me, 'I see here you have signed five ball players in the last two years, in '86 and '87. Now the one in '86, Scott Service, he was a free-agent ball player and you signed him for just five thousand.' And I said, 'Well, is that bad?' and Mr. Giles said, 'Why, no, he might be the best pitcher we've got in our farm system. He won thirteen and lost four at Clearwater and he's only nineteen years old. How'd you do it?' And I said, 'I found them.' There's more to it than that, really, but it only amounts to this: I found them. That's what I'm paid to do."

Tony booked a room for two nights at the Richmond, Indiana, Knights Inn. The Miami University exhibition games we'd attend the next two days were about thirty miles away, in Oxford, Ohio. But Tony said he knew the president of the chain, and he liked to stay in Knights Inns whenever possible.

"Now, are you sure you don't want me to get a room for you, too," he asked. "I can't get you the senior citizens discount they give me, but the rates are still quite reasonable."

"No, thanks. My sister's expecting me." Shari was a senior at Miami, and I'd called from the Fostoria L & K to ask if I could spend the next couple nights on her couch. I wanted to save a few bucks and I wanted to see her, but mainly I didn't want to be stuck without a car in Richmond, Indiana, when I could instead get drunk and sentimental on the grounds of my alma mater.

"That's nice," he said. "I'm glad you'll get to see your sister. Your trip will be worthwhile even if you don't get anything worthwhile out of me, even if you don't decide to write a book about a guy like me."

"I've already decided, Tony."

He shook his head. "That's up to you. You don't know me very well yet. Maybe you'll decide there's not enough here to fill up a whole book, and if you do, fine. You don't owe me any explanation."

The desk clerk was middle-aged with a southern accent, at home in her polyester uniform. She knew Tony and said hi, she was sorry his room wasn't made up yet, it'd be just about a half hour, but she got him the corner suite, the one with the couch, so that ought to be some consolation. And Tony said, "Thanks, no problem," and introduced me.

"A writer, huh?" the woman said, sizing me up as if I were the first of the breed she'd yet seen. Being a real, published writer was new to me—my first book wouldn't be out for three months—and I liked the attention even though I knew enough to pooh-pooh it. "Boy, I could tell you things that would fill a book," she said. "My kids alone, what they've been into, could make one of those scary Stephen King books."

"See?" Tony said. "Maybe you ought to be writing a book about her."

Tony and I went to Jerry's, a small, inexpensive restaurant next door. In the days before fast-food franchises, little places like Jerry's once owned the business of American travelers, especially those who found Big Boy and Howard Johnson's overpriced. Jerry's gave you dark plastic water glasses, big laminated menus, and a selection of food for diners undaunted by 1980s health concerns. We took seats at the counter, and I ordered the chicken-fried steak with a side of fries and a chocolate shake. Tony ordered potato soup—"The Soup D'Jour of the Day (Just Ask)"—and I requested the story of how he'd come to be a baseball scout.

"It started this way," Tony said. By 1942, Tony's playing career was over. It was time, he figured, for him to get on with a grown man's life, and with a young bride and a new baby and a mortgage, Tony Lucadello's best option seemed to be the Fostoria Screw Company, which had been converted into a defense plant. His brother Johnny got drafted, leaving the St. Louis Browns infield for a gunnery position in the Pacific theater. Tony missed baseball, and he missed his brother, and he felt a little guilty being on the home front. At times, he even missed delivering those heavy cases of Chicago olive oil.

"One night there was a knock at my door," Tony said, "and here was Jack Sheehan, who had just been made farm director of the Chicago Cubs, the first time that the Cubs ever had any ideas about developing their own talent—they'd always bought their talent. Their players either played for the Cubs or they played for the one minor league team in Los Angeles, and that was it.

"And Jack Sheehan told me, 'I'm looking for five scouts to start with, and I wanted you here in the Midwest, but I don't want you to work now. Just be on hold until this war is over.' And so he gave me his home phone number and his office number, and he told me, 'Keep in mind now, we don't have any contracts and we can't pay you. We just have this handshake agreement.'

"Later that year, 1942, when all the top major league players were in the service, I got a call from a dear friend of mine, an elderly person who lived in Mishawaka, Indiana, and his name was Franco. I called him Pop. Pop Franco would have been about eighty then. 'Tony,' he said, 'my wife and I have a little problem here, and we'd appreciate it if you'd come and help us out.' He was doing some bird-dogging for me, see, for the Cubs, working as a part-time man until the war got over and they could pay us.

"I said I could come up over the weekend, as soon as I can get some coupons and get some gas, and so I did, and I helped him solve his problem. Pop was managing what we used to call semipro ball, and he invited me to see a pitcher by the name of Ed Hanyzewski, a young right-hander Pop thought I ought to see.

"The pitcher was twenty-two years old, and he was married with a couple of kids, working now in a defense plant somewhere. And he threw the ball *real well*. I got all the dope on him, and I called Jack Sheehan when I got home, and I said, 'Jack, I saw a pitcher today that really can throw.'

" 'Tony,' he says, 'I thought I told you, we don't have any contracts. Until the war's over, we're not going to have any farm clubs.'

" 'I got another idea,' I says. 'I think that this guy can pitch right now in the big leagues.'

" 'Oh, come on.'

" 'Well, I can make it cheap for you. All you have to do is next time the team's home get Charlie Grimm'—he was the Cubs' manager then—'to come out some Saturday morning, and I'll have the kid there to throw to some of the players. And then you can all see for yourself.'

"So we set it up, and I called the kid, picked him up at six o'clock in the morning, and we got into Wrigley Field about eight-thirty and put a uniform on the kid. There were four players working out, three fielders and a catcher. Charlie

Grimm said he'd be the umpire, and he sent those players up to the plate, and the kid struck all three of them out, one two three. No sooner than he did, Charlie Grimm went crazy, and the way he acted, he scared me to death, running around like a madman, and I thought he didn't like the kid. 'Get off the field,' he screams at us. 'Everyone get off the field and get dressed.' And he came over to the backstop, and he called me up to his office, handed me a contract and told me to go back down there and sign him right here, right now, and he joined the Cubs roster that day.

"The next year, the same thing happened, and this time it was easier. That pitcher was a young man from Battle Creek, Michigan, named Bob Rush. Bob went on to pitch thirteen years in the big leagues, and Hanyzewski—he hurt his arm— just pitched five.

"When we signed Bob Rush, Mr. Wrigley was there. Charlie Grimm was ranting and raving, saying we had to sign this kid Rush, right here, right now, boy, can he pitch. And Mr. Wrigley just said, real quiet, 'Sit down, Charlie.'

"Mr. Wrigley commanded attention in a room. He was a tall, thin man, a quiet man who wore small wire-rimmed eyeglasses and expensive black suits, a man who could get more attention with a whisper than most men could with a scream. 'Before you sign this pitcher here,' he said, 'if you want him that bad, you better sign that young man right there,' and he wheels around and points his finger right at me. 'He brings two guys up here who can pitch in the big leagues,' he says, 'and we don't even have him signed to a contract. You sign him to one *today* and pay him a salary, even if he doesn't work a day,' and that's what they did: three thousand six hundred dollars a year, that was my salary.

"And I'll never forget what Mr. Wrigley said as he walked out the door of Charlie Grimm's office there in Wrigley Field, and I heard him say it later, again and again: 'This young man was born to be a scout.'"

* * *

Fall baseball is more than just the World Series, although not much more. While Reggie Jackson gives himself the nickname "Mr. October," while Carlton Fisk waves his extra-inning homer fair and a journeyman pitcher named Don Larsen pitches a perfect game, pro prospects work out in what's called the Florida Instructional League, dreaming of spring training. But about the only people playing baseball in October not receiving paychecks for their time are college kids.

With the school year barely underway, college coaches convene their teams, the returning lettermen, the new hotshots on scholarship and the walk-ons. For the upperclassmen, it's a time to get reacquainted, to find out how their friends did in the summer leagues and to see if any of the newcomers are going to be worth knowing. For the new recruits, it's a time to make first impressions on new teammates, to wonder how much playing time they'll get this coming April and to imagine how their varsity status will impress the Tri-Delts. For the walk-ons, it's a time to glance for acceptance on the face of the coaches, after every catch, every throw, every swing of the bat. For the coaches, it's a time to think about lineup cards yet to be, about teaching that tall lefty how to throw a decent change-up, about making that new shortstop into a center fielder, and sadly, about how to tell some of the new freshmen their extracurricular time might be better spent in the glee club.

For Tony Lucadello, it's a time to get the last look of the season at the players in his "follow" file and to see if any of the new kids ought to join that file. At colleges all over the Midwest, many of those freshman, though new to other scouts, aren't new to Tony; when he finds a high schooler he likes but who isn't developed enough to risk money on, Tony calls up the coaches of the programs he admires, and tells them, Hey, son, there's a catcher up north of Ft. Wayne who might fit into your program.

We got to the ballpark early. Miami had an intrasquad doubleheader planned on this October Sunday, when most of the student body was in the dorms watching the Cincinnati Bengals on black-and-white TVs, having a few bagels delivered, drinking Hudepohl beer, and worrying about that Western Civ test tomorrow. Tony and I were the first people there, even before the team. The sun glinted off the aluminum bleachers at Stanley G. McKie Field, and we sat down behind home plate, chatting about the weather, taking in deep breaths of fall air and reveling in the joy of a green ball field encased by a preposterously beautiful university.

Miami University looks like a seventh-grader's idea of college. A land-grant institution established in 1809, Miami is a campus of wooded commons, ivy-covered walls, redbrick Georgian buildings and fifteen thousand scrubbed, toothy undergraduates who wear bright clothes adorned with Greek letters and hate people who call their school "Miami of Ohio." "Miami was a university before Florida was a state," we'll tell you, adding that our average SAT score towers over that of those tanned boneheads at the other Miami. One of the bookstore's best-selling T-shirts reads, "Miami Is in Ohio, Damn It!"

Tony began walking around the perimeter of the field, scouring the ground with his eyes, like a man who's lost his car keys. "I do this before every game."

"Do what?"

"Look for money. I'm known for it. The other scouts, when they see me at a game, they'll ask, 'Hey, Tony, you find any money?'"

"My dad used to have one of those metal detector things. He used to go out in public parks and dig up bottle caps and rusty spoons."

"I just got into the habit of it. I can't even remember how.

At first I guess it was just something to pass the time. Scouts are alone quite a bit, you see, and since I don't drink or chase the women, this is what I use to pass the time. Now, it's a little more than that. When I can't find any more pennies, that's when I'll know I don't have the eyes to be a scout. That's when I'll hang it up."

Tony and I had covered the third-base side of the ballpark, and we wound our way around the backstop and up the first-base line. Tony said he usually had the most success under the bleachers.

I'm terrible at stuff like this. When I was a kid, I got involved with this outdoorsy group in my high school, at my grandfather's urging. On field trips it was always other people who'd say, Hey, look at that elk, and I'd always be the guy going, Where, where, show me. "How much money do you find?"

"Depends," Tony said. "My best year was 1972. I got almost twenty-seven bucks then." He walked to the end of the bleachers, then shook his head. "Don't look like there's much here." He pulled up the furry collar of his overcoat and thrust his hands into his pockets. "What do you think I do with all this money? Come on, guess."

"Buy your wife a present?"

He smiled. "No. I keep it all in a jar and then, on September fifteenth of every year I give it to the first church I happen to see."

"Oh."

He shrugged. "I'm not a religious man. I don't know why I do that. I just have, for years and years. The first church I see, no matter where I am that day, no matter what denomination. Makes me feel good, that's the only explanation I got."

Tony slapped me on the back, and we took a seat in the bleachers. "You didn't know what you were getting yourself into, did you, traveling with a crazy old man like me?"

* * *

The first batter for the White team was a tall, thin, left-handed sophomore center fielder named Fred VanderPeet. "He's been lifting weights and eating good," Tony said. "Look at him. How much would you say he weighs?"

"One seventy."

"About right. He's six three, so he could gain a little more. Last year he played at one sixty. I see him filling out to about one eighty-five."

The pitcher for the Gray team, a stocky junior with a herky-jerky motion, was behind VanderPeet, 2 and 0.

"Now, look at the good live body that batter has," Tony said, as VanderPeet took a ball. "Eighty-seven percent of the game of baseball is played below the waist. Just look at the way that lead knee of his twitches back and then steps into the pitch. But not so soon he commits himself. He's tall and skinny, but his body position is good and his center of gravity is about right."

VanderPeet walked.

"Good," Tony said. "Now we can see him run the bases."

Next up, the second baseman looked like a good batter—at a glance. But everything VanderPeet had below the waist, this kid lacked. Both legs were stiff and locked into position, and when each pitch came, he stepped into it, committing himself before he had any idea where the ball would be. He checked his swing even on a wild pitch. VanderPeet advanced to second on the pitch and then, trying to stretch it to third, was caught in a rundown and tagged out by the shortstop.

Tony just nodded.

"Good runner?" I asked.

Tony nodded. "I scout by looking for pluses. This boy has an awful lot of pluses, and speed may be the biggest."

"Yeah, but he was tagged out because he was greedy."

"That's a minus. On the other hand, it shows good competitiveness, trying to take an extra base in a meaningless game like this. Look, you can talk yourself out of any player. But what I do is add up the pluses and see if that's enough for me."

The batter lined out, and the next guy up was the White team's shortstop, Tim Naehring. Even I knew that the best athletes, the best prospects, are likely to be those playing the most demanding positions: catcher, pitcher, shortstop, and center fielder. Most big-league second and third basemen are converted shortstops; most right and left fielders are converted center fielders. The media guide said that Naehring had been all-conference last season. "How about this guy, Tony? Is he on your follow list?"

"*Oh, yes.*" Tony watched Naehring more carefully than he had the first two batters, talking less, studying more. Naehring swung and missed.

"Good hard swing, though?" I said, looking for acceptance.

"Oh, yeah," Tony said. "This is the place to study right-handed hitters, about a third of the way up the first-base line. Here, you can see their face and six of their eight sides."

Naehring struck out swinging to end the inning. If I hadn't seen Tony study Naehring so intently, I might have dismissed him. The pitcher had nothing: no speed, no control, no technique, yet here he struck out an all-conference shortstop with ease.

"We'll never get him," Tony said. "He's going to go in the first three rounds next year, but I'm afraid he'll be gone by the time we pick. He may have struck out, but this game means nothing. He showed me good body control. Let's move."

Tony walked up the line, almost even with first base, and sat down. We were probably the only people there not related to or dating one of the players.

"What'd you mean," I asked, "about the player's eight sides?"

"That's how I analyze their body, by looking individually at the top front, back, right and left sides and the bottom front, back, right and left sides. That makes eight."

The Gray team had a little rally going, but Tony wasn't really paying attention to that. His eyes were on Naehring. When the cleanup hitter smashed a grounder deep into the hole—a ball I'd thought was a base hit—Naehring knocked it down and fired it to first, beating the runner by a full step. Tony whispered, "Third base."

"Excuse me?"

"That was a good play—for this level. But he don't have soft hands. What he does have is quick reactions and a strong arm. Hits for power, too. I'm projecting him as a third baseman."

Tony jockeyed himself all over the field, even under the bleachers, and I made a mental note to ask later what his method was. I didn't want to distract him any more than I already had, so for the rest of the game I kept quiet and tagged along.

In the third inning VanderPeet hit a triple, but Tony talked more about his good running form than the hit itself. The next inning he began to study the White team's left fielder, a kid named Tim Carter, who had made two good catches already and whose batting stance raised the old scout's eyebrow.

"I don't know him," Tony said. "In between games of this doubleheader, I'll go ask the coach."

For the rest of the game, Tony studied the every move of VanderPeet, Naehring, and Carter. Two other players hit home runs without getting Tony the least bit interested in them, yet Carter drew a walk that made Tony sure he'd discovered a prospect.

I flipped through the media guide and read that Mike Mungovan, a big first baseman, had led the team in hitting last year. VanderPeet and Carter had hardly even played. In between the fifth and sixth, I asked Tony about that. He didn't even know who Mungovan was. I pointed him out, and Tony nodded. "He doesn't do anything for me. His body isn't live, he can't throw. He can hit with a little power, *at this level*, but that's the only plus I see."

VanderPeet homered in the seventh.

"I've seen all I need to see for today," Tony said. "That wind's blowing through me now. Let's go say hello to Jon Pavlisko, and then we'll go home."

Pavlisko, Miami's coach, a stocky forty-four-year-old who had played a few years in the Red Sox system, met us at the fence. He tried to get Tony to accept a dinner invitation, but Tony said he didn't want to intrude. "A young man like you, Jon, should have dinner with his family. We'll have dinner in the spring."

Pavlisko figured Tony was there to see Naehring, and he talked the shortstop up, extolling his virtues as a player, a student and a human being. VanderPeet, apparently, is something of a flake, though Pavlisko didn't come out and say so. When Tony asked about Carter, Pavlisko was clearly surprised. I don't think he wanted Tony to see that surprise. Pavlisko stammered some, said, "Yes, he's got some potential."

The coach again offered to buy the scout dinner, but Tony said he had a place to stay in Richmond. He shook hands, waved good-bye and headed toward his white Chevy.

I asked Jon Pavlisko and, yes, Tony Lucadello was the first major league scout to see something in Tim Carter. Jon smiled. "I'll tell you what: he's not ever the last."

The next day was a raw preview of midwestern winter, complete with an annoying mist and steady winds that worked in concert to make you remember how much you hated last winter and forget why you didn't move. Tony and Jon Pavlisko sat in the coach's small office in the basement of Miami's basketball arena, discussing catchers. A blackboard and framed pictures of past teams covered the walls. Jon had missed out on a catcher from Troy, Ohio, who'd wound up at the University of Michigan, the biggest, most successful college program in Tony's territory. Michigan was perceived, by scouts and other college coaches alike, as the Evil Empire, and the Michigan coach, Bud Middaugh, as Darth Vader.

"Go after that kid Styles," Tony said. "You know him?"

"Yeah."

"Better future. Better arm, better hitter. Better kid."

Pavlisko nodded. "I'll take another look at him."

The two continued chatting about players all over the Midwest, speculating about how high they'd go in the draft, filling each other in on which players had improved during the summer, which players graduated, which players hurt their arms and knees. Coaches and scouts both are in the business of finding baseball talent, and to some extent, they're rivals: a kid who enrolls in college and then accepts a signing bonus from a pro team is a star lost. Likewise, a college player drafted high who opts to return for his senior year is a wasted draft pick. And a player who *does* turn pro as a junior is a cocaptain who never was. Still, it benefits the coach and scout to work together, and the most honorable men in each profession cooperate, never losing sight of what's in a kid's best interest. Jon said he could keep a kid in his program by telling scouts that he's an attitude problem, but he'd have to face that kid, knowing the lie had cost the young man thousands of dollars. He'd like to be able to tell Tony that Tim Naehring's not ready to play pro ball, because that might win Miami a conference championship. "Some coaches will do that, tell scouts a kid's not ready and then turn around and say to the kid, 'I can't believe you weren't drafted.' "

"It happens," Tony said.

"Up north, right?" Jon asked, invoking the Evil Empire. "I can't do that; if a young man's ready to play pro ball, I'll tell anyone who asks. Otherwise, I'm taking money out of that young man's pocket. Unfortunately, in the case of Timmy, he was ready when he was a sophomore, attitude-wise—and probably ability-wise, though that's for the scouts to say. Personally, I think he may have the tools to be a Mike Schmidt–type player."

Jon smiled. "Let me tell you a story. When I was the assistant coach at Virginia Tech, a guy I'd played some ball with called and said, 'Listen, our organization is interested in this kid on the team you're playing tomorrow, and we'd like you to take a look at him.' Now, I'm a young kid, too, just out of ball and starting my coaching career, so I don't know much, just what I see. So I look at this kid, and he's a nice player, hit two home runs off us. And I said, 'Well, I think he can play. But you said he's a potential high-rounder, and he's going to have to work *awful* hard to make it as a major league player.' I saw him boot a couple balls, and overall, he wasn't real smooth. There were some scouts sittin' around by me, and they said, 'That kid's never gonna be a player,' and being young, I nodded and said, 'Yeah, I don't think so, either.' But he had some catlike athletic ability that a young guy like I was would never see. He still has that ability, and Tony must have seen it all along, because that player was Mike Schmidt, and now he's on his way to the Hall of Fame."

"Oh, you'd see it in him now, Jon," Tony said.

"I sure would. A lot of other coaches asked me, 'What'd you see in Tim Naehring?' and he's a lot like a young Mike Schmidt." He glanced at Tony for a reaction.

"Could be," said the old scout. "He has a lot of pluses."

The pitcher for the Gray team was a kid from Ft. Wayne named Snow, who was hit pretty hard right from the beginning. VanderPeet led off with a sharp single and was eventually driven home by Naehring's deep sacrifice to right. In the second, both Carter and VanderPeet homered.

"Ninety-nine percent of all scouts sit behind home plate," Tony said, as we jockeyed all over the field, watching ballplayers as an appraiser might size up a sculpture. "That's about the worst place to be, to be honest with you. There's a minimum of six positions that I find on a field, every game I scout. First, about ten to twenty feet up the first-base line, so I can see the face of the right-handed hitters. Second, almost behind first, so I can see the strength of the infielders' and outfielders' arms and have another look at the right-handed batters. It's a good angle for left-handed pitchers, too, but a better place is my third position, about halfway up the right-field line.

"My other three positions are the opposite ones on the left-field line: ten to twenty feet up the line to see the left-handed batters, almost behind third to see the arm strength, the right-handed pitchers and more of the left-handed batters, and up the line to see behind the right-handed pitcher."

I was grateful for all the movement, as cold as it was, and I was even happier when Naehring was robbed of a homer to left field in the top of the seventh and Tony suggested we go.

"You know, I met Tony on a real cold fall day like this, about 1970, when I was still an assistant up at Central Michigan," Jon Pavlisko told me, as we said good-bye. "He was sitting up in the corner of the bleachers watching somebody, I can't remember who, and all the other scouts were clustered around taking notes from each other, and Tony was working the field. I watched him a little bit, and I was always impressed: he got along with all the other scouts, but he was able to sit alone and do his job. Most of the other scouts are followers, but Tony's his own man."

"Well, Jon," Tony said. "I told this young man I was different."

Tony pulled his scarf close to his throat and shuffled toward his big white Chevy and his purple room in Richmond, Indiana.

I walked back across familiar quads, to my sister's apartment. In the middle of Central Quad is a large brass Miami seal, and legend says that he who steps on it will fail his next exam. I stopped in front of it and jumped on the seal with both feet.

Meanwhile, Tony sat in his slippers and pajamas, alone in his motel room, hunched over a little table, carefully making out reports on Naehring and VanderPeet, but not Carter, whom he hoped to hide from other scouts as long as possible. He also wrote letters on Knights Inn stationery to a dozen prospects. Then he called his part-time scout in Columbus, Ohio, to find out where the mother of an outfielder Tony signed two years ago would be having her operation. Then Tony called a florist and sent a bouquet. And then he called his wife, who told him to stop worrying about her bruised back, for heaven's sake.

3

It's Great in Dayton

The next morning, Tony picked me up at my sister's apartment building, and we headed for Dayton, where Tony wanted to see Wright State University and Sinclair Community College. He let me drive, and I stopped for coffee at a convenience store in Camden, Ohio. "This is the way I used to go, driving home from college," I said. "I probably know this road better than anything I learned in school."

Tony nodded, looking out the window down a side street, past a lumberyard, an antique store and the post office. "I signed a good ball player out of this little town," he said. "Don Elston, you ever heard of him?"

"Sure. Right-handed relief pitcher for the Cubs for about seven years, late fifties, early sixties."

"I believe he pitched nine years," Tony corrected. "It would have been more, but he missed from '54 to '56, fighting in Korea."

I pointed the Caprice toward Dayton.

"Quite a story, Don Elston was."

I smiled. "Oh, yeah?"

"I had a tryout camp at Mansfield, Ohio, and we had

about sixty kids attend it. This was around the latter part of June, in probably 1953. After every boy had registered and I collected the registration cards, why, I made an announcement to 'em that, now, I don't want to talk to anybody after the camp is over. I'll contact the players I'm interested in directly. If you don't hear from me, that means I'm not interested in you for the time being.

"After the camp I gathered them together in the bleachers, and I made the same announcement. 'I know that some of you might want to know this, you might want to know that,' I says, 'but I haven't got the time for this or that. Let's do it the way I said: I'll contact you if I'm interested.' And so they all left the field but one—this sorta tall, skinny kid. Tall for that time, that is, about six foot. He came up to me while I was putting the bats and balls and equipment in the car, and he says, 'Mr. Lucadello, I came from a long ways, and I heard what you said, but I feel that I ought to know right now what you think.'

" 'Young man, a lot of kids come from a long way,' I says.

" 'Maybe so, but I'm not like a lot of 'em. I'd like to know now.'

"So being a young scout, and not qualified to handle situations such as that, I bluntly came right out and told the kid he couldn't throw hard enough. But his mechanics were good, and I told him to build himself up and try to get stronger and maybe he'd improve. He argued with me, but I stuck to my guns, and that's the way we left it.

"From that day forward, right through about the seventeenth of September, he wrote me a letter every day. Every day. My mailman made jokes about it. Every twelve or thirteen days, I responded back to the boy and told him to quit writing to me, that the results were the same and I hadn't changed my mind. But he never let up.

"About that time, I had to meet my boss and go to Buffalo, New York, by train, and I met him at the train station in Toledo. On our trip, after we ran out of conversation, I told him about this kid Don Elston. And the boss got quite a kick out of it, thought it was very interesting, very unusual. He'd heard of kids writing a couple times a week, but not every day, and not for almost four months. I didn't accept it that way; I was upset about this kid putting the pressure on me. And I told my boss: the kid can't pitch.

"After he got over his chuckles, the boss said that when I got back, he wanted me to go sign that kid. 'Any boy that would do what he did deserves a chance. Can't give him any money, but we'll sign him.'

"Well, when I returned back, I drove down to that little town back there. The family didn't have a phone, so I couldn't let them know I was coming, and I had to take my chances that he'd be home. I knocked on the door, and the mother answered. I told her who I was, and Don, he was in the next room, and he heard my name mentioned. *Boy.* He jumped right up, ran over. 'C'mon in!' he says. 'You come to sign me, huh?'

"So I signed Don Elston, and he made it to the major leagues and was one of the best relief pitchers of his time. And that's the story of Don Elston."

We were beginning to hit the suburbs. Dayton is one of those peculiar landlocked midwestern cities, like Columbus and Indianapolis, which seems to be all suburb and no downtown. Painted on the side of an office building was the city's new motto: "It's Great in Dayton."

"What happened to his fastball?" I asked. "Did he develop, or did you just miss seeing something about him?"

"Well, both. He got a little bigger, but mostly I didn't see the most important thing about a player, and the kind of thing that a young scout, like I was then, probably wouldn't see. My boss made me sign him; I didn't want to. But I learned a valuable thing from Don Elston." Tony's voice hushed. "*I could not see what was inside of him.* Even though he wrote me every day. But when I started to think about it, after he started to develop, I realized he may not have the talent, but he's going to make it up with guts, and that's what happened."

Tony directed me north, toward the Little York Road Knights Inn.

"So you see, Mark, scouting is always talent in combination with what's inside of a ball player. We can't see that. We can guess at it. The kid was trying to say, 'There's more of me than you saw today, and I won't give up until you see it.' Now, to me, that's a key to my business: guessing what's inside, and guessing right."

We reached the Knights Inn too early to check in, so our first stop in Dayton was a ballpark. "Sinclair Community College might be practicing here later. I want to see what shape the field's in."

Howell Field was tucked into the front corner of a green public park in a neighborhood of clean, white frame houses and small, perfect, fenced-in backyards. The outfield fence was deep enough—about 320 down the lines—to make it plain this was no softball field; Howell Field was a baseball diamond. A hillside behind the backstop provided natural seating. The dugouts and press box were freshly painted. A backhoe was parked at second base.

"I wouldn't say the field's in too good of shape, Tony. Looks like the outfield's dug up a little, too."

"They always used to practice here in the fall. Let's see if we can find someone to ask."

I looked around. There was only one other car in the parking lot, which I presumed belonged to the woman in the distance pushing a toddler on a swing.

In the home team dugout, Tony found a man eating an Egg McMuffin. Over his shirt and tie he wore a blue windbreaker with a Dayton Parks & Recreation logo.

"Is Sinclair going to practice here?" Tony said.

"I'm sure they're not," the man said. "I got a crew coming in here to finish putting in a sprinkler system, and then we're going to try to resod the infield before the weather turns on us. We didn't get any rain here in August or September, so we had to wait until now."

Tony and the man speculated about the several fields where the community college team might be practicing. We left him to finish his McMuffin.

"You want to know another thing about Don Elston," Tony asked me. "His first year, he was assigned to Class D, Janesville, Wisconsin. But in spring training that year, in Jacksonville, Florida, a strange thing happened: the boy had a ruptured appendix."

Tony stopped where the third-base bleachers had been, and began studying the ground. "This is always a good place to look, underneath people's seats. Anyway, I was in camp there, and I rushed the kid to the hospital, and the doctor said the boy had to be operated on *immediately* if we're going to save his life, and even then it's only fifty–fifty. We couldn't call the parents, of course, and I had to sign all the papers."

We made our way down the foul line, heads down, looking for change.

"Don asked me to stay in the operating room with him, and they allowed me to put a mask on and do that. After I'd been watching that operation a little while, holding on to the boy's hand even after he was under, the nurse kept wiping my forehead, and she finally said I better go sit down. I did, but I stayed with him in that hospital."

The parking lot was paved with dull white gravel, but all I could find were bottle tops.

"For five days, I hardly left the hospital. Ten days later they let him out, and you know all the rest. Now would that story be of any value to you, writing a book?"

We circled the parking lot, splitting up now. I got discouraged, and though I pretended to keep looking, I watched Tony instead. The most successful scout in the history of baseball shuffled slowly through a public park, eyes fixed on the ground as if he'd lost something: car keys, a watch, maybe an Elks Lodge ring. He bent over, and I found myself rooting for him to come up with a coin. Behind us, the backhoe's engine roared, and it began to dig, about where a good shortstop would play a left-handed power hitter.

"For my curveball, I've been working on bending my chest a little more so it's got that sharp break," the big young lefty said. Tony and I were waiting in the hallway of the Wright State fieldhouse for practice to begin. On his way to the locker room, the pitcher, Mike McCall, spotted Tony and hustled over to tell the scout what he'd done on his summer vacation. "I'm learning a slider, too."

"Good, good," Tony said, nodding, face blank.

McCall grew up in Ft. Recovery, Ohio, a village of 1,370 on the Ohio–Indiana line. He hadn't been heavily scouted or recruited; Wright State took him on Tony's report. He'd pitched for Muncie that summer in the Great Lakes Summer Collegiate League, one of the increasingly popular amateur baseball summer leagues, along with the Alaska, Shenandoah Valley, Jayhawk, Central Illinois leagues, and the Cape Cod League, the best known. Mike told Tony he'd lost twenty-eight pounds, lifted weights, and added velocity to his fastball. "I hope you get a chance to see me throw while you're here. You know, that is, if you have time and all."

"Oh, yes, I want to see you. We'll be here for three days. I want to see Sinclair and Ohio Dominican, too. How are your parents?"

"They're fine, doing great."

"Your dad's new car running okay?"

"Super. Hey, I saw you on TV this summer."

"You did?" Tony grinned, spoiling his mock surprise.

"Yeah. It was when they had that celebration in Philadelphia for Mike Schmidt's five hundredth homer. You were there, weren't you?"

"Oh, yes. Tell me, how did you recognize me?"

"Well, the hat, I guess. I think you were wearing your hat."

Wright State is one of those prefab commuter colleges that looks like a giant Monopoly piece—arbitrarily set down fully formed on a desolate square of undeveloped land. Like many of these schools with traditions that go back all the way to Tuesday, the place has grown faster than snobs like me would have imagined, bridging the gap from glorified community college to a Division I, seventeen-thousand-student university in what seems to occasional visitors a long weekend. The school is constantly building, hiring and expanding and before long will have a full-time baseball coach with a real office. That probably won't be the immediate boon to the program you'd imagine, since this will also spell the end of the coaching career of Ron Nischwitz. A former big-league pitcher, now owner of several successful Dayton businesses. Nischwitz won't have the time to be a major-college coach.

Nischwitz got tied up at the office and missed all of the jayvee workout, but fall baseball is a relaxed affair, and the coach loped into the athletic department smiling and unhurried. Lean and athletic, Nischwitz is fifty but looks a decade younger. His injury-plagued career was noteworthy for two Hall of Fame footnotes: he was cut by Cleveland to make room for Early Wynn—brought out of retirement as a publicity stunt to win his three hundredth game—and he was the informal personal pitching coach in the late sixties of a young Mets right-hander with perfect technique, Tom Seaver. Nischwitz and Tony shook hands and exchanged chitchat about each other's family. Towering about a foot over the old scout, Nischwitz doted on Tony's every syllable, as if greeting a beloved, seldom-seen uncle. "Well, I promised I'd see a young man work out," Tony said, introducing me to Nischwitz and heading out to the field.

We stood watching Tony. "If there was ever a living institution," Nischwitz said, "it's that man right there. You know, if I have a good player, Tony'd be the guy I'd like him to sign with, since he's done so many favors for me. One time, he signed a boy in late May who was thinking of coming to school here. The latter part of July, Tony calls me up. 'Say, Ron, are you still looking for a catcher?' 'I sure am,' I said. And he told me about a boy up in Michigan named Wayne McCann, who came into our program, took the leadership of our ball club, and last year we ended up second in the nation in Division II. Wayne ended up becoming an all-American. I never knew anything about this young man. I would *never* have known anything about this young man if it wouldn't have been for Tony. Tony didn't have to do that, but he said, 'Well, you got me a ball player, and now I got you one.' That's how he works."

Nischwitz shares office space with several other coaches. His cubicle is about the size you'd expect for an entry-level management trainee with Mead Paper, not the head coach for a Division I baseball team. He has to change clothes in the cavernous locker room with the coaches and players of all the other sports. "Tony's different from other scouts. There was a young man that we had signed, a six-foot-five left-handed pitcher, who was going to be a big part of our program. About two weeks before school starts, the young man calls and says he signed with another ball club. That scout who signed him has yet to say, 'Hey, sorry I took this guy. I know you were counting on him and that you had scholarship money extended to him that you're not going to be able to replace, but I'll find you someone else. I'll make it up to you.' I'd expect that. And this scout's not a bad guy, but he's just not the class act Tony is."

"How long have you known Tony?"

Nischwitz laughed. "About as long as I can remember. Maybe since about 1952, when I was a sophomore in high school. I went to Dayton Fairview right here in town, and Tony scouted me real hard, got to know my mom and dad, took a real interest in me. When I decided to go to Ohio State, he respected that—and kept scouting me. I would have really liked to sign with Tony, but my dad thought we ought to go with the highest offer, and that was from the Detroit Tigers, for a thirty-five-thousand-dollar bonus, which was a lot of money in 1958. How many big leaguers has Tony signed, do you know?"

"Forty-nine."

"Well, I'd have liked to have made it fifty, and if it wasn't for the Chicago Cubs, I would have. If the offer had been close, I would've signed with Tony."

Nischwitz finished dressing, and I walked with him out to the field. An intrasquad game was underway: the second inning, according to the scoreboard. I asked if he agreed with Tony that the game of baseball is imperiled.

"I consider it a crisis, yes," he said. Nischwitz has seen good players who've rarely thrown a ball outside of an organized practice or league game. "Young men simply don't throw the ball enough. Whether this is a reversible trend, I just don't know."

We stopped at the edge of the dugout, and as he spoke, his left fielder threw a ball in the vague vicinity of the cutoff man with scarcely enough on it to be governed by the laws of gravity.

The coach shrugged. "I just don't know."

I asked him about Tony's wall theory.

"That could well be the answer. I know I did that, as a kid. And you know, we had an outfielder here, Fred Felton, who just signed with the Phillies, who came in here all last winter and hit two hundred of those little plastic golf balls *every day*."

I looked around for Tony, but I didn't see him anywhere, not in the bullpen, the bleachers, the press box, the outfield, nowhere. I watched a lackluster inning and then noticed the white Caprice parked in the access drive near the first-base line, engine running, Tony Lucadello behind the wheel.

I got in the passenger side. "Ready to go?"

"Yes. I saw what I came to see today."

"Oh, did Mike McCall warm up for you?"

"Yes, I saw him pitch, too."

"So what was it you came to see today?"

"Another young man. A freshman. No one knows about him but me."

Knights Inns are made up of what is called "modular housing," which means that they're manufactured in chunks in a Columbus, Ohio, factory, then delivered and assembled on a vacant lot. *Voila!* Instant motel. Inside, the carpet is scarlet shag, the furniture black Naugahyde, the curtains and bedspread purple velour. Festooned on the wallpaper are swords, shields, crests and murals of shuttered windows opening up on a view of a purple sky. Still, the rooms are clean, functional and reasonably large. The overall effect is a wholesome Canadian whorehouse.

The next morning when I went to the front desk to buy a newspaper, the desk clerk stopped me. "Hey, are you the one traveling with Tony?"

"Yeah. I'm, uh, writing a book about him."

She smiled. "Good. Tony, he's my favorite. I've known him five years, ever since this place opened. Lots of scouts stay here, but Tony's the tops. They're all kinda lonely, see, and they'll come down here and talk. Some of 'em talk about women, bragging and all. Some talk about drinking. Some talk about all the famous people they know. Tony, he just talks nice. When Tony says he's going to bring you something, like a Phillies hat or a baseball for your little boy, why, he brings it. Not like some of those other knuckleheads."

The clerk showed me a snapshot on the bulletin board behind her. She and Tony stood with their arms around each other, her in a Phillies cap and Tony in a corduroy fedora.

"He's a sweetheart, a good man," she said.

At breakfast, I told Tony about the unsolicited testimonial. "Oh, that Ernestine. She's on the day shift now. Isn't she nice? It's like that wherever I go. When you travel like I do, you like to see familiar faces, so I stay where they like me, see."

My biscuits and gravy came, and I wondered just where Tony Lucadello had been where people didn't like him. But as we were walking out, with Tony insisting on leaving the tip, I got an idea. He left only fifty cents for checks that totaled about eight bucks. I had neither the gall to ask if he thought he should leave more nor the presence of mind to slip a buck under my plate to make things right. So we walked, and when we reached the car, a teenager busing the table caught my eye, held up the two quarters, and glowered.

About then the morning's cold drizzle turned into real rain, and we returned to the motel, doubtful the game would be played. In Tony's room, we each read every word of every baseball story in that day's USA Today. We expected to spend the day watching the league championship series games between the Twins and Tigers and the Giants and Cardinals. The rain fell ever harder.

In the Giants–Cards game, Will Clark hit a two-run homer that almost turned into a pathetic out. If base runners pass one another, they're out, but Candy Maldonado, on first, didn't even look at the ball, figuring it would be caught, and trotted back to the base. Clark, elated, didn't look at Maldonado. They spotted each other just past first—and came within inches of passing.

"For heaven's sake!" Tony said. "Do you see what I mean? Now do you believe me? You shouldn't be seeing plays like that in Little League, and here these teams are, in the playoffs. Sixty-seven percent of the players in the major leagues today aren't first-division ballplayers, even on the good teams. Now do you see why I say our game's in danger?"

The phone rang. It was Ron Nischwitz. The game with Sinclair was on, despite the rain. Tony grabbed his overcoat and gloves, flicked off the television, and we set out to see a ball game in a cold, autumn rainstorm.

Carl Loewenstine aimed the radar gun at a small pitcher with poor mechanics, then checked the display and wrote "68" on a printed scorecard on his clipboard. He shook his head and tapped his World Series ring on the press-box desktop. The next pitch was hit, and Carl timed the runner with a stopwatch, watching him churn bits of mud for far too long. "Not much talent out here, Tony."

"Yeah, maybe Sinclair don't have much this year."

"Neither team. Mark, look out there. Do you see any players that impress you?"

"Not really."

Tony walked to the other end of the press box.

"Maybe it's the weather," Carl said. "This ain't exactly the best conditions to judge baseball talent."

Although the Los Angeles Dodgers make him use a radar gun and a stopwatch, Carl Loewenstine is one of Tony's many protégés, one of the dozens of men who've become full-time major league scouts after being brought along slowly by the master. Carl's own playing career had fizzled in the low minors, and he was an assistant coach at a Cincinnati high school when, in 1975, he approached Tony Lucadello and told the old scout that his ambition was to be a full-time scout. The next year, Tony made Carl one of his part-time men and accompanied him to scores of games. Tony got Carl a full-time job with the Phillies, which led to his current job as chief midwestern scout for the Dodgers. The most important lesson Tony taught, Carl said, was not to sit on the fence with a player. Although any sign of talent should make you take notice, "There comes a point in time where you eventually have to pull the trigger and say, 'This guy's a prospect,' or 'He's not a prospect.' " Tony pointed out countless things to be evaluated in order to make the decision, everything from throwing motion to ankle circumference, from good manners to square shoulders.

A lesson almost as important, Carl said, was the sight of Tony in action signing a player, "the most difficult part of our job nowadays." Tony sits down with the whole family and explains the Phillies organization in great detail, beginning with the owner and general manager and proceeding to the coaches who will be overseeing this particular young man, and then to the contract itself, provision by provision, codicil by codicil, line by line. At signing time most scouts are strangers to the parents, but Tony, trained in the years before the draft, usually gets to know the family. When it's time to sign, they trust him, and their son signs that contract.

Though Carl is in his late thirties, with a drawl, a bushy red mustache, a chaw of tobacco, a Dodgers World Series ring, and friends in the country-music business, he has more in common with his mentor than appearances suggest. After Tony secured him the full-time job with the Phillies in 1979, Carl was first assigned to the Deep South. As we sat in an unheated press box in rain-soaked Dayton watching mediocre players flail about on a muddy field, Carl started telling stories. The best involved a quest into deepest bayou country on the trail of a huge high-school dropout with a blazing fastball, no shoes, a drinking problem, and a pregnant twelve-year-old girl friend. Carl ended up signing the kid, whose can't-miss fastball couldn't save him when he left his minor league team in

Oklahoma to rob a bank, trying to get enough money for the girl friend to buy her own house.

I asked why baseball has always been such fertile territory for stories and storytellers. My theory is that ball players, coaches, and scouts have so much time to kill that those who can tell the best, funniest, most ornate stories are naturally the most popular, which helps them stay in baseball, which allows them to amass and embellish more stories. Carl nodded, spat, and said maybe so. "My own theory on that," he said, "is that every player in major league baseball has overcome the odds. Only a tiny fraction of the players who are stars in high school or college ever get signed. Then, probably only one in two hundred of *those* players make it to the majors. Then, only about half of *those* players stay around long enough to say so. Of the ones who do, most are out of the game in five or six years. Your players who make it, really make it, are one in several million. Everybody's a long shot. But there's always that chance. And that's the great equalizer, the thing you'll find in most every real baseball story."

At the other end of the press box, Tony was pacing, ostensibly for warmth, but partly out of frustration at being confined in one place during a ball game. He had been talking to a woman wearing a huge green Wright State windbreaker, the mother of the new pitcher. Tony introduced her to Carl, who stood up and tipped his cap. The pitcher had thus far pitched two perfect innings, and a week ago I would have thought more of him. But after a few days with Tony, I could see that he was a good pitcher only above the waist. The kid's knees were stiff and he was landing on his heel and he wasn't pushing off well, and I dreaded the mother's inevitable question.

"So," she said. "Do you two think he has talent? Do you think he might make it?"

Tony and Carl stared straight ahead toward the soaked field.

"This," Carl finally said, "is no kind of weather to judge talent in."

The woman nodded, then turned to Tony. "Thank you," she said. "I'll tell him about the wall."

Mike McCall entered the game in the fifth inning, and Ron Nischwitz came up to the press box to see if McCall was lighting up Carl's radar gun.

"How was that second pitch?"

"Eighty." An average major league fastball is eighty-five.

"Thought it was faster."

Tony walked as far away from the ray-gun conversation as the press box would allow.

Nischwitz handed me some faded envelopes. "After I talked to you yesterday, I thought you might be interested in these."

They were letters from Tony.

The first, dated April 26, 1955, was written on the station-ery of the Anthony Wayne Hotel in Hamilton, Ohio, under-neath a line reading, HAMILTON PRODUCTS ARE FAMOUS THE WORLD OVER.

Dear Ron,

Was thinking about you to-day and wondering about the play-off game with Kiser and if it has been played. Since I left Dayton I ran into nothing but rain. I am just getting ready to leave for Oxford, Ohio and see Miami Univ. & Cincinnati play.

I was very proud of your fine pitching in both games I saw. You looked like a big leaguer and I sent a fine report to my home office about you. Well, Ronnie, take good care of yourself and watch that arm. Give my best to your wonderful mother & father.

Sincerely,
Tony Lucadello.

The next, dated May 1, 1955, written on Cubs stationery, read:

Dear Ronnie:

Now that I have arrived home for a few days, I feel that I should thank you and your wonderful family for the nice way you received me in your home. This is perhaps the nicest thing about my job and that is to meet people like you and yours. . . .

My plans call for me to see your game of May 9th, against Wilbur Wright and I hope that you will work this game.

I certainly was impressed by you as a person and also with your mother and father. With this back ground and your fine ability, I can see that you will enjoy success in your goal.

Yours in Sports,
Tony Lucadello

The third letter was dated May 13, 1955, and was written on the crest-topped stationery of the Indiana Hotel in Ft. Wayne.

Dear Ronnie:

Would like to let you know that I have been thinking about you and hope that everything is fine at your home. I certainly did enjoy my visit last week with your fine father. He really is tops and a wonderful person to talk with.

Sorry that I didn't get a chance to see you more, but I did enjoy our talk over the phone. Take care of yourself and give my best to your family. Good luck and health.

Sincerely,
Tony Lucadello

The fourth, written five days later, was from the Hotel LaSalle in South Bend, Indiana. The embossed stationery featured a drawing of the nine-story hotel and, across the top, "250 COMFORTABLE ROOMS • WONDERFUL BEDS • MODERATELY PRICED DINING ROOM • AND COFFEE SHOP."

Dear Ronnie:

Just a few words to let you know that I am thinking about you and hoping that you are having nothing but success. Just saw Purdue play Notre Dame University. I am now listening to the Cubs and Phillies game. Won the first and still winning the second game of a doubleheader.

Plan to phone you about Sunday to find out where your next game will be next week. Take care of yourself and lots of success, Ronnie.

Sincerely,
Tony Lucadello

Nischwitz showed them to Tony, who chuckled. "You saved these letters all these years? Hmmm. I must have been a pretty good little letter writer back then."

The ex-phenom told the old scout he could keep the letters if he wanted. Tony thanked him.

Down on the field, Mike McCall gave up a long line drive. The center fielder slipped, and the ball rolled to the fence. McCall slapped his glove against his thigh as the runner circled the muddy base path and scored standing up.

"I signed Mike Schmidt in that Holiday Inn right there," Tony said. "June of 1971. Room 308. It was the culmination of six years of some of the most intense scouting I've ever done."

Dayton's morning rush hour was over and we were driving down a rain-slick, deserted I-75, on our way to see Jack and

Lois Schmidt, the parents of the man Tony calls "the best all-around third baseman in the history of the game of baseball."

"Just about the time I started scouting Mike, in 1965, the draft came in and changed scouting forever. In the old days, what I would have done was get in good with Mike and the family, knowing that if my offer was close, I could get him to sign with me. But now I had to change my strategy. Now, if other scouts knew my feelings about a player, they could recommend him to their front office, and all my hard work would be for nothing.

"But Mike was special, and I used a special approach to signing him. In the spring of 1965, one of my part-time men, Ed French, called to say there was a talented sophomore at Dayton Fairview high school that he thought I should see, an infielder by the name of Mike Schmidt. I went to check him out, and right away I could see he was an excellent athlete and an above-average prospect. Sometimes he would do things that would amaze me. Other times he would make errors or look just terrible up at the plate. This gave me an edge right away, see, because other scouts, they'd see him and they'd pick at all those flaws. But I sensed Mike Schmidt would be a late bloomer.

"So from then on, I mapped out my strategy. While he was in high school, I never once contacted Mike, or Jack and Lois, or his coach, or anyone close to him, for fear other scouts would find out. I saw him play several more times before he graduated, but always hiding behind the other team's dugout or in trees or bushes. I got to know a janitor there and he'd let me up on the roof of a building that overlooked the field. Sometimes, if I got to the game and saw other scouts' cars, I'd just drive on.

"I was pleased that when he graduated, Mike went to college at Ohio University, which at that time was coached by one of the best baseball men in my territory, Bobby Wren. Bobby and I were friends, and he'd always been fair with me, so I confided in him and told him I was interested in signing Mike. Bobby knew I was a target for other scouts, and he never once tipped my hand.

"His freshman year, Mike hit only .260, with just one home run, and he fielded poorly. Other scouts cooled off on him then, but I still knew he'd be a late bloomer. The hardest thing about scouting is projecting if a player's mind is ahead of his body or if his body is ahead of his mind, and guessing when they'll get together. With Mike, his mind was ahead of his body, which I knew from watching his face and from talking with his coach.

"When the shortstop for Ohio University who started ahead of Mike, Rich McKinney, was drafted and signed, Mike stepped in and became a two-time all-American. Every scout knew about him now, of course, but they could still remember how hard a time he had adjusting, and they wondered if he could adjust to the switch from shortstop to third base. Also, Mike had operations on both his knees while in high school, and that made some scouts shy away. Mike's name would come up, you see, and I'd say, 'Well, there's his knees, you know,' and other scouts, they'd nod in agreement, and I could just see them mentally moving him down a notch on their lists. What they didn't know is that Mike had been on a strict weight program, lifting twenty pounds, then forty, then sixty, until his knees were as good as new.

"At the end, the California Angels had Mike as high on their list as we did. I tried my hardest to convince Paul Owens, our general manager, to draft him first, but they took a pitcher instead, and my heart just sank. But when the California Angels picked, they took a pitcher, too, a young man named Frank Tanana. Fortunately, in the second round, the Phillies picked Mike.

"So in that Holiday Inn back there, I met with Mike and his dad, Jack, and signed a Hall of Fame ballplayer for thirty-five thousand dollars. His first year in the minors, in Reading,

Pennsylvania, Mike had a terrible year, and I caught a little heat for it. 'This kid's a late bloomer,' I said. 'I've seen it before. He'll develop.' Sure enough, the next year, he moved up to triple-A ball in Eugene, Oregon, and just tore up the league. The same thing happened in the majors: his rookie year, he hit for some power, but he also struck out a hundred and thirty-six times in three hundred and sixty-seven at-bats. 'Just hang with him,' I said. And one year later, Mike Schmidt won his first home-run title and was on his way to Cooperstown."

We pulled into Jack's Drive-In, an aluminum building with a white awning and a parking lot pitted where the curbservice consoles used to be.

"An interesting thing about the signing of Mike Schmidt," Tony said. "In his first All-Star Game, who do you think the pitcher was? Frank Tanana! And I believe Mike was the first batter he faced."

"What happened?"

"Mike singled."

Jack and Lois Schmidt sat down for a cup of coffee with us. They'd spent more time with Tony at the celebration to honor Mike's five hundredth homer than they had in the six years Tony had scouted their son, and they were amazed to learn how many games the old scout had attended. Jack, a tanned, relaxed man in an Izod sweater, was clearly the bigger baseball fan, and he and I chatted about Mike's career statistics for a while. Jack asked if I'd played baseball. "Poorly," I said. "I'm destined to be more of a fan than a player. The only sport I was ever particularly good at was swimming."

Lois, who ran the small indoor pool next door, brightened. "Mike swam, too," she said. "His best was butterfly."

"Mine was breaststroke."

"Did you swim in college?"

"Just a year."

Lois and I talked about swimming for a while as Jack's

eyes wandered to the dining area's lone wall decoration, a poster of his son. Then he and Tony rehashed the day in 1971 when they negotiated Mike's first pro contract, and we all joined in speculation about how much longer Mike would play.

"He'll miss it," Lois said. "After he quits, there's nothing anyone can give him that'll be like the charge he gets from the cheers of a packed stadium."

"I'd like to see him go out on top," Jack said.

"I think he will, Jack." Tony Lucadello broke into a grin. "But as long as a man has fun doing his job, and as long as he does it well, I don't see any reason he'd want to retire."

Fred Felton had eyes on his bat.

During the fall and winter, the young Phillies prospect lived in a dorm room at Wright State, finishing up his business degree. On the walls of his cement room were inspirational Bible verses and posters of Steve Garvey and Roberto Clemente, Fred's two baseball heroes. Of the two, he was built more like Clemente—tall, thin and graceful, with a good arm and great speed—and Clemente had been Fred's idol since his childhood in downtown Pittsburgh.

Fred and I went to his room to grab a Hefty bag full of plastic golf balls, his batting glove and his favorite Louisville Slugger, on which Fred has drawn a pair of scowling eyes. "You've heard the expression 'That ball had eyes'?"

"Sure," I said. "For balls that go right between fielders."

"Well, this bat has eyes. It lets me see the ball with my hands."

I wondered if this idea came from a baseball coach or a power-of-positive-thinking Bible-study leader. Fred Felton, an effusive, personable young man, was a defensive standout during his years at Wright State, but his bat hadn't come around until he devoted himself to Tony Lucadello's plastic golf ball drill. He didn't get hits right away, either, but that summer, while playing for an Athletes in Action team in Oklahoma, something clicked, and the eyes on Fred Felton's bat began to look out on line drives sprayed to all fields. When Don Williams, the Phillies scout in Oklahoma, Texas and Louisiana, found out that Fred had gone to school in Tony Lucadello's territory, he called the old scout and convinced him that the team should sign the speedy outfielder.

Fred and I went to a study lounge on a women's floor. "There's never anyone in this one during the day," Fred said, moving the furniture around. "Now, you just kneel there and toss them into the strike zone."

It took me a few throws to get the hang of it, but I quickly reached the point where I could challenge Fred by placing balls high and low, on all corners of the imaginary plate. Fred swung hard at every ball, never missing, sending the tiny things whistling into the wall and ricocheting all over the room, into pizza boxes, ash trays, couches, chairs, tables, framed starving-artist oil paintings. This was the first time I'd seen a grown man do the drill, and it was a little scary, especially when the force was confined to such a small space. While he didn't have the fluidity of young Matt Stone, Fred Felton slapped the balls around with manly, unrestrained grunts, and sweat flying off his brow.

After Fred had hit the bag of balls twice, never missing a single ball, and we had retrieved stray balls from beneath couches smelling of stale beer, I made a crazy, hubris-propelled request. "Let me try that."

I took savage swings at the first ten balls Fred tossed, missing them all. "That's my fault," Fred graciously admitted. "Those were bad throws. But, boy, do you have a nice powerful swing."

I missed the next toss, and the next, and the next.

"I think you have a little uppercut there," Fred opined, echoing the Little League coaches of summers past.

By now, I was sweaty, ashamed, and a little pissed. On the next toss, I relaxed. *Just meet the ball.* Whiff.

"Hoo! That was close! If you'd have connected with that, you'd've taken that pizza box out."

I hadn't seen Matt Stone, Jason Myers, or Fred Felton swing and miss *even once.* "I can't believe I can't do this," I said. "This is awful embarrassing."

"Aw, a tree'll never grow if you keep choppin' it down."

When I finally managed to foul off a couple balls, I hung it up. "I'm getting a blister," I said, between huffs and puffs.

"That last swing was close."

I handed the bat back to Fred Felton, who rubbed it with a towel, gently, a firearm returned to the custody of a marksman.

By the time I returned to the field, the Wright State–Ohio Dominican game was in the second inning. "You didn't miss much," Carl Loewenstine told me. "Last year, I signed the shortstop off of Ohio Dominican. Fourth-round draft. But it don't look like they got much to replace him this year."

Wright State batted around on the Ohio Dominican pitcher, a stiff-legged little guy with a shot-put throwing motion. "He's what we call a short-armer," Carl told me. The pitcher used only the range of motion from his elbow to his wrist, rather than taking advantage of his entire throwing motion, from shoulder to fingertips.

I looked at Tony and he nodded in agreement.

In the bottom of the inning a tall redhead came in to pitch for Wright State. His first pitch lit up Carl's raygun at eighty-four miles per hour. "We may have something here, Tony," Carl said, clicking his mechanical pencil and making notes on his little cards.

"Could be," Tony said, opening the door of the press box and making his way down toward the field.

"Eighty-four's pretty doggone good for a freshman," Carl said.

"Do you think he looks so good just in contrast to Ohio Dominican's pitcher?" I asked. "I mean, does context ever play tricks on you?"

"Yeah, that happens. But this kid here's six four, and throwing hard is throwing hard, period."

Tony stood near the Wright State dugout, chatting with a coach.

The pitcher, Mike Mathile, finished the inning with another eighty-four-mile-per-hour fastball. But in the next inning, Mathile began to slow into the high seventies, and Carl began to point out flaws in his pitching motion. The worst, Carl said, was that Mathile's arm was too far back when his front foot hit the ground. Ideally, the arm should be halfway through the range of motion when the foot makes contact; Mathile's was just getting started. Carl kept making notes and glancing at his radar gun. Finally, an inning later, as Ohio Dominican began to hit Mathile a little bit, Carl put his pencil down. "There's just no way this kid can throw a major league fastball with a motion like that." The Dodger scout sat back in his chair and sighed.

Tony Lucadello opened the press box door. "Well, I've seen as much as I need to," he said. "Are you ready, Mark?"

"Too bad about that Mathile kid," Carl said. "I thought we had one there. Maybe he'll still come around, who knows?"

"Who knows?" Tony said.

Tony and Carl shook hands, the last time that season that they would see each other. Each man seemed tired, each happy that the off-season was near.

On our way to Tony's car, behind the bleachers and out of Carl's view, a woman intercepted Tony and introduced herself as Mark Mathile's mother.

"I know who you are," Tony said. "I've seen you at other

games of Mike's. He's a fine young man, Mrs. Mathile. You deserve a lot of credit."

And then it clicked: *this* was the pitcher Tony had worked out yesterday. The freshman no other scouts knew about was Mike Mathile.

It turns out that Tony had convinced Mike, a Dayton resident, to go to school at Wright State rather than the University of Michigan. He thought Ron Nischwitz would do a good job with a big-league pitching prospect, and Michigan coach Bud Middaugh has a reputation for wrecking pitchers' arms. Also, though Tony didn't come right out and say this, he wanted to hide Mike at a more obscure school.

"I'm glad, as a mother, that he stayed close to home," Mrs. Mathile said. "Mike really likes it here, too. Thanks so much for your help, Mr. Lucadello."

"I want to tell you something," Tony said, his voice hushed. "Your son has a *really* good chance to make it all the way. He really does."

Mrs. Mathile took a deep breath. "We hope so," she said. "That's all he's working for, and he's working hard."

Mike came over to shake hands with the old scout.

"I have to ask a favor of you," Tony said. "I'd like you to keep this to yourselves, what I've said to you today. If other scouts find out how much I like Mike's chances, I won't have a chance."

"We promise," Mrs. Mathile said, and Mike nodded in agreement.

"Please say hello to your husband," Tony said. "I'm so sorry I didn't get to see him today."

"He'll be sorry he missed you, too," she said. "But I'll surely tell him."

In the car, I asked Tony about the reservations Carl had registered about Mike Mathile's mechanics. He shook his head. "Mike's a little out of shape. Plus, he's just a freshman. Those things are easily corrected. Mike has all the good pluses to develop into a first-division major league pitcher. Even when he slowed down a little, his fastball had good movement on it. And he's starting to get a good sharp curveball. It's easy to talk yourself out of a ball player, but the most important thing about scouting is being able to *project* what a player will be able to do. This young man could be a good one. If other scouts don't find out what I think of him, this young man could very well be my fiftieth major leaguer."

As we drove through the redundancy of suburban Dayton, en route to the purple splendor of the Knights Inn, I remembered the looks of puppy-dog loyalty on the faces of the Mathiles. If they have any choice in the matter, I thought, Mike Mathile will sign with Tony Lucadello in 1990, on the way to his major league debut, which Tony projected as approximately July 1993—the month the old scout would turn eighty.

4

The Gravesite
of Pop Haines

In Virginia, where I live now, Indian summer is merely annoying, because it is, in fact, summer. You cannot wear wool clothing. You wish the public pools were still open. You sweat, and because you are sweating in October, you swear. But in the Midwest where I grew up, Indian summer has the graceful fragility of a doomed queen. In a part of the world where a foot of snow may stay on the ground for a month, a warm October day when even windbreakers are optional is a treat. After three wintry, rainy days, Tony and I woke to a day brighter than the penny Tony found on the way to breakfast.

This scouting trip, he told me, was really over, but he had one more important stop, in Coldwater, Ohio. "To give what help I can to a young catcher who's having a hard time of it now," he said. "His father, Louis Brunswick, is a friend of mine. The whole family's a great story. You'll see that for yourself."

We took a two-lane state road, Ohio 49, most of the way there. "I'm taking the backcountry because today we got time to," he said. "And I'm a backcountry man anyway."

I marveled aloud about the weather.

"That's a plus today. Actually, we've had better-than-usual weather on this trip. Up here in the midwest area, the weather is a big handicap. You see players under strange conditions. In fall baseball, they don't replay games that are rained out, snowed out, what have you. I think my success lies here: I realize the weather conditions in my area. One time last year, I'm down in the southern part of Indiana and I'm waiting there to see a ball game, but the way the weather is—rain, snow, sleet, hail—I don't know if I'm going to see one all week.

"So what do I do? I get out all my reports on all the players in southern Indiana, and I call their coaches and say, 'Hey, I'm over here in Bloomington to see Indiana University. I'm staying at the Knights Inn over here, that new one. There's no way I'm going to be able to see a ball game. I know the high schools don't have anything scheduled now, but are you working out indoors?' I tell them who I want to see, and they set it up for me. I spend a few hours calling around, and before you know it, I have seventeen good high-school ball players I'm supposed to see. If you can't judge a ball player indoors, you can't judge a ball player, simply because the fact is that all you want to see is the body control, all you want to see is his reactions. He can show you his arm indoors, his running speed indoors, his hand action indoors, his bat swing indoors. That's all you're going to see if you saw a ball game outdoors. It's a lot better doing that than sitting in your motel room doing nothing, right? And by the time I'd seen those seventeen ballplayers—some good, some not, some I knew about, some I didn't—the weather had cleared up, and I got to see those college games I'd come to see in the first place."

I can see the aging shortstop digging his big car out of a snowbank at the Knights Inn, driving down unmarked roads to rural high schools, parking behind the industrial arts room, and finding the coach in the teachers' lounge. They pull the kid out of Spanish class and watch him work out in a corner of the gymnasium, while puzzled members of a phys ed class are distracted from their killball game long enough to watch their schoolmate turn phantom double plays and the little old man in the hat purse his lips and nod.

"Did I ever tell you The Great Storm Story," Tony asked.

"I don't think so."

"The greatest story in the world. I'll tell it to you. If you ever speak before an audience, you tell that story, and you'll get a hand that'll really shake you up. You can tell 'em the old scout gave you that story. Here it is."

In the driver's seat, Tony sat back, adjusted the brim of his hat, and drove the next mile in silence. He looked straight ahead, northbound on Ohio 49, and his eyes took on a glaze of fond remembrance and judicious embellishment.

"It happened many years ago, in fact it was July the seventh, 1952. I had to go to Edwardsburg, Michigan, to see Edwardsburg play Niles in an American Legion game that would determine which team went to the regionals. It had been raining steady every day. The regionals began just three days later, and they had to get that game in before the three days were up, because if they didn't, they'd have to flip a coin to determine the winner. The first day it was raining, and I went to Edwardsburg—I was staying in a motel over in Niles, only fifteen miles down the road—and stayed in my car until they canceled the game. The next day I went out there again. Sa-a-ame thing.

"Neither team wanted to flip a coin, because they both felt they could win, so the third day, the final day, it was not raining, but it was heavy overcast, still some darkness, still a lot of clouds, but not raining. Well, they went out and got two big truckloads of sawdust and threw it all over that field and they started to play. They were going to play seven innings.

"You could see flashes of lightning way out west, and I wondered how long this would last. Going into the fourth inning of the ball game, the score nothing to nothing, a squad car came out, and the policeman made this announcement: 'There's a tornado sighted in the west, coming this direction, and everybody here should vacate.'

"Everybody left that ball field but the players and the umpires and me. They kept right on playing. Going into the sixth inning of the game, the score was tied 1–1. Now the storm was right over our heads. The lightning was more frequent, the thundering blasted loose, the wind was starting to blow much harder, the rain started falling, and the darkness settled in. Going into the bottom half of the seventh inning, Edwardsburg, at bat, had a man on second base. There was two outs, and the hitter I wanted to see, a big, strong outfielder, was coming to the plate. I knew the odds were against him if it took him two swings, but I thought there might be time for one more pitch. I was just hoping, hoping the pitcher would throw the ball somewhere near the plate and the kid would swing. Keep in mind, there was a runner on second, two outs. The storm was over the top of us and the rain fell harder.

"He swung at the first pitch, which was a high pitch, and hit a towering, major league, short-center-field fly ball—into the clouds. And it looked like it was bouncing around in the air, with all the wind and the darkness and the lightning and the thunder. The runner on second base had to run, and the hitter ran out to first. The umpire ran out towards center field to see who was gonna catch that fly ball, because the center fielder had to come in, the shortstop had to go out, and even the second baseman had to go out.

"Up and behold, just as the ball started to descend, a bolt of lightning struck the baseball and cut it in three pieces. The center fielder caught a piece, the shortstop caught a piece, and the second baseman caught the third piece. And the umpire dashed towards the mound, and when he reached the mound, the storm broke. It was deafening: the thunder and the wind and the sheets of hard rain. And the umpire reared back and *screamed* his decision. How do you suppose he ruled?"

Caught up in the rhythms of the road and the story, I was startled by the question, like an unprepared student in the back of a lecture hall. "I, um, I think that he called him out, but I mean, uh—"

"All right."

I felt a wave of relief, presuming I'd guessed right.

Tony smiled. "But you, see, you only have two guesses. To get that right, you still have to answer why the umpire ruled it that way."

"Because they all three caught it. I mean, it's no mean feat catching three wobbly fragments of an exploded baseball. Maybe if one of them dropped it, then it would've been—"

"Yeah. But you see, you're wrong. The umpire screamed this: 'Here is my ruling on this play. The run counts. Edwardsburg wins this ballgame 2–1. The hitter who touched first base gets a base hit. And now that the game is over, I will tell you why. The rule states that you have to catch all of the ball. I repeat: *all* of the ball. When that lightning struck that baseball, I saw a few fragments of that ball flying in the wind. They did not catch all of the ball. Edwardsburg wins.' "

We laughed together, and Tony slapped me on the thigh and said, "Now, isn't that a story!"

I closed my eyes and asked The Question. "Um, can you honestly tell me if that story is true?"

"Well, Mark, I'm gonna tell you. I'll put it to you this way. Do you think it's humanly possible for me to tell a story like that, to make it up, if I didn't see it with my own eyes?"

"Not a chance."

A flock of canvasback ducks banked down from a cloudless sky and landed in a sun-dappled farm pond. We turned north onto U.S. 127, the site of epic Indian battles and the signing of the Treaty of Greenville.

"I call that," Tony said, "the greatest decision ever made by an umpire in the history of the game of baseball."

* * *

Tucked in a wooded city park, Coldwater Field is clearly the home of a baseball team with the support of its community. Months after the last game of the year was played here, the field, with new outfield fences, crushed-stone warning track, and freshly renovated dugouts, looks like it could be ready for a regional championship game in about a half hour. The infield is smooth and even, the outfield mown and clean, save for the first fallen leaves of October, sprinkled like toasted coconut across the green surface of the field. Behind the center-field scoreboard—which the Kiwanis have pledged to replace next year—is a community center. The coach lives in a white ranch-style that is a 350-foot foul ball down the right-field line. Coldwater, a community of just 4,220, boasts a baseball field which would be the pride of many college programs. Its only quirk is a small, rolling hill in left-center field, so that outfielders must run uphill in pursuit of long fly balls, and long fly balls must clear the top of an eight-foot fence on top of an eight-foot hill to be a home run. This by no means makes the field bush-league. On the contrary, like the Green Monster of Fenway and the ivy of Wrigley, Coldwater Field's hill is a reminder of baseball the way it was meant to be. In an era when every American city seems intent on building look-alike, giant, plastic-carpeted, mutated oil filters and calling them ball parks, the Coldwater Fields of the world remind us that this is the only major sport where the playing field varies from town to town, where individuality trumps conformity.

"Come over here," Tony told me. "I have something to show you." Near the ballpark, past the netting of batting cages, rose huge slabs of cement, each about a foot wide and twelve feet high. "What do you think this is?"

"Handball courts?"

"Walls. Baseball walls. I signed a pitcher named Louis

Brunswick to a contract in 1948, right out of high school. But he played just three years, hurt his arm, and that was that. He fought in Korea for three years, then went to college, got his degree, and got the coaching job here."

We walked around the cement walls as if taking in a provocative Max Ernst sculpture. Tony ran his hand lightly along the smooth surfaces.

"His first four or five years, Louis Brunswick was not a successful coach. So he contacted me and asked me if I had any idea how to help him. I made a special trip down here to talk to him about it, and I told him to build a wall near the baseball field somewhere. This is a city park here, so he went to the park board, but they refused to build a wall. He told me, and I said, 'Well, here's what you do. Go over and tell 'em you're gonna use it for racquetball, tennis balls, handball. For *girls*. And he did, and they said they'd build this wall right away. The girls never used it. But he had all these little elementary school kids started, throwing balls against these walls. And he had them out on the field, hitting plastic golf balls."

Tony bent over to pick up an old baseball with the cover half off, red string puffing out from its seams.

"Eighteen years later, Louis Brunswick had become the most successful coach in the history of the state of Ohio. He's won over six hundred games. He's been to the state finals seven or eight times. And he's coached state champs three of the last five years. He's getting close to retirement now, and it's only been this year that he finally revealed to other coaches about these walls. I'd been asking him to for years, but he was afraid of the competition. Here," Tony said, flipping me the battered ball. "Try it yourself."

I pulled off my sweater and faced the rectangular strike zone painted on the wall. I tried to keep in mind some of the fine points of pitching Tony had shown me this week: the cross-seam grip; the position of my feet; the over-the-top throwing motion; the rhythm of my head, leg and arm. After all, here I was, being scouted by *Tony Lucadello!* Maybe my Little League coaches were wrong! Maybe Tony will see some small flash of raw talent, something which, at the very least, will give me the confidence to tear up my city softball league. With every ounce of strength I could summon, I fired the ball at the wall. It was a low strike, and I scooped up the ground ball, barehanded and clean.

"Start slowly, for heaven's sake! What do you want to do, hurt your arm? Start with lobs."

I threw about a dozen more balls. I booted three of them, and my last chance at becoming a big-league ball player—a dream I thought I'd buried at age eleven—slipped away fourteen years later in the gorgeous autumn of west-central Ohio. I picked up my sweater, shaking my head, sheepish about taking that little tryout so seriously. Tony had only been trying to show me the concept of the wall firsthand. He disappeared underneath the bleachers of Coldwater Field, where he found a quarter, and I sat in the first-base dugout, watching as Louis Brunswick's sons Tom and Mark took the field, Tom with a bucket of balls, Mark with two wooden bats and a catcher's mitt.

Mark Brunswick, in his third year of pro ball, hit just .167 in sixteen games with the Class A Lynchburg Mets. Mark was signed for his glove, though, not his bat, which is why the tendinitis in his right shoulder, his throwing shoulder, is more troublesome to the young catcher than his low batting average. Lynchburg had three other catchers last year, and the Mets had since signed two, a second- and a third-round draft choice. But Mark is just twenty-one, and had he gone to college, he would now be starting his senior year, so for a little while longer, time is still his friend. Mark knows, though, that if his shoulder and his hitting don't come around, next year might be the end. He expected to blossom this season and instead had his worst year ever.

There is a determination to this practice that goes beyond two brothers tossing balls in a small-town ballpark on an idyllic day. No small part of this is Tom Brunswick's own failed big-league dreams. Tom, a middle infielder, inked his first pro contract in 1976 with Tony, the very scout who'd signed his father. Tom bounced from Auburn, New York, to Pulaski, Virginia, to Spartanburg, South Carolina; then the Phillies traded him to the Oakland A's, and he finished his career in Modesto, California. Tom is now an assistant coach in nearby Celina, the biggest town in the area, and three or four days a week he pitches to his brother, offering what advice he can, convinced that this is the year Mark's bat will come around, the year the injuries will go away. They start slowly, as Mark loosens up, spraying ground balls all over the infield. After they pick up the first batch of balls—with Tony's help—Mark steps back into the batter's box and starts swinging with power. Line drives to right-center mostly, but he connects for a homer here and there. Tom bears down and throws harder, cautioning his brother not to overswing. Mark nods, but he starts popping balls up. Tony walks over to him and mutters something I can't hear. Mark still pops the ball up, but he looks at Tony and Tony nods. "That's okay," the scout says. "Try it again." And sure enough, a few pitches later, everything clicks, and the last three balls in the bucket wind up over the fence. The last, to center field, goes over four hundred feet: a major league homer.

As we picked up the balls again, I found out that both Tom and Mark had thrown countless balls off those nearby walls. Tom now has his team in Celina use the drills. Mark had thrown off the walls that very day; the battered old ball there was his. "When we were kids, we used the side of the garage a lot, too," Tom said.

"I wish I'd've had stock in the hardward store," Louis Brunswick said. "All those windowpanes I replaced."

If Mark Brunswick doesn't make the major leagues, he could well have a career as a stand-in for Tom Cruise, for whom he is a dead ringer. But for now, baseball's his obsession. Although a little disappointed that the Mets drafted him ahead of the Phillies, and therefore denied him the satisfaction of signing with Tony (and of being Tony's fiftieth big-leaguer), Mark wants nothing more than to be a major league catcher. "Even if I could get up there *for just one day*," he whispered. "*For just one at-bat. For just one pitch*." That spring, when Dwight Gooden was on drug rehab, he pitched his first comeback game for the Lynchburg Mets, and though Mark didn't catch those four shutout innings, the proximity to the sellout crowd and the big-city media made Mark see what his dream would be like. "I'm serious," he said. "*For just one day*."

Mark got behind the plate, catching pitches, positioning to throw, and then—because a trace of tendinitis lingered—lobbing the ball back. Tony stood aside, stone faced, in his scout pose. Mark belongs to the Mets now, Tony had told me. He was here as a friend of the family, and he didn't want to meddle unless asked. But Louis Brunswick asked. "You see anything, Tony?"

"Two hands," said the old scout.

Louis nodded.

Mark took a dozen more balls.

"How do you feel, son," Louis asked.

"Funny. I don't know. It still hurts."

Louis motioned toward Tony.

"Oh," Mark said. "Tony, what do you think?"

"Use two hands when you're catching the ball," he said, walking over to the young catcher, crouching down and pantomiming catching the ball. "That way, your throwing hand is right there. You don't have to waste time reaching around.

And if you have to throw to second, you can come right up, in position to throw, automatically."

When Tony played baseball, every good player caught the ball with two hands. By the 1970s, for reasons mostly to do with style, virtually all big-leaguers caught the ball with one hand. Tony can't see why a player wouldn't want to do a thing the best way, and the one-handed catch fuels his fears for the game of baseball.

"Look, I know the other guys don't do it that way," Tony said, his voice louder. "Why for gosh sake do you want to be like the other guys? Don't you want to be *different*? You start catching the ball with two hands, and the coaches down in spring training will say, 'Hey, this young man's *different*.' That's how players get noticed. They stand out. They're *different*."

Mark tried it. He did in fact look better using two hands, because he could catch the ball, stand up, plant his feet, and throw, all in one motion. But each time he did it, Mark grimaced. He moved mechanically, while Tony, alongside him, guided him through the motions: the legendary choreographer instructing the headstrong young dancer.

"Something's not right," Mark finally said. "If I throw like this, I wouldn't last a month in pro ball before I'd be hurt again."

As Tom, Louis, and I stood aside, spectators to the little ballet, Tony hung in, barking instructions, insisting that good fundamentals couldn't possibly cause an injury, for heaven's sake. But the motion felt unnatural to Mark. His voice became thin and desperate. "If I get hurt, Tony, they got a dozen guys to replace me."

"Fine," Tony said. "You do what you think's best. I'm only telling you what I think's best."

"It's been the same thing for two years now," Mark said. "Nobody knows what I'm going through."

The sun was low in the west and Tony said we had to go.

As Tony and Mark shook hands, they looked into one another's eyes, silently. On Coldwater Field that day, three men who'd played pro ball came out to do what they could for one man still playing, the one who still had a chance to play in the majors, even if just for one day. Every ball player's a long shot, Carl Loewenstine had said, and I wondered if three-to-one was a good bet. Tony and I got into his car and headed home. Behind us, even with the windows rolled up, I could hear the pop of the ball in the glove, fading.

On our way home, we stopped for gas at a Sohio station in Phillipsburg, Ohio, population 700, where full-serve cost no more than self-serve. Tony calculated his mileage on a weathered notepad that featured the Phillies 1983 spring training schedule. "There's something I've always meant to see in this little town," Tony told me. "Have you ever heard of Jesse Haines?"

"Right-handed pitcher for the Cardinals in the twenties and thirties, right? He's in the Hall of Fame, I think."

"That's right. He won about two hundred and ten games for them. Well, he was a boyhood idol of mine, and he lived his whole life right here in this little town. That big stone house up the street there, he built that during the Depression, after the Cardinals won the World Series one year. When I was a young scout, I finally got to meet him once. I was scouting an American Legion game here, and he came up and introduced himself to me. A nice man, a good man. It was a thrill for me."

Haines had pitched for the same team that had signed Tony Lucadello, and while Tony's playing career fizzled out in Fostoria, Haines had gone to the World Series five times, the Cardinals winning in '26, '31 and '34. Haines was no small part of those wins; his career Series record was 3 and 1, with a 1.67 ERA and a .444 batting average. Tony told me he listened to Haines shut out the hated Yankees 4–0 in the second game of the 1926 Series—helping his own cause with a two-run homer. After giving up a homer to Babe Ruth, he won the seventh game 4–3, with relief help from Grover Cleveland Alexander. The Cardinals lost the 1930 Series 4–1 to the Philadelphia A's, Tony said, but that one win was a Jesse Haines four-hitter over the great Lefty Grove, in which Haines pitched no-hit ball the last six innings. "I was seventeen years old at the time," Tony said. "A couple years later, when I signed with the Cardinals, Jesse Haines was one of the guys I hoped to meet someday."

Tony handed his Sohio card to a middle-aged man in coveralls. "Young fellow, you wouldn't maybe have heard of Jesse Haines, have you?"

"Sure I have."

"Do you know where he's buried? I'd like to pay my respects."

"I sure don't. We have three cemeteries around here. Might be any one of them. Could be that those gentlemen inside would know."

We went into the Sohio. Four guys, all about Tony's age, sat on metal chairs clustered around the counter, talking high school football.

"The young man out there said you'd know where Jesse Haines is buried."

As one, all four rose to their feet.

"Did you know him?" asked a guy wearing a hat emblazoned with the logo of the Phillipsburg Volunteer Fire Department.

"Just a little."

"Bethel Cemetery," said a gaunt man in overalls. "You know where that is, don't you?"

"No," Tony said. "I'm not from here."

A man with a Gro-Mor Feed patch on his windbreaker gave Tony directions, and Tony nodded his thanks.

"It's atop a little hill," said a man with a dark hand-carved cane.

"I believe his tomb has two iron Cardinals perched on it," said Phillipsburg Volunteer Fire Department, and Overalls agreed.

"He's buried next to his wife, Carrie," said Dark Cane. "She died here in '81. Pop Haines died in '77."

"No, '78," corrected Gro-Mor Feed.

"Do you remember the year he had in '27?" said Phillipsburg Volunteer Fire Department. "The Pirates nudged the Cards out for the pennant, but old Pop Haines was 24 and 10 that year, with an ERA of about 2.70."

"2.72," corrected Gro-Mor Feed. "Pitched six shutouts and twenty-five complete games."

"Whatever," said Dark Cane. "This was back when the whole league batted close to .300. The Cards should've gone to the Series that year. Shoot, the Yankees swept the Pirates. The way Pop was in the clutch, I think the Cards would've had a chance."

"Against Murderer's Row?" said Overalls, aghast. "Son, it's one thing to root for the hometown boy. It's another thing altogether to be a fool."

Tony and I backed out the door, waving and expressing our thanks. The men waved back and returned to arguing and reminiscing. It was easy to imagine them, sixty years ago, riding their bicycles down to the corner store, buying a couple packs of bubble-gum cards, stuffing the brittle gum into their mouths, and Gro-Mor Feed offering Overalls Hack Wilson, Sunny Jim Bottomley, and Lloyd "Little Poison" Waner for a new Jesse Haines.

We passed a vacant building with "Haines Brothers: 1921" carved into the stonework, turned right, and we were on a county road, already out of town. As instructed, we made a left on Diamond Mill Road and there, on the right, was Bethel Cemetery. Tony pulled the car into the gravel drive, and at the crest of a rise, we found the gravesite of Pop Haines. Beneath the sundial on the top of the stone was carved:

St. Louis Cardinals
National League Pennant-Winners, 1928, 1930
World Champions, 1926, 1931, 1934

"The man was right," Tony said, removing his tweed hat. "Old Jesse Haines passed away in 1978. Nine years ago. I can't tell you how many times I come through this town since then, and I was going to stop and see him. Hey, what was the name of that great pioneer woman who shot so well?"

"Annie Oakley?"

"Yes. She's buried along this road. I always wanted to see her, too. But Jesse Haines, boy, I'll tell you, he was an idol of mine."

We stood facing the tombstone, hands at our sides, shadows cast long across the grave.

"Go ahead and take a picture," Tony said.

I pulled out my camera, and Tony walked to the other side of the stone. The day's last rays of sun shone in his face, and his white hair became transparent. Tony touched the sundial lightly.

"You were one of the great ones, Jesse," Tony whispered.

I took the picture.

Tony put his arm around me and we walked back to the car. "Now you have a picture of the old scout looking down at the great ball player. How about that?" Tony looked out across flat land and fallow fields, white barns and brick farmhouses. "The old scout," he repeated, smiling, rolling the phrase around in his mouth. "The old scout."

5

Talent Is Where You Find It

A slick third baseman for eight years with the New York Yankees, a cardiologist and, now, president of the American League, Dr. Bobby Brown set out in 1984 to reverse the decline in the game of baseball. He saw the paucity of the baseball skills a new generation of players had brought to the big leagues, and he decided that something needed to be done on a grass-roots level to produce more talent, more ball players, and a better ball game.

Dr. Bobby Brown paced about his Park Avenue office, mulling over the problem. Commissioner Peter Ueberroth agreed that something must be done, and told the league president to do what he could to help amateur baseball. Dr. Bobby Brown had talked with the top brass from all the teams, and as this is America, everyone had an opinion. Raise more money for amateur baseball. Change the number of balls and strikes. Develop high-tech training tools. Establish a think-tank to research baseball training methods. Opinions everywhere. But Dr. Bobby Brown wanted a grass-roots solution, so he sent a letter soliciting ideas from major league baseball scouts, the people who spend the most time watching baseball at that level.

From another flood of opinions came this modest proposal: Players who keep improving will never lose the desire to play baseball. Young basketball players, shooting at hoops on garages and barns and poles, have fun and keep improving. Young baseball players, throwing balls off cement walls, can do the exact same thing. If we get those walls built, a good coach can take five hundred kids, ages six to twenty, on one field, and in thirty minutes every player would throw and handle 180 balls. In thirty more minutes, everyone would swing the bat fifty times. And in thirty more minutes, every kid would run the bases.

You won't believe me, Tony Lucadello wrote. No one does. In a quarter century of trying to spread this idea, the old scout had been consistently frustrated, and he supposed this was unlikely to change. But he thanked Dr. Bobby Brown for the opportunity to express his opinion, and he added that if, by chance, the league president *did* see merit in the idea but needed proof, he should call Dallas Green, who'd seen the idea with his own eyes.

Lucadello, Brown thought. He'd played with a guy named Johnny Lucadello; this must be his brother.

Brown called Green. The former Phillies manager, who had since gone on to become the general manager of the Chicago Cubs, confirmed the effectiveness of Tony's proposal. In the early 1970s, the Phillies sponsored a series of fourteen youth baseball clinics in Puerto Rico, run by Tony and using the principles of the wall and the plastic golf ball. In the first one, Green said, more than eight hundred kids showed up, and still, within two hours, each boy ran the bases, swung the bat fifty times, threw the ball 180 times, and fielded the ball 180 times. Bobby, you should have seen it, Green said. My God, if we'd have filmed it, we'd've made a million bucks.

Filmed it.

Eureka.

A year later, at tiny Anthony Wayne High School, about a half hour from downtown Toledo, Dr. Bobby Brown was sliding in the dirt, and the puff of dust, along with the reaction of 318 nodding kids, was captured by a film crew from Chicago. The little old man with the narrow-brimmed hat ran the clinic, lecturing on enthusiasm and outlining practice methods. Brought along as living proof of the wall's effectiveness was Matt Stone, who starred in a segment of the film and whose skills elicited a low whistle of admiration from the Yankee heart surgeon.

The videocassette—entitled *A Coaching Clinic* and distributed by Major League Baseball—debuted at the 1987 winter baseball meetings, and orders have been brisk. The league office targeted Youth League and high school coaches, but orders came in from all over the world. When officials from the Soviet Union came to spring training in 1988 searching for methods that would help their nation build a competitive team in time for the 1997 Barcelona Olympics, they were presented with a copy of *A Coaching Clinic*. Rumor had it that the old scout might be asked to stage a clinic himself somewhere behind the Iron Curtain.

"Oh, for heaven's sake, I'm too busy for that," Tony says. "I have my job to do. And I'm not so sure I'm happy about the Russians getting into our game. What's next? Can you imagine?"

Tony Lucadello has no off-season. He'd been invited to Dallas, where *A Coaching Clinic* debuted, but he told the Phillies he couldn't make it. He needed to spend December—and January, for that matter—writing letters to coaches, finding a new part-time scout to cover the Cincinnati area, working out his minor league players who hadn't been invited to the

Florida Instructional League and preparing his schedule for 1988.

The weather in Tony's territory in March, April and May—the crucial months before the annual draft—ranges from erratic to arctic. To have a fighting chance to see the players he wants to see, Tony gets the schedules from every baseball team in Indiana, Ohio and Michigan and plots out where he needs to go and when. The spring is a short season for the old scout, with time enough only for players eligible for that year's draft, but Tony is rarely seeing a player for the first time then. In fact, some players eligible for the 1988 draft have been in Tony's "follow" file for nine years.

At the end of the 1987 season, Tony made a list of players he thought he might recommend that his office draft in 1988. Then he studied the schedules of those players' teams, trying to find days the teams played each other and making sure that whether it rains or snows or drops cans of Bartlett pears from the sky, he'll have a player to see. Sometimes he'll see them in a gym or a barn—or a coal mine.

"I had to do that once," Tony told me. "Back when I was with the Cubs. It happened in West Frankfort, Illinois, in mine number 3. I heard about a kid down there that they said could *really* throw hard. When I got there, it was raining cats and dogs. They didn't have no gyms around, or no barns neither. I contacted the kid. His brother was a catcher, and they both worked in a coal mine. I waited there for three days for the rain to break, and finally I decided I couldn't waste any more time on a ball player I knew about only on reputation. So I went over to the mine, and I talked with the man who worked on top of the shed there—you know, had control of everything in the mining operation. I told him about my problem, and I asked if there was any possible chance I could go down in the mine and have him throw to his brother along the side of the track. He knew the pitcher I was talking about, and he called into the mine and okayed it.

"I brought a ball and a couple gloves with me, and the man and I went down in the shaft, all the way down to the bottom, four hundred feet below the surface of the earth, and there they were waiting for us. And we picked out a spot alongside the track where the coal cars go, and we had to get twelve miners with those lamps on their heads. I put four of 'em behind the catcher, four of 'em between home plate and the pitching mound, and I put four behind the pitcher, and I warmed him up for about thirty minutes.

"After it was all over, I thanked everybody, and I picked up my gear, and the guy who brought me down there took me back upstairs. When we got to the top, he asked me what I thought. 'He don't throw hard enough,' I told him. 'He's no prospect.' "

As I was listening to the story, I expected it to come to a fairy-tale ending—"And I signed that pitcher, and now he's in the Hall of Fame." But I learned a better lesson than that from the coal mine story. Talent is where you find it. Scouts have to do everything they can to see as many good ball players as possible, including acting on tips and finding some place to see the players play. Ultimately, though, baseball scouts are slaves to the athletic skills or shortcomings of the ball players they see. Unless that talent is developed at a young age, there's nothing a scout can do except get in that company car and head down the highway toward the next prospect.

At 8:00 A.M., Friday, March 4, 1988, for the forty-sixth consecutive spring, Tony did just that. He emerged from his small house in Fostoria, backed his Caprice out from beneath the carport and drove down snow-blasted roads to Huntington College, south of Ft. Wayne, where he had reason to believe he might see a good pitcher. Or two.

Meanwhile, I was in Clearwater, Florida, the Philadelphia Phillies minor league training site since 1945. Ballparks are sprouting like kudzu all over Florida, and obscure burgs with goofy names like Plant City and Port St. Lucie have lured teams away from their established homes in Tampa and St. Petersburg by building—at no charge to the team—large complexes with multiple fields to allow teams to keep all their players, both major and minor league, in one facility. But the Phillies will stay put at least until 1996, which means that Phillies minor leaguers will continue to train at the four-field Carpenter Complex, a geographically short but metaphorically long three miles from Jack Russell Stadium, where the major league club trains and plays.

All four fields have precisely the same dimensions as Philadelphia's Veterans Stadium, although here the grass is real. Behind each backstop small sets of metal bleachers offer less seating than at a suburban high school. In the center of the complex is the cement clubhouse, where the players dress, the trainers tape ankles and dispense sun block, and the scouting director can stand in the shade of the doorway and, for better or worse, size up the Phillies of the 1990s.

The players wear hand-me-down uniforms from the big-league team, which gets new polyester each year. Except for some of the coaches who are obscure ex–big-leaguers, the names stretching across their shoulders are unfamiliar, and many must suffer the ignominy of wearing numbers in the seventies, eighties, or nineties. Some players already have big-league legs. Others have big-league arms and shoulders. Even at a glance, all but a few *look* like minor leaguers. They're too short, or their voices crack, or they wear their hats funny, or their butts are too big, or their chests are too narrow, or their postures still have vestiges of adolescent clumsiness, or they wear frozen, nervous smiles which reveal that even *they* aren't sure if they belong here.

Seven players at the Carpenter Complex were signed to their first professional contracts by the old man in a straw hat. I left my Cincinnati Reds cap in the car and stood on the sidelines of the four fields, trying to get interviews with each of Tony's players. Minor league coaches are unaccustomed to nosy reporters disrupting their practices this way. One coach would give me the okay, but then another coach would find it particularly important that the player take a lap of the field just then. In the brief time I stole, I got the same story from everybody. Each player had heard from the old scout within the previous week. Each talked about the personal interest Tony had taken in him, both before and after signing. Most said that Tony's courtesy, honesty, and consideration were what made them sign that pro contract. Each knew Tony Lucadello had signed forty-nine big-leaguers; each wanted to be the fiftieth.

At the head of the class was Scott Service, a blond, six-foot six-inch pitcher who went thirteen and four the previous year with the Class A Clearwater Phillies, and whom several baseball publications rated as one of the Phillies' best prospects. Except for his translucent mustache, Service, twenty-one, could pass for a big-league pitcher. I talked to him on the field with the players ticketed for AA Reading, and he stood taller, threw harder and with better control, and carried himself with more balance and confidence than anyone out there. The Phillies' scouting director, Jack Pastore, told me he expected Service to break into the Phillies rotation by 1990 or 1991. Yet, if not for Tony, Scott Service might now be pouring concrete in Dayton.

Tony found him in 1985, pitching in a regional Connie Mack tournament at Miami University. The tournament had more teams than Miami had fields, so two teams had to trek out to rural Edgewood High School to play their game. The only scout who bothered to tag along to watch a game in the middle of dusty farmland rather than in the shade of Miami ivy was Tony Lucadello. Service pitched well and won the game. Afterward, Tony introduced himself and told the pitcher he'd be in touch. But on Tony's way out, Dick Finn, coach at

Ohio State University, caught up with him. "You're too late, Tony," Finn said. "I just offered him a four-year scholarship." Tony knew he couldn't offer a free-agent pitcher that kind of money, so he wished Finn the best and made a mental note to follow Service at Ohio State. Two weeks later, just to keep in touch, the scout called Service at home, who had only that day learned that his scholarship had been revoked because of poor grades. Tony made an appointment to work Service out, then met with the entire family and signed the contract. Don't worry about the money you're getting, Tony told him, or the money anyone else is getting. The real money's in the big leagues. You just go out and play as well as I know you can. "I know he needs a fiftieth major leaguer," Service told me, "and he's hoping I'll be it. It feels great—knowing the kind of man he is and the kind of players he's signed—to have the chance to give something back to him."

An even better prospect than Service, according to Pastore, is Mark Cobb, an eighteen-year-old outfielder from Columbus, Ohio, who "has all the physical tools we look for. He's going to be big and strong and—I hope this won't jinx him, but he has superstar potential. There's no telling how good he could become." The Phillies got him in the fourteenth round in 1987. If Cobb hadn't been injured his senior year, he'd have gone in the first three rounds, but he broke his thumb before any scouts got to see him. Except Tony Lucadello, of course, who'd seen him play not only that year but each of the past three since he first saw him in a Mickey Mantle tournament at age fifteen. Cobb's mother had forbidden the boy to talk to scouts and was in fact wary about him turning pro as a seventeen-year-old. But she eventually introduced *herself* to that sweet old man in the hat who'd been at almost all of Mark's games, and when it came time to sign a contract, Tony had earned her trust. He seemed, in fact, like a member of the family. When Mark's mother woke up last winter from a minor operation, she wasn't surprised that the beautiful bouquet of flowers came from the old scout.

Tony had other highly regarded players in camp, including Chris Limbach, a left-handed reliever, and Tim Peek, a right-handed finesse pitcher. I watched them all work out until tiny blisters of sun poisoning rose on my arms and neck. For relief, I ducked into the clubhouse and crossed its rubber floor to Jack Pastore's office. We stood in the breeze by the doorway, looking out toward field number 2, where Mark Cobb was taking batting practice.

"Tony *is* different," said Pastore, who's known the old scout almost twenty-five years. "He's like a gardener; he cultivates his players. He takes an interest in them at a younger age, maybe at fourteen or fifteen years old. And he keeps in touch, maybe by sending a Christmas card, and he really gets close to the player *and* the family, probably closer than most scouts today. You know, most scouts would just say, 'Well, the kid's going to get drafted. What's my chance of getting him?' They can find twenty reasons why not to, but Tony takes the one positive reason and he does it the other way. If we draft one of Tony's players, the negotiations are a lot smoother, the probability of signing that player is a lot better, because the families appreciate that personal touch."

The attrition rate among minor league players is high; for every player who makes it to the majors, scores fizzle in the minors. Pastore said he couldn't even calculate the odds of a scout averaging more than a major leaguer a year, as Tony has. As we stood and talked, one of Tony's players, a stocky and crude eighteen-year-old outfielder, a player from Tony's hometown of Fostoria, was jogging when he should have been running, and he would be released the next week. Tony would still have seven players. While I was in Florida, getting a tan, living out a dream, seeing two ball games a day and checking in on his prospects, Tony Lucadello went out in two pairs of long johns and a wool hat and found a six-foot-seven, 210-

pound right-handed pitcher, Todd Elam, whom no one else knew about. Tony had him throw up against a gymnasium wall until his mechanics improved, then signed him and sent him to Florida, in the middle of spring training.

Ann Arbor's Ray Fisher Stadium—a scrubbed, stately ballpark of weathered brick and optic green—contained a dozen or so baseball scouts. In today's Michigan–Michigan State doubleheader would be at least five players projected to go in the early rounds of the 1988 draft—including Jim Abbott, the star lefty born without a right hand. Every time we ran into other scouts, Tony told me I ought to talk to them. "Maybe you'd rather write about someone else," he'd say. "At any rate, you can find out for yourself if I'm telling you the truth. I'm *different*."

That he was. By and large, the other scouts were paunchy, middle-aged white guys with World Series rings on their fingers, radar guns in one hand, stopwatches in the other, sitting behind home plate and shaking their heads. Bellies, rings, guns and watches notwithstanding, the sitting down and head shaking guarantee these men are scouts. *Nah*, they say, seated, *this kid doesn't have it.* Or, *Boy oh boy, we can't believe what a player this kid is; we can't believe how much money we're going to be offering him soon.* On this day— which would have been more suited for football—the sitting down was interrupted by standing up, foot stomping and voyaging to the right-field concession stand for hot chocolate.

Tony and I sat five rows back from the first-base dugout. Tony waved at some of the scouts as they stomped by. Few waved back, because few recognized him. Tony was swaddled in a heavy black overcoat, a houndstooth hat with Elmer Fudd earflaps, and a shocking-pink scarf, which circled his head thrice. Only his eyeglasses were visible. He had no gun, no rings, no charts. By the fourth inning, he'd seen the players he wanted to see from all of his favored vantage points. Abbott had been scheduled to pitch that day, but rain-outs—and snow-outs—had thrown the Wolverines' rotation off.

"That's the hardest part about scouting here in the midwest territory," Tony said through the scarf. "The weather. Up here they play half as many games as the teams do in places like Florida and California, places like that. Up here, too, the weather we get for the high school and college seasons—in March and April and early May—is just dreadful. Sometimes you can go days without getting a ball game in, but yet you have to keep trying so that you're ready for the draft in June." Tony gestured toward the Michigan shortstop, an aggressive, good-fielding player with mediocre body control. "That's why scouting's a year-round job. I've seen this young man since he was a sophomore up at Bay City Western High School, over in Linwood, Michigan. I already have an opinion about him, and now I just check in to see if anything's improved. But if I don't see him, I still have something to go on."

I nodded, blue-lipped and shivering. The wind had picked up and tiny flecks of hail stung my cheeks. Before leaving Virginia to join Tony, I'd been wearing a T-shirt and shorts. Now, in a sweatshirt and down vest, I was able to quote whole paragraphs from "To Build a Fire."

"We'll leave after this inning," Tony said.

I wanted to kiss him but feared he'd offered to leave for the sake of my pathetic blue lips. "Are you sure? It's okay with me if we stay. I'm fine, really. Do you want some hot chocolate?"

"You can take some with you." Tony said. "We have to go. I can see Abbott pitch another time."

Michigan took the field in the bottom of the sixth, and I closed my eyes and wished for three quick groundouts.

"Back in the early fifties when I was just a young scout, I was at a high school game in Portsmouth, Ohio. It was a cold, brutal day, colder than this. I was in some rickety bleachers, and here comes this guy up to me and he says, 'You mind if I sit here, young man?' And I said I'd appreciate it. He introduced himself. It was Branch Rickey, Sr., who, of course, had owned the Cardinals when I played, and this high school game was in his hometown."

The first batter struck out.

"Well, Mr. Rickey sat there with me for about three innings, and the wind just blew harder and harder. He turned to me and he said, 'Have you seen anything out there that impressed you? Have you seen any talent?'

" 'No, I haven't.'

" 'Well, what are you doing here?'

" 'I don't know,' I says."

The second batter lined out to third.

"I was just a young scout, see, and I thought I had to stay for the whole game to be doing my job. But on the way out to the parking lot, Mr. Rickey put his arm around me and told me just the opposite. 'Don't ever stay. If there's nothing there, go home."

The third batter, one of the players Tony had come to see, hit a fly ball to the warning track in center field.

Tony put his hand on my shoulder. "Go get that hot chocolate," he said. "I'll warm up the car."

By mid-April, Tony had driven more than five thousand miles. He had seen fifty-five games and fifty-nine teams. The Phillies supplied him with a new Chevy Caprice, this one burgundy with burgundy interior, but within weeks the car looked as used as the old white one.

The draft was just six weeks away, and Tony's territory was shaping up as the best in the United States. Baseball insiders were predicting Midwesterners as the first three picks in the draft: pitcher Andy Benes of Evansville University, shortstop Mark Lewis of Hamilton High School in Ohio, and pitcher Steve Avery of Kennedy High School in Taylor, Michigan. The Phillies, picking eleventh, had no chance at these three, but still Tony did his job and scouted them. In the days before the draft, he could have charmed these players' mothers and fathers enough that he might have signed all three. Now, he saw the three obvious but unattainable blue-chippers early, then followed down every lead he had, trying to find that long shot, that sleeper.

Now his months of scheduling paid off. He had a briefcase full of schedules and an intricate but flexible itinerary. "The worst kind of scout, what I call a 'poor' scout, is one who drives up and down the highway just looking for a ball game," Tony told me, driving through southern Michigan toward Toledo. "That's no way to scout."

"Poor" is one of Tony's four kinds of scouts, all of which begin with the letter p.

"The picker," he said, "picks on the ball player's one particular weakness. He might have three pluses and one weakness, but the scout picks on that one weakness so that he don't even like the ball player, even though he could be outstanding. Then you have performance scouts, guys who go on the basis of what the kid did. If he hit a home run or made a good play, why, they go strictly on that. Finally, you have the scout who's the projector, who projects what the boy will do two or three years down the road."

Tony Lucadello is a projector. He thinks about 5 percent of scouts are poor, 5 percent are pickers, 85 percent are performance scouts, and only 5 percent are projectors. "More of them would think of themselves as projectors than *are* projectors."

After only a few weeks of traveling with Tony, I'd have to agree. Every time a player made a good play, hit a ball a long way, made a good throw or pitch, I couldn't help but be impressed. It's one thing to know that a player's performance on the amateur level is irrelevant, that what counts is his body control, his instincts, his attitude, his raw tools, and his chances of improving. It's another thing to make yourself believe it.

Tony slid the Caprice through rain-slick Toledo neighborhoods, stopping in a junior-high parking lot. "We can see from here," Tony said. "That's Rogers High School on the other side of the field. That's where the kid I'm looking at goes to school. He's a right-handed pitcher, name of Gallendar."

We were parked along the first-base line, about a hundred yards from the field. The rain and wind picked up and after a few minutes mixed with hail. People in red and in blue warm-up jackets scurried around under umbrellas, and two older guys in parkas—the umps—walked around the infield. The wind blew so hard now that the car rocked.

"They'll never play this one, Tony."

"You never know. They have to get in what games they can in this part of the country."

The hail stones grew, but the rain slowed and, to my chagrin, players from both teams began playing catch on the sidelines. Minutes later, the field lights went on, and Gallendar took the mound. His first pitch sailed four feet over the catcher's head. The car shook, and I wouldn't have been astonished if it flipped over.

Tony turned on the windshield wipers and swept away the hail. "They should call this game," he said. "Someone's going to get hurt. I don't even think he warmed up." After an inning, Tony shook his head and drove away. "Daggone," he said. "Now I'll have to see him another time."

How, I wondered, could a man have signed so many major leaguers scouting this territory? He sees fewer games than Sun Belt scouts, under far worse conditions. His cross-checkers—scouts from the home office who look at the top prospects in every territory—understandably prefer spending time with the scouts in Florida, Texas and California, scouts who'll never sign half the major leaguers Tony has. Yet the cross-checkers see their players, and consequently the team drafts twice as many kids from those territories. You couldn't blame Tony if, in frustration, he gave it all up. Yet there he sat, the most successful scout in major league history, a decade past normal retirement age, bundled up inside his car, straining to catch glimpses of a high school kid throwing wild pitches in a sleet-slinging typhoon.

6

Two Barns in a Rainstorm

During spring training, Phillies President Bill Giles called Tony and asked him to take a couple days off and fly to Florida.

"What for?"

"You can come down and visit with us and enjoy yourself."

"Under those conditions, no, Mr. Giles. I've got work to do, schedules to double-check, letters I just sent out. I'm trying to get organized and make my plans. This would be a poor time for me to leave my territory."

"Oh, what the heck. You can miss a couple of days."

"Well, if you say so, I can. But I don't want to."

"That's okay, Tony. If you don't want to, you certainly don't have to."

"What's on your mind, Mr. Giles? You've got more in mind than me coming down there and having a good time."

The president paused. "You're right," he said. "I was down in the Instructional League last fall, and you had five kids there, all five of them better than our top five draft choices. I couldn't believe it. What you paid those five kids wasn't half what we paid any one of those high drafts."

"Well, Mr. Giles, anyone can scout the cities. You can find those ball players just by reading the newspapers. Everybody in the country knows about that kind of guy. You have to look in the background, and some of them *will* surprise you. Some of them have more talent than the number one, two, three, and four in my territory—after I find them."

Bill Giles thanked Tony, who went back to work. The draft loomed near, only two months away now, and he had ball players to see.

Tony kept wanting me to talk to other scouts, so he invited Whitey Hafner to meet us at the Toledo Turnpike Inn, a low, yellow, cement-block motor court of small, dark rooms carpeted in olive shag. Tony had stayed here since Whitey was in high school when Tony correctly decided that the hustling catcher had no chance of rising above Class C ball. We sat in Tony's room on laminated furniture, talking first about the trend toward signing good athletes in the absence of complete ball players, then changing the subject to talk about the cute girl who swims in the lane next to Whitey at Vic Tanny's. Tony lost interest and seemed relieved to get a phone call that provided a graceful exit from the conversation.

Whitey Hafner, Toledoan, is perhaps the most relentlessly and sincerely happy man on the planet. In the late 1950s, he played pro ball, but the fates of baseball have rarely looked kindly at 155-pound catchers with mediocre arms. By the mid-sixties his playing days were over. He wanted to be a scout, but he had a family to feed, so Whitey joined the electricians union and quit baseball altogether. After twenty years in the union, a divorce and some lucky real estate investments, Whitey retired and spent his time going to ballparks and flirting with young women at his neighborhood Vic

Tanny Health Spa. He scouted all the baseball teams in Greater Toledo, putting a stopwatch to every player's every move and then giving his information to any scout who'd listen. Finally, in 1988, he landed a job as a part-time scout with the Chicago White Sox, and now the only time he quits smiling is when the tobacco juices well up in his mouth and he has to pause to spit in a Pepsi can.

"That was Dr. Brown," Tony said afterward. "They're really going to get the word out about the wall, about the film." He grabbed his hat and coat. "Enough of this. We have to go see a ball game, and then I'll show you where that film was made."

We piled into Tony's burgundy Chevy and crossed Toledo without driving on a four-lane road for more than three blocks. When I was a junior in high school, I swam for the Greater Toledo Aquatic Club in meets all over town, and I thought I knew the city well, but I hadn't a clue where we were until we surfaced among the putting-green lawns and brick three-car garages of Ottawa Hills, where the Genoa Comets had come to play the Ottawa Hills Green Bears.

School had just let out, and the players trickled onto the field, gloves under their arms, adjusting the bills of their caps on the way. The coach, a thin, thirtyish man with the carriage of a career Army captain, raked the infield and—while his players limbered up—rolled powdered lime down the foul lines. The metal scoreboard just off the third-base dugout proclaimed the Green Bears the 1986 Ohio Class A Baseball Champions. "This is a little school," Tony said. "But they always have a player or two."

"You bet they do," Whitey agreed. "I referee basketball games in the off-season, just to see what kind of athletes some of these boys are. Did you ever think of scouting that way? Huh!"

From the time we'd met, Whitey had been clutching his idle red stopwatch in his left hand, but now he began to click it, timing windsprints and warm-up throws and, for all I know, the coach's speed from home to third with the lime bucket.

"See if you can pick out the player we're here to see," Whitey said. "See if the athletes stand out to you. Huh!" He and I sat on the bleachers; Tony, his face swaddled in a scarf, had wandered behind the backstop.

I looked over the players on Ottawa Hills, now taking infield, and on Genoa, which had just piled out of a schoolbus and begun to loosen up. A few weeks with Tony had taught me at least this much: *baseball is played 87 percent below the waist.* So I tried to figure out who had the best lower-body control. I settled on the biggest kid on the field, Ottawa Hills' first baseman, who seemed to position himself well during infield and who was startlingly broad shouldered for an eighteen-year-old. Wrong, Whitey told me. But I felt redeemed that I *had* found an athlete; the first baseman had led their basketball team to the state finals. Just then a throw sailed in from the center fielder, level and true, a one-hop strike to the catcher.

"That's him."

"He's a good one, isn't he? Huh! I like him, but I've seen him strike out a lot this year."

Everything is obvious in retrospect, and as I studied the center fielder, I couldn't believe I'd missed the grace with which he planted his feet and threw, the precise drive of his rear leg during his swing. But he'd looked a little small to me through the chest, where I shouldn't have been looking anyway. He was seventeen; how big was his chest supposed to be?

Tony had been talking to the Ottawa Hills coach, and I followed him as he went to talk to the chain-smoking coach from Genoa. Tony greeted the man by name, shook his hand, and asked about his family. "How many games have you played this year?"

"Eleven."

"Tell me: in those games, did you see anyone who really *impressed* you? Anybody who really shook you up?"

The Genoa coach scrunched up his face, pulled another Marlboro from his maroon warm-up jacket, lit it, stuck his lower lip out and said, "Not really. To be honest—and I'm not just saying this because he's on my team and because he's such a good kid—I haven't seen anybody who's half the player my catcher is." He pointed at a stocky kid leading the rest of the Comets in a lap around the field.

Tony thanked him and went on his way. "Now that's how you cover a territory," Tony whispered. "These two coaches just gave me a scouting report on almost three hundred ball players. You can't go on this alone, for the simple reason being that you have to see the top players yourself. But this is one way I find out about that one player no one else knows about." He looked me in the eyes, beaming. "I have one this year. A player no one else knows anything about. A sleeper."

"Who is it?"

"I can't tell you. I can't tell anyone."

"Where is he?"

"In Ft. Wayne, Indiana. Just be patient. If you promise not to tell anyone, even your wife, I'll show him to you on Sunday."

Tony moved around the perimeter of the field, changing his vantage points while Whitey sat in a lawn chair and clicked his stopwatch. Tony ruled out the Genoa catcher, who—though he was a good high-school player—was twenty pounds overweight, hit off his front foot and wore glasses. "I've never signed a position ball player who wore glasses. They can't hit that low outside breaking pitch. And as they get a little older, their vision's only going to get worse."

During the game, Tony got the name and address of the Green Bears center fielder and talked briefly with the boy's mother. He's a good student, Tony learned, who'd start at

Miami University that fall, to play baseball and—Tony's face fell when he heard this—to punt the football.

"The signability's not there," Tony said to me. "And besides which, the kid's not ready yet. A good follow. But the football coach probably will make him go to spring practice, and that may ruin him for baseball. But you have to keep your eye on him, because he definitely has the talent. At least he's staying in my territory."

Whitey Hafner looked down at his stopwatch and up at the field, so fast and twitchy that casual onlookers might have pitied him for his affliction.

Bruce Edwards looks and sounds like the beloved president-for-life of a tradition-laden bowling league: a middle-aged, dark-haired guy with a slight air of self-importance, a touch of Appalachian drawl, and an overstuffed physique. Edwards actually works part-time in a grain elevator and part-time as the Anthony Wayne High School assistant baseball coach. He's also a self-taught author and Tony Lucadello's unofficial chief disciple. When Tony blew the dust off those yellowed sheets in his rusty footlocker—the papers outlining his ideas about the walls and the plastic golf balls and the future of the game of baseball—he gave them to Edwards, who turned the collection into *The Lucadello Plan*.

Tony and I met Bruce in Whitehouse, Ohio, at Anthony Wayne High School, a consolidated school surrounded by fields, either fallow or in soybeans. Behind the school, next to the baseball diamond, is a low white wall, about the size of the side of a garage for short people with low-slung cars. Painted across the wall in red and blue block letters was ANTHONY WAYNE. "This is some place," Tony said. "This is where they made the film."

When we parked the car, Bruce Edwards was waiting, clutching a briefcase full of manuals and videotapes. He broke into a smile when he saw us and extended his hand fifty yards before he was close enough to shake ours.

Bruce and Tony shook hands with all four hands clasped together, the manly midwestern father-son hug. "You two talk a while," Tony said. "I'll look around some. I wanted Mark here to see the wall, Bruce. You tell him about the film and about the wall. He's a book writer, so he'll be looking for the kind of information he can put in a book." With that, the old scout shuffled off to the ballpark bleachers, head down, looking for coins.

Bruce shook his head, watching Tony stoop to examine something. "I love Tony Lucadello, that's the bottom line," he said. "I'll tell you what: if Tony Lucadello told me to play baseball in the middle of the ocean," he said, setting his bulging briefcase on top of the wall, "Bruce Edwards would be out in that water with gloves and spikes, playing baseball. He's done more for me than . . . than I can tell you. He won't take a cent for all the help he's given me. I said, 'Tony, how much do you want from the sale of this manual?' and he said, 'Nothing. I want you and your family to get by.' "

When Dr. Bobby Brown called Tony and asked if he'd be interested in putting his ideas into a videotape, Tony agreed, but only on the condition that they dropped the idea of doing it in Florida. Tony wanted to stay within his territory, with coaches he knew. Brown thought, Sure, why not? Let's do it with everyday people in an everyday place. Eager to help Bruce Edwards, Tony suggested Anthony Wayne High School.

At that time, their wall had been up for a year, Edwards told me. The players dug the footer by hand, poured the concrete, hoisted the cinder blocks and painted it with brushes. Edwards swept his right arm toward the nearby concession stand. "Now you notice a little graffiti on that wall over there." It read, Speed Metal Rules. "You notice you don't see it on this wall. The kids built this themselves, by hand, and everyone respects that."

Across the field, between first base and a trash can painted with a smile face, Tony Lucadello blew the dust off something in his palm.

"To have major league baseball come to Whitehouse, Ohio—" Bruce said. He laughed, unable to complete the sentence for the scope of the concept. "And it's all because of that man over there. This whole thing—the manual, the clinics, the film, the whole bit—has been a labor of love. But the bottom line on it all is that *it works*. Our first year with it, we cut our errors in half. People had fun practicing, and the word got out. The first year, we had twenty-eight kids come out for baseball. This year, our third year with the wall, we had sixty-three.

"That's all because the wall *works*. Anybody can do it. It's not some gimmick, it's not a scheme, you don't have to run it through a computer, you don't have to graduate from college or be a rocket scientist or even have any money at all to do this. Granted, it's simple and it's unconventional, and some coaches I've talked to say, 'Yeah, yeah, good idea,' but they don't follow through and implement the wall into their program. But I'll tell you what: if you have a problem—and we do have a problem producing baseball talent in this country—well, you don't solve that problem by doing the same tired old things you've always done. But a lot of these coaches, the only nonconventional ideas they'll listen to are these high-tech gizmos. The wall's too simple for them to place their faith in. I don't know why. But I do know that when they see it with their own eyes, they change their tune."

Bruce stood with his back ramrod straight, chest thrust out, thumbs in his hip pockets—confident, coachly gestures—but he also shifted his weight from left to right, a contrapuntal and nervous tic.

"You know what else: this idea makes practice fun for the coach. It's not just the players, you know, that don't want to practice anymore. But if you can make practice so you can

107

finish in an hour and a half, make it fun, make it where everybody contributes, then the coach starts havin' fun, too, and he wants to practice. You can't coach from behind a fungo stick, anyway, and what the wall does is get the coach out from behind that fungo stick to where he's having more fun than just throwing a ball in the air and hitting it himself. This way, I've got a line of kids fielding ground balls right here. I can stand here and watch those young men field ground balls, and if one of them does something wrong—boom—I can take him right out of line, while everyone else keeps going and show the boy what he's doing wrong, and—boom—he goes back in the line."

Tony sat in the bleachers now, counting change in his upturned palm, his back to the setting sun.

"This idea has got to get out. Tony's had this idea for thirty years, that's what we told Dr. Brown. But without the help of Major League Baseball, this thing's not going to go. They're the only people big enough. I told Dr. Brown in a letter, I says, 'All you got to do is call someone on the phone, and you can open up doors that I'll never see.' "

Bruce rocked on his heels, his tone evangelical. He told me about a clinic he hoped to organize that fall in Toledo, a clinic on the wall which would feature Mike Schmidt and another friend of Tony's, Pittsburgh Pirates manager Jim Leyland. The proceeds from the clinic would benefit the city's recreation programs. "I don't want any money from it," Bruce said. "I could use it, you understand. I'm not a rich man. But all I want is recognition for the training manual and the film. And, one other thing, I told the city. You build a wall out there and you call it the Lucadello Wall. You do that and I'll do anything you ask.

"I'm not in this for the money, if you haven't guessed," he said, laughing. "I took this program to Ohio Special Olympics—severely mentally retarded children—and in fifteen minutes you could see the difference in them. That is probably the most enjoyable day I ever had as a coach, and I didn't make a penny, and I'll never ever forget that.

"Listen, I don't have the money to do this thing justice, I know that. If it wasn't for my wife being as understanding as she is . . . She told me she'd give me five years on this thing, to do what I had to do. I can't even advertise my book, because I have no money to do it with. I call it a book; It's not a book, it's a training manual. I'm not an author, believe me."

Bruce broke up into a windstorm of nervous laughter, and I tried to reassure him—in the pose of a real writer guy who'd published all of one book—that I thought he had nothing to be ashamed of.

"Well," he said, breathless and still laughing, "when I set out to do this thing, I went to the library and read every book on writing that I could find, and then I typed it out—and I type with two fingers—*tap, tap, tap*. It took me two years. Every one of those books there, I paid for."

Bruce ran his hand across the wall. I stood, humbled and inadequate, alongside a man willing to sacrifice so much of himself for the love of a game and the unwavering belief in another man's ideas, and together we watched the sun disappear behind the bricks of the high school.

Tony walked over and asked me if I was ready to go. "Look here," Tony said. "My best day this year. I found a dime, a nickel and four pennies."

"It's been a good day all around," I said, and I wished Bruce good luck with his manuals, and Tony sent his best to Bruce's family.

The next morning, Tony told the waitress at Miller's Restaurant that we were in a hurry. It was only nine, and the Toledo University game wouldn't start for another four hours. "I'll have my usual," he said. "You know what that is, don't you?"

The waitress shook her head. She was about twenty. "No, sir, I sure don't."

"Well, I always order the same thing: canned peaches, a bowl of Raisin Bran with skim milk, wheat toast, and Sanka." The waitress nodded, took my order, a Denver omelette, and ambled to the kitchen. "She's new," Tony said. "And she looks slow. All the waitresses who used to work here are retiring now. They treated me nice. They knew what I wanted."

Miller's had the dark formica ambience of a sixties turn-pike plaza restaurant. The booths were covered in harvest-gold vinyl, and cypress-wood wall clocks were for sale behind the cash register. Tony has slept at the Toledo Turnpike Inn and eaten at Miller's since before I was born.

Tony Lucadello conducted his business with monastic devotion and inviolable consistency. To enable his septuage-narian body to handle forty thousand miles a year on mid-western roads and eight months in modest motels, he ate at eight, noon and five, and he ordered the same thing every day: a fast-food salad or a fruit plate with cottage cheese for lunch; soup and salad bar for dinner. To ease the boredom between games and to keep his eyes sharp, he went to the ballparks ridiculously early and scoured the ground for loose change. The desk clerks in his motels provided him with an extended family. Every day, at breakfast, he bought USA Today but read only the Phillies score, the scores of their minor league teams, and the front page. He spent off-hours in his rented rooms, filling out expense reports, calling his part-time men, working on his schedules and writing a letter a week to all "his boys" in the minor leagues. In any town, he never forgot to stop in to see old friends—coaches, parents, scouts, players and ex-players—having learned well the principles of networking forty years before there was any such term. When he chatted, he chatted baseball. In a year together, he and I never had a conversation about any other subject that lasted more than five minutes. When he sat and thought, he dreamt of walls and diamonds full of prospects. And he wondered if there was something he'd missed: something else he could conjure up that would help save "our game."

We reached the Toledo University baseball field at ten, three hours before game time, and parked the car just beyond the right-center-field fence. The player we'd come to see was Tom Marsh, the center fielder, a fast, aggressive senior with good speed and a powerful arm. "He'll be high on my draft list," Tony told me. "I doubt I'll be lucky enough to get him, but if the office is smart and if they have any faith in me at all, they'll draft him."

As the teams arrived, Tony sought out the coaches of both Toledo and visiting Ball State, paying his respects and asking about players they had and players they'd seen. Stan Sanders, the Toledo head coach and a longtime friend of Tony's, had once taken a leave of absence to scout for the Yankees, a job Tony had helped arrange. A first-year Ball State assistant, Kyle Reiser, had been a high school coach and had appeared in the Dr. Bobby Brown–instigated videotape. His association with Tony, he told me, probably got him his job. Next year, Ball State is building a wall.

Still in the car, shielded from a stiff wind, Tony cast an assiduous eye on the infield and outfield drills, dissecting the rote tosses and fungoes and concluding that, yes, Tom Marsh was the one. For now, the only one. But the game itself proved a disappointment. Marsh also pitched—he had four wins, no losses—and to rest him between starts, Sanders used him not in the outfield but as a designated hitter. We stayed for his first at-bat, a line drive to short center field which Marsh stretched into a double.

"His future isn't as a pitcher, for heaven's sake," Tony said as we drove south down I-75 to catch a game at a rural high school. "I understand that Stan's trying to win games, but I'm afraid that it's going to hurt Marsh. He won't be seen."

111

Then Tony smiled. "Of course, that might help me. I've seen him since he was in high school, and I *know* how good he is."

The high school game was in Celina, a little town of big houses on the largest man-made lake in the state of Ohio. The ballpark is only a few blocks from the lake, set in a wooded city park where utter tranquillity is disturbed only by the muted whine of a small machine shop nearby, about a five-hundred-foot dinger to right.

The game was in the third inning. Tony had come to see the pitcher for visiting Elida, a skinny and stiff-kneed righty named Joe Renner. The Celina coach bragged up his pitcher, too, a five-nine short-armer named Noll. The change from the relative polish of college baseball to the flailing gawkiness of eighteen country boys was abrupt, but despite the obvious flaws of most of these players, Tony was clearly more excited at this level of baseball. The average player here was immeasurably worse than the average college player, but Tony wasn't interested in the average. He knew that most scouts look at this as the back of beyond, so he figured that if he could project one of these crude players as someone who can be helped and who can make steady and dramatic improvement, then he'd found a player no one else knew about. Like a reporter on the trail of a scoop, Tony got his biggest day-in, day-out kicks from finding sleepers. It's nothing like hearing about the major league debut of one of his boys, mind you. But it was a thrill.

Renner got hit hard in the second inning, and Celina went ahead. Noll had a shutout going, but the Elida players were swinging at bad pitches. *Project,* I thought, keeping Tony's voice in my head. *Don't be swayed by performance.* The two right-handed pitchers in the big leagues as short as this guy throw far harder. He doesn't extend his arm enough, he's a poor student, and he's wild. Had Elida been more patient at the plate, they'd have either lit him up or filled the bases with walks.

Renner had a little nod in his delivery; as he came through his windup, he looked down and he looked up, and by not keeping his head steady, he finished off balance and staggering. When he pitched from the stretch, the flaw was less pronounced and his fastball had more movement. He threw hard for a high school kid, but I wondered how easy it'd be to improve his mechanics. As Celina touched him for two more runs, I studied Renner's flaws more thoroughly, and by the time Tony motioned me to go, I'd written off both pitchers.

Tony had been tucked in between the press box and the dugout, hidden from the view of parents and girl friends in the grandstand. He'd seen what he needed to see, and he was ready to leave. But Tony has a self-imposed code of scouting etiquette. One cardinal rule prohibits talking about players within earshot of anyone who might be a friend or relative of that player. This rule frustrated me at first, but I learned to wait for the full rundown in the car as we drove away. Another cardinal rule decreed that a good scout sneaks away from the ballpark, so players and coaches won't know precisely how long he stayed and try to infer something from that.

Tony slipped to the edge of the Elida dugout, got the attention of the coach, and whispered, "When will you pitch him again?"

"Tuesday."

"Good. I might be there. One more question, Mike, real quick. Of all the games you've played this year, have you seen any outstanding kids? Any one particular kid that stands right out?"

He hadn't seen much. Tony thanked him for his help and made his escape, snaking his way behind the press box and under the bleachers to the car. I had the engine running. We pulled away slowly.

Tony was happy. He'd just received a scouting report on more than a hundred players, and he'd just seen a pitcher he liked.

"Really?" I said. "I thought his mechanics were kind of poor." And I told Tony about the flaws I'd seen. As I went through them, I started stammering a little and belaboring my points, nervous about presenting an extemporaneous scouting report to history's most successful scout. He didn't say anything until I'd dug my grave as deep as I could and finally shut up.

"Well, I'm going to look at him again, I'll tell you," Tony said. "All I have to do is give him a ball and have him throw it up against that wall, and he'll learn how to spread those legs out and bend that knee to get down on it, or it'll go by him. It won't take him five minutes to improve. If he does that, he might be a pretty good pitcher. So today was worthwhile, seeing him. He was more impressive tonight than he has been, because tonight he threw strikes. He kept the ball down. But he stands straight up and throws across his body. Now, if he was to spread those legs out and bend his back, then he'd really have something on his fastball."

"He may not be ready for the draft this year," Tony said. "But I found out that he hasn't made a college connection yet, so there may be something I can do." At Toledo, Stan Sanders had told me Tony must have a list of colleges and the players he's sent to each. He finds players for everyone, Sanders said. And I realized that I'd been with Tony as Joe Renner's name was added to that list.

We stopped at a salad bar, then drove on to the Van Wert L & K Motel. I thought about Tony's Four P's of Scouting. I had tried not to be swayed by *performance* but rather to cleave to the ideal of the *projector*. Instead, I had been a *picker*. Left to my own devices, I knew, I would be a *poor* scout, driving up and down the highway, looking for ball games.

The next morning, as we were driving into Indiana, Tony pointed to two red barns. "You see those barns there?" he said. "Quite a story behind those barns."

I smiled. To think some people have to get their drive-time entertainment from the car radio. I asked Tony if he'd tell me the story, then I sat back and pointed the Chevrolet west, eager for another gem from the scout's past.

"Gene Martin was our farm director then," Tony said. "Every once in a while he wanted to get out of the office and go visit the scouts. He loved to travel with me, and we got to be pretty good friends. One year, I told him I thought I might have a pretty good pitcher. The reports I had on him were excellent, and he was supposed to pitch the next day, over in Hicksville.

"The next day it looked like rain, and when we got to the ballpark, the coach was there, and he said the game was canceled, but they were going to try to play it tomorrow. So the next day it rained like cats and dogs, and I called the coach and he said the game had been postponed until ten days later. So I said, 'Well, do me a favor, willya? Meet me at the ballpark with a catcher and that pitcher.'

" 'What for?' he says. 'You can't work out in the rain.'

" 'We'll work out if you'll just bring him out there for me.'

" 'Fine,' the coach said. 'I want the kid to be looked at.'

"I hung up, and Mr. Martin asked me how I was going to work the kid out. 'I'll find a way,' I says.

"All the time, as we were driving down there, he was grumbling. 'Whoever heard of working out a ball player in weather like this,' he says, under his breath like.

"We got to the ballpark, and I rolled down my window and told the coach to follow me. We drove to this farm that had two barns with sliding doors, facing each other. The barns were short and about twenty feet apart. I pulled in the driveway, ran up the steps and asked the farmer if I could use his barns. I explained the whole thing, and he said sure, grabbed his coat and unlocked the sliding doors for us.

"I put the catcher in one barn, and the pitcher in the other. It was raining even harder now. I had five baseballs in my pocket, and I gave him one to warm up with. After about fifteen minutes, I gave him another ball and told him he could cut loose if he wanted. He threw a few pitches and I could tell Mr. Martin was impressed. Then I stopped the boy, and I handed him three brand-new baseballs. 'Now, wait until I walk over to that other barn,' I says, 'and then show me your best fastball.'

"So he wound up and he cut it loose. I took the ball from the catcher and motioned for the kid to throw again. He got another ball and he cut that loose, and he got the last one and he cut that loose. I looked at all three balls, then I gave one to the catcher and one to the pitcher, for souvenirs, and I told them they could go. I thanked the farmer and I thanked the coach, and me and Mr. Martin got in the car and drove off.

"Mr. Martin don't say nothin' for a while, but finally he couldn't stand it anymore, and he said, 'Now, tell me what did you prove back there?'

" 'Didn't you see the kid,' I says.

" 'Sure I saw him. He looked pretty good to me. But how could you tell how good he is under those conditions?'

"And I told him that when the catcher handed me those balls, they were wet. All three of them. If the kid could really throw hard, they'd have been bone dry."

7

The Sleeper

"I never go to a game just on what you might call the off chance of seeing a player," Tony said. "Either I've seen the boy before, or I've had him recommended to me, or the team I'm going to see is one that always has a player or two. Sometimes, of course, I'm just paying my respects to a coach even if he don't have nothin' for me—this year. You see? That coach might have a player I'm interested in next year, and he'll remember that I came to see him at least once, even in lean years, and that I took an interest in him personally and asked about his family. And then, you see, when they do have a player, they'll help me out. But—and I want you to put this in your book—I couldn't do any of this without my part-time men."

We were bound for the Wildkat Baseball Klassic—a high school tournament in Kokomo, Indiana—and we stopped on the way, in Ft. Wayne, to pick up Norm Kramer. For the past twenty-one years, Norm had been Tony's part-time scout for Indiana, seeing more than three hundred ball games a year, checking out players' backgrounds and pointing the old scout in a direction that might lead to a major league ball player. Tony also had part-time scouts in Cincinnati, Louisville, Cleveland, Columbus and Detroit. Together, they saw well over two thousand games each year. None was paid more than twenty-five hundred dollars. Yet most had been with Tony for decades. Some taught high school, some were retired, but they covered the cities for Tony and helped prevent him from going to games on what you might call the off chance of seeing a player. "I've told this to everyone, to my bosses, to other scouts, everyone," Tony said as we pulled into Norm Kramer's tortuous driveway. "The secret to my success is that I owe everything to my part-time men."

Tony got in the backseat, told Kramer to drive and told me to interview Kramer. Then he took off his hat and pretended to go to sleep.

Norm Kramer, unlike Tony, wore his 1980 Philadelphia Phillies World Series ring. As he waved his hands to illustrate various points, the ring clicked against the plastic steering wheel. Kramer had been a minor league pitcher in the Phillies chain, but a sore arm hastened his progress toward a job coaching high school baseball and basketball at Shelbyville, Indiana. He was a jovial, round-headed, ex-jock teacher, as eager for the end of the day as his students. One day, he heard that a Phillies scout was at their game, and Kramer introduced himself to Tony, who asked if he'd seen any good players lately. Yes, Kramer said, a big first baseman. Tony asked him to see the player again and then call him collect. Kramer did, and though that player never made it, Tony Lucadello had himself an apprentice.

Over the next few years, they attended a handful of games together, and Kramer sat in Tony's car during rain delays, learning how to be a good scout. At first, Kramer rated the players too high, comparing them against one another, but Tony finally taught him how to compare the players against the major leaguers. The next year, they were at a game when a scout from another team said, "That second baseman isn't any good. You don't like him, do you?" Tony frowned, elbowed the scout, and pointed at the second baseman's parents, who were within earshot. "Don't ever make a parent or a coach mad at you," Tony told Kramer. "You don't gain nothin' from it, it's discourteous, and it's just bad technique." The year after that, Tony taught him the 87 percent rule, and Norm Kramer signed a contract as a part-time scout.

Kramer, now retired from twenty-seven years of teaching anatomy and driver's education, negotiated the sunny drive to Kokomo, down roads flanked by failing farms and budding trees, past adjoining billboards that advertised Jesus Is The Answer and Harley-Davidson Cigarettes, to the scrubbed green and aluminum of Highland Park Stadium. The park seats more than two thousand and was built by the city to attract the American Legion World Series, which it did. Though the facility is better than many AA pro parks, the city allows it to be used only by high school players.

Kokomo, Indiana, once had an American Legion team with three pitchers who went on to make the major leagues. The best of these was Tom Underwood, who played eleven years in the majors and was signed to his first professional contract by Tony Lucadello. It was Tony who convinced the Phillies to draft Underwood. It was Tony who convinced Underwood to sign, rather than go to college. But it was Norm Kramer who saw Underwood first, and it was Norm Kramer who, for two years, saw every game Underwood pitched. "I think of Tom every time I come to Kokomo," Norm said. "Tony had me chart every pitch Tom threw: what kind of pitch and exactly where he threw it. By the time we signed him, I'd charted over five thousand of his pitches. This park here was almost like a second home to me then."

The first game of the tournament pitted the Marion Giants against the host Kokomo Wildkats. We saw both teams take infield and batting practice. Tony and Norm went their separate ways, wandering around the stadium, casing the joint. I sat down in the bleachers. The sun was out now, and I took off my sweatshirt. Spring had come to central Indiana. I leaned back and stretched, my feet on one row of bleachers, my butt on the one above, my head on the one above that, and my arms on the one above *that*. On the adjoining youth league diamond, it was opening day. The muffled sounds of fussy, herding parents and glee-shrieking children drifted dreamlike into Highland Park Stadium, where the stands held a couple dozen much quieter parents, some Kokomo baseball boosters and four or five other scouts, all of whom were camped on their ample haunches behind home plate.

Norm had gotten lineups from the two coaches. Tony came back, too, and asked for my program. We stood for the playing of the national anthem. The record was scratchy, and Tony and Norm took off their hats. I might have sung along. I was too suffused with springtime and Americana to remember.

The Marion pitcher, a six-three blond senior named Eric Persinger, who seemed to wind up all the way back to second base, fired a knee-high fastball to begin the game.

"So, scout," Tony said, slapping me on the back. "What have you seen so far?"

"That was a nice pitch."

"Aw, that's not what I meant." Tony looked disgusted. "I mean *all* the players, for heaven's sake. Have you seen anyone out there who really impressed you?"

I stammered that the game had just started.

"Well, sure but we've been here an hour now. If you're going to learn about scouting, you're going to have to learn how a scout uses his time."

I looked at the program in his hands. Tony already had these two teams narrowed down to just three players who interested him. He had little tiny "n"s—for "no prospect"— penciled in next to the names of all the other players on the rosters. I shook my head in disbelief.

"You can do this after forty-six years," Tony said. "I don't often rule someone out and then have them change my mind. If I see even a hint of someone who might develop major league tools, then I don't rule them out. But this way, you see, I do a number of things. I see if the players Norm's brought me here to see are the only players worth looking at. And then I can concentrate on just those ball players that have pluses."

The game was a tight pitcher's duel between Persinger and Kokomo's pitcher, a shorter, smaller kid with decent mechanics but little velocity, little control and little movement on the ball. There was an "n" beside his name on Tony's program. "He won't get much better," Tony told me after the game, as we went in search of a salad bar for lunch. "He gets batters out at this level, sure, but that's not what a good scout looks for."

The East Noble Knights played the Elkhart Central Blue Blazers in the second game. Elkhart's coach was a bird-dog scout for Tony and Norm, so they already knew that the Blue Blazers didn't have any pro prospects this year. But the East Noble pitcher was a player—a six-three, 185-pound sophomore named Ben Vanryn. In the third inning, Norm leaned over and whispered, "This kid has the best daggone fastball I've seen all spring." As a Greek chorus to this, an obnoxious, middle-aged paunchy guy with a radar gun and a red "Major League Scouting Bureau" golf shirt swaggered underneath the stands directly behind home plate and, without asking anyone's permission, swept back a piece of green canvas and trained the beam of his gun toward the big fifteen-year-old. "He's got nice big hands, too," Norm whispered. "And a good grip. I shook hands with him before the game to find out. That's something Tony taught me."

The rhythm of Vanryn's motion was erratic, and his fastball was higher than it should have been, although the umpire was calling the pitch for strikes. The kid's curveball rarely caught the plate, but he threw the heat every time he got in a jam, and he walked only one batter. When he threw his best fastball, Vanryn grunted. He wasn't old enough to drive, and he was born about the time of Watergate, but when Ben Vanryn grunted and let fly, he sounded like a man. This boy, who probably doesn't yet shave, can throw a baseball hard enough to kill you.

In the seventh inning, Tony tapped me on the arm. "We're ready to go," he said. "I'm going to wander down the first-base line and go out that way. Kramer'll leave the other way. You sneak out down by the concession stand, okay? I don't want anyone to know we're going until we've already left. I don't want to hurt anyone's feelings."

Tony headed toward left field, a little old man in long johns, a turtleneck, and a wool suit on a hot April afternoon, looking for money on aluminum bleachers. I knew he was eager to get a look at Vanryn from yet another angle. A casual onlooker would have figured Tony for a bored retiree or perhaps the grandfather of one of the players, not a living legend out to assess a young pitcher's follow-through with a diagnostician's cold, impassive eye.

I left by the prescribed route and waited for Tony and Norm by the outfield fence of the Kokomo Southside Youth League Diamond, where the umpires were fatter, the parents more shrill. The players were smaller and more enthusiastic, pounding their mitts and hopping around. No one had yet been forced to explain to them that this game is supposed to be *fun*, damn it. A parade through the outfield grass featuring every team in the league had just ended, and the players from all but two teams scattered like uniformed blowing leaves into every corner of Highland Park. The two remaining teams started their game, and the pitcher walked the first batter on four pitches.

Tony waved me over to the car, where he and Norm were standing. He put his arm around me and pointed toward an asphalt basketball court. Six players had found a red rubber kickball and started a full-court pickup basketball game. Tony winced at the sound of plastic spikes scraping across the pavement. "Now will you look at that!" he said. "Godalmighty! Will you look at those kids, shooting buckets in baseball uniforms? If that doesn't tell you something about the problems we have with our game today. . . ."

When Tony was that age, he told me, kids would have been more likely to run from basketball practice and start a pickup baseball game.

"But, Tony," I said, "this is Indiana. Parents here put hoops in their kids' cribs."

"That's just my point! Can you imagine—now just *imagine* this: what if parents felt that way about the wall? If those boys had a wall to use, they'd have more fun practicing. I don't have anything against basketball, really I don't. But when boys in baseball uniforms would rather spend their summer practicing basketball . . ." His voice trailed off, and he dismissed them with a wave of his hand.

Norm headed us back to Ft. Wayne. Tony made Norm wait until we were out of the Kokomo city limits to begin his scouting report. Marion's center fielder was fast and a good athlete, and though he swung one-handed, Norm was a little interested. Tony told him not to waste his time. They agreed that the Kokomo shortstop was the best position ball player, "the only one I'd see again," Tony said. Vanryn was the player who interested Tony most, even though he said the kid didn't know how to pitch yet. "He's got the best raw tools," Tony told us, and though Vanryn wouldn't be eligible until 1990, Tony wanted Norm to continue to see him regularly. Persinger, Norm said, was a sophisticated pitcher for his age, but he had a full ride to Michigan. Persinger's long, overextended motion bothered Tony, who wanted to see the Marion pitcher cut down on his stride and get some snap in his delivery. He'd be a good draft, Tony said, but he'd sought out the kid's father and learned Persinger wouldn't sign for any less than a hundred thousand dollars. "That's a first- or second-round draft," Tony said. "I can't see that. I can't see more than thirty thousand dollars, if that. Let him go to Michigan. If he doesn't get pitched to death or completely ignored, maybe he'll develop and interest me more. We'll see on him."

The scouting report took about an hour. It neared five, and Tony asked Norm to stop "somewhere where I can get a nice soup and salad." We pulled into a chain restaurant in Huntington, Indiana. On the way in, Tony found a nickel Norm and I had walked right over.

We picked up plastic trays and plates, filled our glasses with iced tea and headed for the salad bar. On the other side of the sneeze guard from me, Tony Lucadello frowned. "Those kids shooting buckets back there: it still bothers me. You know, it's things like that that make me worry about our game. Maybe it's too late to save it." He ladled up a cup of vegetable soup. "But think about this. Those cribs you were talking about?"

"The ones with basketball hoops?"

He nodded. "Imagine what would happen if the same number of fathers built little walls in those cribs."

Imagine.

Tony has stayed at the Hart Motel for almost thirty years. Tucked in a small lot on the west side of Ft. Wayne amidst the strip zoning of always-open donut shops and package stores, the Hart Motel features ash-colored formica on the dresser, the nightstands, the countertops, and the walls. On the night-stands are battered copies of *Guideposts* and *People*. The bedspreads are skimpy white chenille, classic material for slipcovers in the musty houses of old-maid aunts. The indoor-outdoor carpet is an indeterminate dull shade. The phone has no dial. You must pick up the receiver and wait for Mr. or Mrs. Hart to connect you with an outside operator. A soda machine near the office sells ten-ounce drinks for forty cents, and it works only with four dimes. Predictably, the sign for the place is in the shape of a heart, but the otherwise humble marker is easy to miss in the glow of neighboring minimarts.

The Hart Motel is clean and costs only twenty-four dollars a night. It's run by nice, steady Mr. and Mrs. Hart, who live in a suite of rooms behind the office and treat Tony Lucadello like a member of the family, always giving him number 14— literally, a room reserved in their own house.

Tony told me to be ready for breakfast at seven the next morning. Against every law of my nature, I was. "We've got a big day today," he told me, warming up his Caprice in the dewy haze of morning. I felt like I was eleven years old, roused from a deep sleep by my grandfather to go fishing in borrowed hip waders.

I yawned and nodded and tried to get him to tell me what was so big about today. "It's a surprise. I'm not going to tell you until it happens. And then you can see if it's worthwhile to you. You know, if it's the kind of thing you'd want to put in a book." He found a restaurant where he could get his peaches, Raisin Bran, wheat toast, and Sanka, and we seated ourselves. "I don't know what kind of thing you're looking for," Tony said. "I'm no book writer. I'm just trying to do my job and show you some things that may be of interest to you."

Again I tried to coax the surprise out of him, but he was steadfast and turned instead to his *USA Today*, eager to see what Mike Schmidt did last night and to find the scores of the Phillies' minor league teams' games, scanning the columns of agate type for mention of Maine, Reading, Clearwater, and Spartanburg.

We drove back to the Hart Motel, and Tony stopped in the tiny front office to let Mrs. Hart know he was about to make a call. He held the metal screen door open and chatted for a while, asking about family members and dissecting the vicissitudes of the weather.

Back in the room, Tony worked his toothpick around in his mouth and called Norm Kramer. "Do you have it set up?" the old scout said. "Does he have a catcher? . . . Good. No one knows about this, right? . . . Oh, that's okay. Anyone other

than your wife? . . . Good. Why don't you pick us up here? . . .
More like noon, I think."

When Tony hung up, he turned to me, deadly serious.
"I'm going to tell you now. This is all about my sleeper. I try
to get one every year, a good player no one else knows about.
But I can't tell you his name, and you have to promise me you
won't tell anyone about him. Not even your wife."

"I promise."

"Because if you do, it'll hurt me. It'll kill me. Another
team could find out about this, and they'd steal my sleeper
right out from under me. I may sound like an old man about
this, but I know how rumors start, and I've lost many players
that way."

"I promise."

Last fall, Tony and Norm went to see Huntington College
play an intrasquad scrimmage. Huntington is a small Christian
college, and Tony and Norm were probably the only scouts
within ten counties. The player they'd come to see was Tim
Dell, who had pitched for the Canadian Pan-American Games
team, beating Japan, and whom Tony projected as a very high
1988 draft. He had already filed a report on Dell that called
him "another Fergie Jenkins"—no idle comparison, since Tony
signed the 284-game winner and since Jenkins himself had
been Dell's Pan-Am pitching coach. And while Dell pitched
as expected, the find of the day was a skinny freshman with
raw mechanics but a hissing fastball. The kid had much to
improve, but Tony decided there were many reasons to believe
he *would* improve. For one thing, the kid had played for tiny
Ft. Wayne Christian High School, with an enrollment of 130
and a baseball team coached by one of the dads, a team whose
schedule was filled with the jayvees from public high schools.
Since Tony liked the Huntington program and coaching staff,
he was confident they'd teach the kid much of what he'd need
to learn, at a pace that wouldn't be intimidating. Of course, he

wouldn't be eligible to sign until after his junior year—in 1990—but Tony told Norm to put the kid in his "follow" file.

That winter, Tony was calling and writing for schedules. Because he wanted to see Dell early, before other scouts invaded, he called the Huntington coach to see when Dell would pitch his first game and to ask how things looked for the season. You ought to have an awfully good pitching staff, Tony said, what with Dell and the new kid. Not really, the coach said. The new kid hadn't liked college much. His grades weren't there. He dropped out and moved back home. It was a shame.

Tony put down the phone. His hands were shaking. His sleeper had just fallen into his lap. Another scout might have balked at the list of ifs that stood between the sleeper and the draft. *If* no other scout found out about him. *If* the kid and his parents were willing to keep the project a secret. And the biggest if: *if* the kid improved. But Tony Lucadello called Norm Kramer, who arranged a meeting in room 14 of the Hart Motel between the Sleeper and his parents.

Tony drove to Ft. Wayne. The Sleeper had been working construction, resigned to a blue-collar life and certain his baseball days were over. His parents came, knowing only that this had something to do with baseball. Mrs. Sleeper—a pretty and optimistic woman—had decided that it was God's will that her son's sports career was over. Mr. Sleeper was tight-lipped and skeptical. They got to the old gray room, and Norm Kramer introduced them to a tiny old man in a yellow cardigan sweater. Tony greeted them and offered a seat on the edge of his double bed.

"Young man," he said, raring back to deliver a sublimely hypothetical question, "how would you like to play for the Phillies?"

The Sleeper and his parents looked at each other. The Sleeper couldn't understand how this could be happening to him, but his face had opened into a preposterous grin. "I'd like it a lot."

"Well, I'm giving you a chance," Tony said. "But all of you have to do exactly what I tell you."

Tony swore the parents to silence and directed the Sleeper to meet with Norm Kramer three or four days every week. They went to the basement of the Sleeper's church. Outside, the ground was covered with snow, but the Sleeper threw baseball after baseball off the basement walls as Norm studied him, correcting flaws in his stance, his grip, his arm position. After one week the Sleeper could tell that he was a dramatically better pitcher. Every couple of weeks Tony Lucadello would happen by, watching as his Sleeper fired baseballs between the rungs of a ladderback chair, watching as his Sleeper learned to bend his back and his lead knee, as he learned to get down on the ball to field it, as he learned to stop throwing and start *pitching*.

As the weather got warmer, some of the workouts moved outside, and another accomplice was enlisted: a high school friend of the Sleeper's, who became the catcher. Tony swore him, too, to secrecy. He actually made the kid say the words: "I swear."

"He's not ready yet," Tony told me. "We have a little over a month now, and I'm hoping that he'll improve enough that I can sign him. But I'll tell you this: every time I see him, it's like he's a new pitcher. That's what the wall can do for you. This young man is living proof. Today we're taking him out to a field and you can see for yourself."

Tony sat on the bed, fidgeting and chewing his toothpick, waiting for Norm to arrive with the Sleeper and his catcher. Even talking about the Sleeper made him anxious. Here was a kid who played high school ball for a team that nobody saw, whose college career consisted of one scrimmage on a cold October day in Huntington, Indiana, and yet Tony Lucadello was panicky. What if I invest all this work and all these hopes in this young man, and I lose him?

He looked out the window, then sat back on the bed. Norm would arrive in an hour, but the wait was eating at Tony. He kept chewing on the toothpick as the water pipes of the Hart Motel ticked and whined.

"You know," Tony finally said, softly. "These toothpicks are kind of a trademark with me." He folded his arms across his chest and stared up at the ceiling. "It started many many years ago when I was playing with the Fostoria Redbirds. We had a pretty good club. We finished in second place, but we had a terrible time trying to beat the team in Tiffin, Ohio, which was affiliated with the Dee-troit Tigers. They had an outstanding pitcher, the best pitcher in the league by far, a cocky, ruthless player who'd just as soon throw at you as look at you. Anything to win. He put on a big show before he pitched, walkin' in front of the dugouts and poppin' off about how he was going to knock our ears off or pick our noses off, and so on.

"We never could beat this guy, so I decided it's about time for me to try to do somethin', because our players gave up every time he threw his glove out there. I was a cocky young ball player myself—I had to be because of my size. Every time I got into trouble with somebody, why, I'd jump on him real quick and hold on real tight until some big guy'd come in and break us up. Anyway, this pitcher was warming up along the side of the dugout, and there was an outhouse in that corner. I walked over there, pretending I had to go to it. I had a toothpick in my mouth that I'd been chewin' on. I stood there and watched him throw. I made a wisecrack at him, and he told me he was gonna hit me right between the eyes with the first pitch of the game. That's because he wasn't man enough to strike me out, I said, and we exchanged some more words until he got so mad he tried to jump me, but a couple of other guys broke us up. In the huddle of separating him and me, why, I pulled my toothpick out of my mouth, and I yelled at him, 'I can hit you with this toothpick! This toothpick will prove to you that you're nothin'! You baffled your way through all those wins.'

" 'You try it,' he says, 'and I'll nail you right between the eyes.'

"So the game started, and I stood up there by the batter's box and the umpire asked me where my bat was. 'Right here,' I says, pullin' the toothpick out of my mouth, and I waved it in his face. 'I'm gonna prove to this lousy so-and-so that I can hit him with this toothpick.'

"By now the fans had figured out what was going on, and even the players on his team were in my corner—everybody was—but they didn't think I'd go through with it. But I went up to the plate, and I hollered at him, 'C'mon, you lousy so-and-so, show me that good fastball. You're nothin'!' I thought he might try to throw at me, but he didn't. He came at me with his best fastball. I held my hand steady, with that toothpick over home plate, and when the ball came in, it was out of the strike zone, so I just bailed back a little bit, and it hit that toothpick square. It didn't hit my hand, but it bent the toothpick over and split it. It didn't break, because it was wet. I just raised the toothpick up and stuck it right in front of the umpire.

"And he said, 'Strike one!'

"I went to get a bat, and I'm yellin' at him, 'I told you, you lousy so-and-so, that I could hit you with a toothpick, and I proved it. There's the evidence.' And I asked the catcher if I didn't, and he said, 'Yep, you sure did.'

"The next pitch I hit into right field for a single, and then the big first baseman for the Tiffin Tigers picked me up and carried me to the mound. The umpires wondered what was happening, and they came running over to the mound. The first baseman wanted his pitcher to apologize. He wouldn't, and the first baseman set me down, and I ran back over to first base. Well, after that, the pitcher couldn't throw a strike. For about three or four innings, he walked just about *everybody*, and we beat him for the first time. And believe me that was quite an achievement. But that's a true story and it actually happened, in 1936, my first year in professional ball."

Norm Kramer drove up and tooted his horn. Tony grabbed his hat, cast his soggy toothpick to the wind, and we were off to a baseball diamond and the fuzzy-cheeked hopes for the future.

Carrington Field stands almost in the shadow of the Ft. Wayne Memorial Coliseum, where I saw my first rock concert. Connie Mack League teams play here—baseball for high school freshmen and sophomores—and the dugouts were built by the managers of the teams in that league.

Beyond the outfield fence, cars thundered down Coliseum Boulevard, Ft. Wayne's busiest thoroughfare. We came in on a back street, and Norm parked the car in the shade in a far corner of the parking lot.

"Who's that?" Tony said, pointing to eight thirtyish guys in sweatshirts taking batting practice in the right-field corner of the ballpark. "I thought you said there wouldn't be anyone here."

Norm took off his cap and scratched his bald head, embarrassed that this mission might have hit a snag. "They can't be an organized team," Norm said. "No one's scheduled to be here. I checked it out."

Tony thought this over. The average baseball fan doesn't realize how many thousands of bird-dog scouts there are, guys under contract to big-league teams to refer promising players to the full-time scout in their area. But Tony knew: scratch a man heavily involved in amateur baseball and you'll find someone who gets paid two hundred dollars if the Montreal Expos sign a player he recommends. We sat quietly in the car as Tony watched the men in right field. It was plain he didn't like the situation much, but he decided the risk was infinitesimal—though even that scared him—and, reluctantly, he motioned us out of the car.

The Sleeper and the Catcher jogged to the bullpen pitcher's mound down the third-base line, took off their jackets, and began to warm up.

"I know one of those guys," Norm said. "He owns one of the Connie Mack teams in this league. He's a millionaire."

Tony didn't show any alarm or even look up. "You hide."

Norm laughed.

"I'm not kidding," Tony snapped. *"Hide.* Behind that dugout. You go with him," he said to me. "And don't take your notebook or your camera out. I don't want to create any suspicion."

As Norm and I slipped behind the home dugout, Tony walked down the third-base fence and the Sleeper went behind the mound and warmed up with long and easy eighty-foot tosses, moving up a couple of steps every four or five throws. Tony pulled up the collar of his overcoat and wrapped his lavender scarf around his face.

By the time the Sleeper worked his way to the mound, Norm could take it no longer. Straining for a better view, he stuck his head furtively around the corner of the dugout, which made him look like a skittish desperado in a TV cop show. The men in right field, as far as I could tell, were oblivious.

"He throws what you call a 'cut fastball,' " Norm said, demonstrating the off-center grip that makes the ball behave like a cross between a regular fastball and a split-fingered fastball. In addition to being a little easier to learn than the split-finger, the cut fastball moves more unpredictably and can be more difficult for batters to solve.

The Sleeper threw harder now, and Tony, leaning on the fence, sized up every quirk in the young man's motion and physique. He was six feet tall, a little short for a pitcher, but powerfully built, especially in his lower body, which was a little out of proportion to his torso. He had blond, curly hair, and he hadn't said anything since Tony and I got into the car, answering Tony's proffered instruction with nods and mumbles.

After about twenty minutes, Tony moved the Sleeper and the Catcher to the pitching mound on the field. Norm kept darting his head around the corner, whispering to the Sleeper: "Bend that front knee. . . . A little more. . . . Now show him the curveball. . . . C'mon, get it over the plate. Throw strikes, Mike."

"Mike?"

Norm winced. "Oh, geez, don't tell Tony." He looked longingly out on the field, and he couldn't have been any edgier if the Sleeper were his own grandson. "He comes from a good family. I've checked it out. Real close-knit. They eat together, they go to church together. Real good people."

Tony stood on the third-base side of the mound, trying to get the Sleeper to pull the ball straight back, rather than winding up over his head. But the Catcher kept breaking the Sleeper's concentration—dropping balls, throwing them back in the dirt and over the Sleeper's head. He even flinched on low fastballs. Finally, the old scout stomped up to the plate and gave the boy a two-minute catching summary, crouching in the dirt alongside him, reaching behind him and positioning his arms and his shoulders, pantomiming a smooth throw back to the pitcher. Tony went back to the mound, and the Catcher did well for the next several pitches, until one got away from him and sailed over second base.

"C'mere," the old scout barked, waving me over.

"I don't have a cup, Tony."

"No, don't worry about that. I want you to have a chance to really see my boy throw. Stand in the batter's box."

The fastest pitcher I've ever faced is probably Hurricane

Hank, a since-destroyed batting-cage machine in Bryan, Ohio, where I grew up. The sign on the cage said Hank threw at eighty-five miles per hour. I stood on the right side of the batter's box, without a bat or even a toothpick. The Sleeper fired the pitch in, low and inside and hissing. I bailed out and the Catcher winced and the ball glanced off his mitt and rolled to the backstop.

My heart beat faster. The Sleeper looked twice as fast when I stood that close. The next pitch, a curve, came in high and tight. I couldn't have hit it with a barn door.

I moved to the left side and calmed myself as the Sleeper bore down and threw his best fastballs of the day, three darting blurs low and inside. All three pitches broke downward, strikes that almost landed in the dirt.

The Catcher's throws kept rolling into the outfield, and the Sleeper, annoyed and perhaps tired from chasing the ball, began to get wild. I backed out of the batter's box, and I was relieved when Tony told us to pack up and get in the car.

"Go say hello to your friend," Tony told Norm. "You don't have to lie to him, but tell him something to throw him off."

The Sleeper's parents had pulled up on the service road, and they'd been watching the workout from about a hundred yards away, obscured from view by the bleachers of Carrington Field. Tony ordered the Sleeper to put his coat on, and then he introduced me to the boy's parents, although not by name. Tony told them their son was progressing just fine. Mrs. Sleeper told me that this secrecy was testing her discipline. She was so excited, she wanted to share the news with all her friends and relatives. She wanted to hire a town crier to announce to all of Ft. Wayne that her son was being scouted by the Philadelphia Phillies. Whether he got drafted or not, she could hardly believe the good fortune that had befallen her family that day in the Hart Motel, and they were all pinching themselves that Mike would at least have a chance.

Mr. Sleeper nodded his assent.

"Mike always dreamed of playing baseball," said Mrs. Sleeper. "He used to say to me, 'Mom, no one's ever going to watch Ft. Wayne Christian School play,' and I kept telling him that if the Lord wanted him to play baseball, He'd find him."

The Sleeper blushed and shrugged. "Yeah, well, when I quit school, I thought my baseball days were through," he said in a whisper that was almost a prayer.

Mrs. Sleeper showed Tony her kitchen wall calendar, which had the days until the draft marked off.

Tony laughed. "You do that, too?"

"Just one more month," she said. "I don't know if I can stand it."

"It'll come up quick," Tony said. "I only hope the office will draft some players for me this year."

The April sky had grown gray, and the first sprinkles of a spring shower dotted the windshield of the Sleeper family's car. For Tony Lucadello, years of work were narrowing to a three-day bottom line: the draft, June 1, 2, and 3. During the past few years, he has seen tens of thousands of players eligible for the 1988 draft. He has filed reports on a hundred or so. Of those, about twenty will appear on his final draft list. Of those twenty, if he's lucky, he'll get four or five. Some years the Phillies haven't drafted any of his players, and the old scout, through no fault of his own, had nothing to show for a year's hard work. He feels like a player who has hit .300 or won twenty games, only to find his season erased from the *Baseball Encyclopedia* by a cruel technicality.

The Sleeper, his friend, and his parents went home, visions of pro ball dancing in their heads. Norm Kramer handed Tony a stack of reports and went home to his wife. But Tony Lucadello struck out on U.S. 24, destined for more nights in places like the Hart Motel, more days in places like Carrington Field, looking for more players like those forty-nine young men he had correctly foreseen as major leaguers. Time was short, and the seventy-five-year-old scout wanted to find one or two more players for that draft list—big, raw, loose-limbed young men whom he could project in the home whites and maroon caps of the Philadelphia Phillies.

8

The Signing of Dick Drott

The first three players taken in the 1988 draft were all from Tony Lucadello's territory. Drafted first by the San Diego Padres was Andy Benes from Evansville University, a six-six right-handed pitcher, who had just this year found some extra velocity—and the plate—with his fastball, transforming him from a marginal prospect to the nation's top draft choice and a young man with two hundred grand in his pocket. The Cleveland Indians picked next, selecting Mark Lewis from Hamilton, Ohio, whom Tony called the best shortstop prospect he'd ever seen—this from the man who recommended that the Chicago Cubs sign Ernie Banks. Picking third, Atlanta took Steve Avery, a six-three lefty from Taylor, Michigan's, Kennedy High School. Avery was committed to a full-ride at Stanford, but drafted that high, he stood to get about a quarter-million bucks.

Tony would have drafted Lewis first ("a position ball player will help you more than a pitcher"), Avery second, and Benes third, but he had every confidence that all three were future big-league stars. He'd quit going to their games a month ago, certain of his assessment and equally certain that they'd be gone by the time Philadelphia picked, eleventh. He was right. The Phillies took a pitcher from Baylor.

We heard the first-round selections on ESPN in Tony's living room in Fostoria.

"Texas!" Tony scoffed. "There, you see? They're always drafting those players from Texas and California and Florida. But where are they? I don't know, but they're not in the major leagues." He picked up the remote control and snapped off the TV. "How can it be possible for a scout with my record not to get a player in the first twenty rounds for the last ten years? They make me get by with sleepers and free agents, never the top kids in my territory."

Phillies officials I'd talked to at spring training had assured me this was just one of those things, that it was the fault not of Tony but of the luck of the draft and the bounty to be found in the territory. It happens to every scout, they told me. "Maybe so," Tony said. "But then how come players I recommended, players we could have drafted, are playing in the big leagues for other clubs? And how come the magazines are rating our minor league system the worst in baseball now?" I'd just shown Tony an article from *Inside Sports* that rated the Phillies system as the most devoid of talent in all of baseball.

He put his hands in the pockets of his cardigan sweater and walked to the window, as angry and nervous as I'd ever seen him. At home, Tony didn't wear a hat, which made him seem smaller. But he did have on a shirt and tie, red socks and dress shoes, though he had no intention of leaving home, even for a second. The phone might ring anytime over the next three days with the news Tony waits a year to hear: "We've drafted a player for you."

But the black rotary-dial phone on the wood-paneled kitchen wall was silent. Tony paced back and forth, from his living-room lounge chair to the kitchen table, where he'd arranged several neat stacks of papers, all the information he'd need for any call that might come. Occasionally Tony would pick up the phone. "It's still working," he'd say. "At least there's a tone. I hope people can get through." Then he'd rub his hands together, pace back into the living room, switch on the TV for another few seconds, and then pace back into the kitchen.

The baseball draft is a different species from the football and basketball drafts. For one thing, it lasts three days and goes as many rounds as the teams want, usually about fifty; basketball, by contrast, now last only two rounds. Also, baseball drafts players out of high school or after their junior or senior years of college. The football and basketball drafts take players at the end of their college eligibility, and if you don't like the team who drafted you or the money they offered, well, son, enjoy your new job down at the exit 4 Jiffy-Lube. In baseball, unless you are an abysmal student or a college senior, you can always opt for another year of school and hope you'll be drafted higher next time.

Perhaps the biggest difference is that the baseball draft is held in private. Only the first-round selections are announced; the remainder of the draft is kept secret until the scouts have time to sign the players. Baseball officials fear that college coaches would descend, scholarships in hand on drafted high-school kids, using the professional teams as a free resource for finding talent.

So for three antsy days Tony Lucadello flits about his little house as if someone had dumped bennies in his Sanka, afraid the phone won't ring, afraid it will ring and the news will be bad. When he heard about Benes, Lewis, and Avery, he hung his head, walked to the kitchen, and picked his draft list from the piles of papers. With a face as somber as a sensitive general recording troop casualties, Tony placed a small "x" in each of the first three boxes on his list, pausing to whisper the comments he'd written.

"Has outstanding pluses in all areas.

"Will be a first-division major league pitcher.

"Cannot miss. Born to play shortstop."

All afternoon we sat in the house, staring at the telephone while Tony wondered how many more players from Texas the Phillies had drafted now. "They're probably in the third round," he said at about two. At four, he guessed the draft was in its eighth or ninth round. "They're not drafting anyone for me," he said. "Again this year. I guess they just don't like me. Maybe I should quit."

At five he asked his wife to take me out to dinner. "I'd take you myself," he said. "But I've got to stay by the phone. And besides, I'm just not hungry for some reason."

Virginia Lucadello took me to the Golden Corral, where we each had the salad bar and she snuck a cigarette. We talked about her daughter's success in graduate school, about her granddaughter's high-school tennis triumphs, and about her own upbringing as the daughter of a poor and black-lunged coal miner in the hills of southeast Ohio. Virginia Lucadello is the smart, doting aunt we all wish we'd had, engaged with the world but taken up by the lives of her relatives. I enjoyed the chance to drift away into the daily circumstances of her life, and we were each a little relieved to be freed from eight hours of intense baseball speculation.

Tony greeted us at the door. "One more's gone," he said. "The Boston Red Sox took Naehring in the ninth round." So Tony had lost the Miami University shortstop he'd coveted, a player he thought had the potential to succeed Mike Schmidt as the Phillies third baseman. "I told them to take him in the second or third round, but they didn't. We could have taken him all the way up until the eighth round, but they didn't. They can't say we never had a chance to get Naehring, now can they? But Boston knows their hitters. He'll be a good one. He was my number five."

"Nine rounds already?" I said.

Tony nodded. "They're done for the day."

"Did you get anyone?"

He closed his eyes and shook his head slowly. "No one from my office called. I heard about Naehring from the Miami coach."

"Who was your number four?"

"Oh, he must be gone by now. It was Tom Marsh, the center fielder from Toledo University. He can do it all, great arm, great speed, excellent body control. Somebody got themselves a good ball player. And number six is Dell, that right-handed pitcher from Huntington. I'm afraid he's gone too. I need to go for a walk."

He put on his hat and walked down the tree-lined side streets of Fostoria, down to the town's twin reservoirs. He looked across their smooth surfaces, black with reflected dusk, and he figured that half of the players on his own draft list were gone. In all, 260 players had been drafted. Some of them will play in the big leagues. A handful will help their teams win a pennant someday. Maybe one or two will wind up in the Hall of Fame. But none would be signed by Tony Lucadello.

The next morning, Tony greeted me at his door with what I took to be good news, although he didn't seem particularly elated. The day before, right after I'd left, the office had called Tony with the news that they'd drafted Indiana University shortstop Mickey Morandini in the fifth round. Morandini was tenth of eighteen on Tony's draft list, yet the Phillies drafted him ahead of players five through nine, all but one of whom were still available. Tony knew why. Morandini had played last summer in the Cape Cod collegiate league, where he'd led the loop in hitting and caught the attention of Dick Lawlor, the Phillies' eastern cross-checker.

I would have thought that whatever the circumstances, Tony would have been delighted to get a player drafted this high, the highest he'd gotten in a decade. But he knew this was not his accomplishment but Lawlor's, who was in Philadelphia with all the top brass. And Tony worried how difficult Morandini would be to sign, since he'd been invited to try out for the 1988 Olympic team. As far as Tony had been told, players who signed would forfeit their amateur status.

"I called and offered him twenty-five thousand dollars, which isn't bad. Now, on him, we just have to wait and see how bad he wants to play. If they let me handle it the way I want to handle it, I'll just say, 'Look, if you don't want this offer, go ahead and play in the Olympics. Take your chances that you may get the same offer back. But you're wasting a year, right down the drain. You play all summer with them, what's it gonna get you?' "

Baseball in the Olympics has gotten a glowing reception by the press, as 1984 Olympians like Will Clark, Mark McGwire and Barry Larkin have become big league stars. Tony contends that those players would have been just as good without the Olympics, probably better, and reached the majors at least a season sooner, which would have bagged some of those players a million bucks or so. Plus, Tony told me, you don't hear much about that kid John Hoover, the ace of the 1984 pitching staff, because he pitched so many innings that he hurt himself and has had a hard time getting out of AA ball.

"You don't think Morandini'd improve close to as much as he'd improve in the minors?" I said.

"*Improve!*" Tony scowled, aghast that after several months with him I could ask a question so ignorant. "There's no possible way he'd improve more. The Olympics is just a show. It's just a rah-rah type of thing and that's it. But in professional baseball he's playing against pros, under much better instruction. See, he has to change positions, too, from shortstop to left field, so the instruction's important to how fast he progresses."

But there was more to Tony's frustration. He fidgeted in his gold corduroy recliner as he explained. "Tom Marsh still hasn't been drafted. With the scouting report I sent in on him, they should have taken him in the second round, at least."

"Well, if he's still available," I said, "you guys might just get a bargain."

"Yes, but the thing is, if they get drafted high, the team will play them automatically, no matter what they do, because of what we have invested in him. That helped Mike Schmidt, remember. He struggled at first. If we'd have gotten a 'bargain' out of him, why, he might have never had the chance to play. Now, I like Morandini all right, and the fifth round's about right for him. But Marsh is a much better defensive ball player. Marsh has got a better arm—there's no comparison with their arms. I would have to say that Morandini's got a little bit of an edge on speed. But just a little, and he's not as aggressive as Marsh. Marsh has got real bat power. You know, I can't understand it. But they think they can get Marsh, or whatever, so we'll just wait and see."

The phone rang.

Tony's face opened into a grin, and he popped up from his La-Z-boy. "Watch out!" he said, and the seventy-five-year-old scout jogged into the kitchen.

The call was from Toledo coach Stan Sanders, who said a Toledo pitcher named Sager had been drafted by the Padres in the twelfth round and that Marsh, inexplicably, was still available. Tony was crestfallen. "I thought that was the big call," he said. "At least he's still available. Why they don't pick him is completely beyond me."

He sank into one of the hard chairs at the kitchen table. The only sports memorabilia in the room was behind him, sixteen clippings touting his granddaughter's high-school tennis exploits, taped to the side of a wooden hutch.

"If I was with another organization," he said in a reverent whisper, "I could get a dozen players drafted *real quick*. But I'm just with an organization that . . . Well, I don't know. I just don't understand it. Maybe you can tell me. Don't hesitate to tell me what's wrong with me. You could say, 'Well, Tony, the reason why they don't draft any ball players for you is because you don't do this, you don't do that, you're not a good scout.' Come right out. What the heck's the difference? At my age, it doesn't matter any more. What am I gonna get out of it, a medal?" He laughed. "I don't even wear those rings, for heaven's sake, and I got four of them."

He was happier now, enjoying the opportunity to poke fun at himself, and I had to beg shamelessly to get him to show me those rings: two Scout of the Year rings and two World Series rings, four heavy nuggets of precious stones and metals, all stored in a drawer, swaddled in folded handkerchiefs, far from the danger of easy, ostentatious display to strangers.

The phone rang. He left me with his 1980 World Series ring in my hand and snatched up the receiver. Dick Lawlor said yes, the Phillies had drafted Tom Marsh.

"Sixteenth round! Well, okay, Dick. At least we got him. Tell me now what I can offer him."

I looked at Tony's draft list, where Marsh's "$ Evaluation" blank read "$90,000."

"Naw. Aw, for cripe's sake. Godalmighty, is that *all*? I hate this offer with Marsh. His brother's a cripple and everything. . . . Jesus criminy. Who told you this, Jack? . . . No, Jim didn't see him, for heaven's sake. . . . Well, that's ridiculous. I hate to even make an offer like that to him. Here I got him up there as high as I have him. . . . Well, they don't think much of me. . . . If I could offer him that, I'd be satisfied. But ten!"

Tony talked with Lawlor about signing Morandini. Apparently, Major League Baseball had signed an agreement with the Olympic Committee which allowed players to sign and still play in Seoul, as long as payment was deferred until after the games. Tony said he'd call Morandini and set the record straight and, furthermore, that he'd meet with him tomorrow and try to sign a contract. "But so what?" Tony said to Lawlor. "What's the Olympics? . . . Yeah, but he's twenty-two years old, and he's gonna waste another year on the sandlots, huh?"

Tony was silent for a while as Lawlor detailed the proper procedure for signing the prospective Olympian.

"Dick," Tony said. "Let me ask you something. Don't the people like me in this office? . . . Well, how can they possibly like me, Dick, when you don't even draft my players?"

After a few more minutes of mumbling "OK" into the receiver, Tony hung up. "That daggone Scouting Bureau. They put Marsh down for a bonus of five thousand. Well, who'd the bureau ever sign? Nobody, that's who. They're wrong about Tom Marsh, you wait and see. They must have seen him pitching or playing DH and not been able to project him as a major league center fielder. Now I'm not criticizing them, really. That should have helped me. But what I don't understand is how my own team can take the word of the bureau over mine."

He stood by the phone with his hands on hips, the career employee who'd done his job so well for so long that his bosses had begun to underestimate him. "They told me the reason why is that he's a twenty-two-year-old player and he has to sign or else. Oh, my. This is gonna be embarrassing."

But he turned to one of the neat stacks of paper on the kitchen table and picked up a form with Tom Marsh's phone number.

"Hello, Mrs. Marsh. This is Tony Lucadello with the Phillies. We drafted Tom. Yeah, I'll hold."

He turned to me. "That daggone bureau."

"Hi, Tom. It's Tony Lucadello. Well, I got some good news and I got some not good news. I want to be honest with you. First is that we drafted you. That's the good news. You've been drafted in the sixteenth round. Now, the other thing is, I can't offer you a whole lot of money. That's the bad news. I'd like to get together with you, and when I do, I'll explain the whole thing of why the bonus is not extensive. But it is an opportunity for you.

"Now if you signed, I want you to leave Sunday. I'll buy you a plane ticket at my travel agent's here in Fostoria. We have a minicamp in Florida, and you'll spend seven days there at our complex, and then they'll assign you to a team, probably Batavia, New York, which is our high rookie league team.

"I just wish it was more money, but that's beyond my control. Look at it this way: we thought more of you than anybody else did. This gives you the opportunity. All you have to do is go out there and wear that ball out, and you'll make the money. It'll be there."

Tony set up a meeting with Marsh for that night, at the Toledo Turnpike Inn. They finished talking, and Tony gently hung up the phone. His face was drawn and pale. He sat down at the table and put his head in his hands, and we sat there for a long time.

Finally, he gave a resigned nod and produced a yellow contract. You're a writer, he said, you must know how to type, and then he asked if I'd like to type up the first professional contract for a young man Tony expected would play in the major leagues. As any hopeless fan would, I grinned and said, "You bet," wondering if I could somehow get away with typing in my own name on the top line and catching the next Piedmont flight from Toledo to Clearwater. Tony produced a portable, manual typewriter—a blue 1958 Royal Futura 800—and I pecked out three copies of the agreement between the Batavia Clippers Baseball Club and Thomas Owen Marsh, player. The last line was: "This player signed by Tony Lucadello, Scout"—a line I typed slowly and with reverence, until I reached the period, which I slammed home each time with enough glee to cut through the paper to the old, pitted platen.

* * *

"That offer to Marsh is going to kill me," Tony said later that afternoon, still waiting for the phone to ring. "This office shows no real deep affection for me, but they claim this: this Current kid, my catcher, we're going to have to give him some money. See, he's got a four-year football scholarship, so they want the money to go there, 'cause they know how much I like him." Tony tapped his hands arrhythmically on the armrests of his La-Z-Boy. "If other scouts would have seen this kid when I saw him, he'd have gone in the first two rounds, no question. But he improved late in the season. I would say, 90 percent he's a sleeper, but you never know."

The Phillies office called a couple times to see if Matt Current could really be as good as Tony promised, and Tony told them, "For heaven's sake, yes, and what are you worrying about, anyway? Who are you looking at in the twentieth round that's better than this kid? He's six foot three, two-twenty— the body of a man already, and he's just seventeen years old! After five years of pro ball, he'll still be younger than Morandini is now!"

As Tony's somber kitchen clock tolled the second stroke of two, the phone rang. Tony picked it up and laughed. "Oh, great, Dick! Twenty-second round? And, um, I'm gonna give him twenty-two. . . . Nope. He won't take that. Definitely. . . . Well, he's got his full football scholarship. He wants thirty. . . . You let me have twenty-two and I'll go down there and sign him. But there's no use having me go down there and embarrassing myself offering him twenty, 'cause he won't take it."

Tony told Lawlor he already had arranged to go sign Marsh and would consequently be leaving shortly, though his wife would be there to answer the phone.

In disgust, Tony hung up. "I had a notion to tell them that if they didn't want to give me enough money to sign my ball players, they could have this job. They wanted to give me twenty. He's worth a hundred!"

A few minutes later, Morandini called, and Tony told him

that he could in fact sign a contract now and still try out for the Olympics. "To me, I think you still ought to go and play for us, but you do what you think you have to do. . . . Yeah, I did sign Mike. And forty-eight others. . . . Well, whatever you do, I'd sign, because if you got hurt you'd still have something."

Morandini lived in Leechburg, Pennsylvania, and Tony made arrangements to meet him tomorrow at the exit 10 Holiday Inn, halfway between his home and Tony's.

Tony and I were on our way out the door when the phone rang again. It was Norm Kramer, calling to tell Tony that he'd seen in *USA Today* that Scott Service had been called up from AA Reading to AAA Maine. Kramer told Tony that his fiftieth was only a notch away now. "I've been that close before," Tony said, "But, maybe, this time, who knows? Thanks for the good news."

And then he gathered up his papers and we were off, driving up Ohio 199, past farm-implement dealerships and Sterling stores, to Toledo to sign Tom Marsh. "Way to go, Scott," he murmured. "Make me proud."

We waited for Marsh at Miller's Restaurant, where yet another young waitress knew neither Tony nor his usual order. I ordered a burger and asked if he thought Marsh might balk at the low offer.

"No, he just wants to play ball. I probably feel worse about it than he does. If he plays like I know he can, he'll get his money up in the big leagues. Back before the draft, other teams could have offered him more, but he's a college senior and he doesn't have any choice now."

I asked him if he'd ever had trouble getting his club to authorize a high-enough bonus before the draft.

"Well, one time I signed a boy who had offers from seven

other teams, and my offer was ninety-six thousand dollars lower than anyone else's."

"Who was that?"

"Dick Drott. He played seven years in the big leagues. Won fifteen games as a rookie, but then he hurt his arm. I first saw him at an American Legion game in Lawrenceburg, Indiana, back when he was fifteen years old, pitching for the Bentley Post team. Because he was so young, and because they had an extremely good team, they used him mostly in relief. This was a big game, though, and I thought sure he'd pitch. I got there in the seventh, and I went to a drinking fountain, and Dick Drott arrived there the same time I did. So I told him to drink first. 'Are you going to pitch?' I says.

" 'Yeah, I'm goin' in next inning.'

" 'Great,' I says. 'I came all the way down here just to see you. I'm a scout for the Chicago Cubs.'

" 'You are?' he says. 'Geez, that's great!'

"I got his home phone number, and he asked me for one of my business cards, and I gave him one, and I told him to go out there and show me what he could do.

"He pitched that one inning and struck out the side. From that day forward, I kept a real close relationship with the boy and his family. Every time I was in the Cincinnati area, I'd stop to see him. I got a chance to meet the parents, and they invited me into their house several times for meals.

"During his senior year, he was invited to work out for the Cincinnati Reds, and scouts from every team in the National League were there. They fell in love with him, and they all told him, don't sign with anybody else because we'll give you a lot of money. The father got involved with this, and he'd hear a hundred thousand here, more than a hundred thousand there.

"High school players couldn't sign until one minute after midnight on the day after they graduated, so the father made appointments with all the teams for the morning following the boy's high-school graduation, starting at nine o'clock. I hadn't made an appointment, but I went over to the house just before the graduation ceremonies, and the father and the boy asked me when I would like to come over the next day.

"Baseball had a ruling that year that if you gave a player more than four thousand dollars he'd have to go to the major league club for two years and remain there before they could option him out. I had talked it over with my superiors, and they wouldn't go over four thousand for Dick because they didn't want him to throw batting practice for two years and lose out on the training he'd get with the minor league clubs. So, even though they knew I had a close relationship with the family, all they'd let me offer him was four thousand dollars.

"The parents were asking when I'd like to come in tomorrow, and I said, 'You name it,' and finally the boy said, 'Well, you're going to my graduation, aren't you, Tony?'

" 'Do you want me to?'

" 'You're darn right I want you to! And then after the graduation you can talk to me.'

"We went to the graduation, and we came back, about nine-thirty, and we were just talking baseball, and it gets to be about eleven o'clock, and I realized that now I had to make him my offer. I asked to be excused, to go out in my car and get something. I got a little bottle of onion juice. I soaked the little finger on my left hand with that juice, and then I went back into the house.

"I started by talking about how all this happened between Dick and myself, and how we related to one another all these years, and how much he really meant to me. Then I started wiping my eyes with that little finger, and the tears started floating down out of my eyes. I kept talking—broken, sad, all that bit.

"Then the most remarkable thing happened. The mother started crying. The father started crying. And the boy started crying. They knew how deeply in love I was with this boy, how much he meant to me over the past three years. I told them that I couldn't give them the kind of money the father had told me he'd been offered from other teams. All I could offer was the four thousand, and he'd have to go through the channels of our minor leagues. That was the best I could do.

"The father, in spite of the fact that he had tears in his eyes, came right out and says, 'Tony, we have seven offers here, and every one of them says they'll give Dick more than a hundred thousand dollars.'

" 'Yes, Mr. Drott,' I says. 'I understand that and I agree with you. I know what the boy means to me, and you know what the boy means to me. But you do what you think is best.'

"All at once, the boy jumped up and the mother went into a kind of collapse. That scared us all, and we called the doctor. Back in those days, the doctor still came to your house. He came in there and he gave her a sedative and told her to lay on the couch, and she was fine, a little drowsy, but okay.

"I told Mr. Drott that I thought I better leave and that I was sorry I couldn't offer him what all those over scouts were going to offer tomorrow. I thanked them and told them I'd let them get some sleep before their big day.

"As I was going out, the mother says, 'Dick. Dad. Kneel down by me here.' And they did. 'I don't want the money,' she whispers. 'We're not poor. We're not wealthy, but we're gettin' along fine. Over my dead body is my boy going to sign with anyone but Tony. Tony loves our boy and we love Tony. For three years, he's stayed in touch with us and helped Dick with his pitching, probably more than anybody else. Now, Dad, you get that big money out of your head and do what I said.'

"The father accepted it, and the boy said he wanted the same thing, that he'd never intended to sign with anyone else and that was why he'd invited me to his graduation ceremonies. At about a half hour after midnight, I signed Dick Drott.

"I was getting ready to drive away, and the father asked

me what he should say to the other scouts tomorrow. And I said, 'Just tell each one that he signed thirty minutes after midnight for four thousand dollars.' But all those scouts did not believe it. They thought I'd slipped him money under the table, and they all reported me to the commissioner of baseball."

The commissioner made Tony fly to New York. He didn't believe Tony's account of the signing. But there was no proof of wrongdoing, so the commissioner sent a private detective to follow Tony, looking for any shred of evidence of under-the-table payments. The other scouts started calling Tony a dirty crook, and the detective made it impossible for him to do his job. Finally, Tony persuaded P. K. Wrigley to clear up the matter. Wrigley called the commissioner and told him that if there had been any illegal payments they would have been made with Wrigley's money. No such payments were made, Wrigley said, and if you do not cease your harassment of my scout, I shall seek your removal from office. The next day the detective vanished and the commissioner sent a letter to all the teams involved, saying that the signing of Dick Drott had been accomplished not by hook or by crook but with skill and integrity, and the matter was now closed.

"Onion juice?" I said. "Why did you have onion juice in your car?"

"I don't know!" Tony said, laughing. "I don't remember. It just came to me to use it, all of a sudden like."

Tony picked up the check, and we waited in the parking lot until a battered blue Bonneville drove up. "That's Marsh," Tony said, casting his toothpick aside and hurrying to meet him, hand outstretched.

Tony had rented a room at the Toledo Turnpike Inn just for the signing. I had assumed this would be the same small dark room he stayed in himself. But instead, he'd asked the desk clerk for the best room in the place. Apparently not a whole lot of people make this request at the Toledo Turnpike Inn, and the room was available. It wasn't actually a room at all but a small cottage in the middle of the inn's wide, flat courtyard: a free-standing house, yellow, peak-roofed and seldom occupied, with its own driveway, patio and picnic tables. It must have been designed as a honeymoon suite, but—I mean no disrespect—how many couples honeymoon in Toledo, Ohio?

Oh, honey, let's go see where those scales are made! And we can stay in that darling yellow cottage at the Toledo Turnpike Inn, close to scenic exit 4!

The cottage had been redecorated recently; the bedspread sported a lively pineapple-splotched print and the room smelled of new carpet, Pine-Sol, and hot polyester. Tony opened his attaché case on the dresser and began to arrange his papers in stacks. In the driveway, Tom Marsh pulled a wheelchair from his trunk, opened the passenger door, helped his brother into the chair and wheeled him into the cottage.

"It's okay if my brother Dan watches, isn't it?" said Tom, a quiet six-footer with broad shoulders, a blond flattop and a faint blond mustache. Of Tom's three older brothers, one died in a car crash, one lost two fingers and a thumb in another accident, and the third, Dan, broke his neck diving into a shallow pool.

"Of course," Tony said. "Naturally. This is a big day for your whole family, Tom."

Tom and I sat around the room's small round wooden table. Tom wheeled Dan to the edge of the table, and Tony Lucadello took a seat on the edge of the bed.

"Now, before I even show you the contract, Tom, I want to explain a few things and answer all your questions, and then if you're still interested, we'll talk about that contract, okay?"

Tom nodded.

"Now, there's no question that the Philadelphia organization could use an outfielder with power, and you can play all three outfield positions, so you fit in very nicely as far as being a prospect is concerned. I don't believe that we have enough players in our minor leagues with bat power, good speed and a good arm. There's too many ball players being signed today that have only one plus, instead of two or three, like you have, and the results is it shows, up in the big leagues.

"Now, the Phillies, we have just about as nice a baseball park as you'd want to see. The only better-looking park I've seen is Kansas City, and they don't seat but forty-eight thousand. Our park will seat close to seventy, and it's a better park for that reason. It's not built like these football theaters, like Riverfront Stadium and all those other places, which were built for football first.

"Our training quarters is in Clearwater. We have a complex there, perhaps the nicest complex there is in baseball. We have four diamonds around a big clubhouse, and all the diamonds measure the same distance as our Veterans Stadium in Philadelphia. This year, we have what we call a minicamp, and we're bringing in all the players we sign, and you'll stay there until they assign you to where you'll play the rest of the summer. That'll be about June the seventeenth. But it's a special thing because you get to see our complex, you get to see Russell Field, where the big club will train, and you get to meet a lot of the fellas you'll be playing with.

"Now, you're going to be signed to Batavia, New York, which is in the New York–Penn League, probably the oldest league in baseball. Maine is our triple-A club, but just for the time being. By the time you're promoted there, you'll be playing in a beautiful new stadium over at Scranton, Pennsylvania. Reading, Pennsylvania, is our double-A club. Clearwater, Florida, is our high-A club. And Spartanburg, South Carolina, is our middle-A club. Batavia is our high rookie league club, and Martinsville, Virginia, is where we're sending the high school kids. We're putting all college kids up in the New York–Penn League.

"Keep in mind that all minor league teams operate just like a major league club: they have presidents, vice presidents, business managers, secretaries, everything a major league team has, with the exception that it's on a smaller scale, naturally. You'll be paid on the first and fifteenth of every month, just like everyone in baseball is paid.

"Now, I want to get down to the nitty-gritty of this thing, and that is this: you also have a chance, if you prove yourself up there in Batavia, to go to the Instructional League, which starts September the twentieth and lasts until November the twentieth. That's what you want to shoot for, because if they take you to the Instructional League, they're taking you there to work with you, to do something to promote you to a higher level the next year. They only take thirty or forty men, so you have to earn it.

"Now we get down to the conditions of the contract. Your salary will be seven hundred dollars a month. That's the highest I can give you. Nobody can give you any higher. That's the most any minor league ball player can make in his first year. Depending on what you do, you can get a raise the next year, and the next year, and so on. Your bonus is gonna be ten thousand dollars, cash bonus, five thousand when the contract is approved by the National Association—that's not us. They're the people who are protecting you. And you'll get the other five thousand May the first, 1989. That's to help you with your taxes, see. And then I'm gonna throw in the incentive bonus plan, which will work this way. You've got a chance to make seventy-five hundred dollars. When you play ninety days with our double-A team, which is Reading, Pennsylvania, you get a thousand dollars. When you play ninety days with Maine, which is our triple-A club, you'll get another bonus of fifteen hundred dollars. And when you reach the major leagues, you'll get a bonus of five thousand dollars. Now you'll forget you got that coming, probably, but it's there."

Tony repeated the terms of the contract, the meager monthly salary, the bonus he'd been embarrassed to offer, the *de rigueur* incentive bonus plan. He spoke not like a salesman but rather an elderly, square-shooting uncle taking his inexperienced but hard-working nephew as a junior partner in his venerable lumber business. Nodding at Tony's every sentence, Marsh kept his hands clasped together on his lap. His knuckles were white. Dan Marsh, two years older than Tom, sat with his hands to his chin, a Red Man Chewing Tobacco painter's cap turned bill-backward on his head.

And then Tony tossed the yellow contracts, contracts that *I'd* typed, onto the table. "Do you have any questions?"

"Nope," Tom said, his right hand on the table, shaking, ready to sign.

"Well, how about the brother, do you have any questions?"

"Probably about twenty," Dan said. "But I can't think of a one of 'em."

The contracts sat on the table. Tom hunched over them, rocking gently in his chair.

"Now if you sign," Tony said, "I have a plane ticket here. You leave at eight o'clock Sunday morning, and you'll get into Clearwater about two forty-five. You've been in a plane before, haven't you?"

"Yep."

Tony explained how to hail a limousine to the Phillies clubhouse, how to get reimbursed for the ride, where to report. Tom Marsh's shoulders began to tremble.

Tony set the ticket on the table. "Now, that's your ticket, if you sign."

Tony opened up one of the contracts and handed the other two copies to Tom and Dan. He read the terms outlined there, and the brothers followed along, making sure everything agreed. In the middle of this presentation, Tony stopped and looked up. "Do you want to sign today?"

"Yeah!" Tom shouted, then, embarrassed, he added, almost in a whisper: "Yes, sir."

"Oh," Tony said. "Well, I had to ask, because if you don't, there's no need even reading the rest of this thing."

He finished going through the contract and handed Tom a pen. "I know you're of age, Tom," Tony said, "but I'd like your brother to sign this, too. You know, as a witness like. You can sign it there where it asks for parent or guardian."

Tom signed his first copy, hand racked with the shakes, pen spinning in undecipherable whorls on the page. In a soothing voice, Tony told him to take his time, to make that "2" on the date blank a little easier to read. He rested his hand lightly on the shoulder of the young outfielder.

When the papers had been signed and slipped into stamped and addressed envelopes, Tony snapped his attaché case closed, shook Tom's hand, and said, "Congratulations, young man. Now you're a Phillie."

Tony walked into the bathroom and came out with two new Louisville Sluggers. "There's one thing you have to do to really make it big," Tony said, handing one of the bats to Tom, "and that's lean out over that plate. You're an inside-ball hitter, but they can get you out with those curveballs and sliders on the outside corner." Tony took off his hat and set it on the floor: home plate. Then he showed Tom where he should position his feet and get the fat part of the bat onto an outside breaking ball. "You do that, and you play with that outstanding enthusiasm you have, and you'll go places fast."

Tony handed the other bat to Tom, and they shook hands again. Tom wheeled Dan out the door of the cottage, and Tony and I followed them out to the car. Tom stopped to open the door for his brother, and Tony pressed one of his business cards into the new Phillie's palm. "If you ever need to talk to anybody, if you ever have a problem, you call me—*collect*—anytime, day or night."

"Yes, sir, I'll do that."

"Promise me."

"I promise."

It was dusk now.

Dan looped his arms around Tom's neck, and Tom lifted him out of the wheelchair, cradling his older, heavier brother in his arms and setting him on the bench seat of their parents' Pontiac. Tony handed Tom Marsh a plane ticket to Clearwater, Florida, and we watched the brothers drive away. As the car's taillights disappeared around the corner, Tom tooted the horn.

"C'mon," Tony said, and we turned off the lights, locked up the cottage, dropped off the key at the front desk, found a post office and mailed two copies of Tom Marsh's first professional baseball contract, one to the National Association of Professional Baseball Clubs, one to the Philadelphia Phillies.

In Philadelphia, cross-checkers and club officials talked at dinner about tomorrow, the last day of the draft. In Fostoria, Tony waited.

9

Hanney's Pancake Mix

"You're late," Tony said. When I'd driven up to his house, he'd been pacing through dewy grass, arms akimbo, dressed in a gold cardigan sweater and staring anxiously down the street.

"You told me seven, Tony." It was five till. Steam rose from my cup of convenience-store coffee.

"Well, I'm afraid we may not make it. C'mon, get in and let's go."

We got on the Ohio Turnpike at exit 6. You can count on every toll road in the Midwest being torn up for repairs all summer, but even with several stretches of two-lane road, I didn't see any problem reaching exit 10 by ten o'clock.

"I got big news last night," Tony said. "Really big. They drafted another player for me, and they promised me one more for today. You remember that big right-handed pitcher from Huntington College?"

"Tim Dell?"

Tony nodded. "We got him in the twenty-eighth round. I can't understand how he could have lasted that long. I don't like to compare amateur players to big-leaguers, but in my report on him, I said he could be another Fergie Jenkins. I signed Fergie Jenkins, and Fergie Jenkins was Dell's pitching coach when he played for the Canadian Pan-Am Games last summer. They look just alike on the mound, some of the same mannerisms even. Twenty-eighth round!"

"At least you guys got him."

"Yes, but again, he won't get the kind of money he's worth, and the coaches in our minor league system, they give the most chances to those players down in Texas and California, the ones that get the really big money. This just goes to show you, though, that a lot of other scouts don't do their homework."

Tony had been scouting Dell for years and had been startled to see the pitcher throwing batting-practice fastballs in April games. Other scouts trained their rayguns on Dell, recorded the "68 mph" in their little books and mailed in reports that said "no prospect." Tony wasn't satisfied; he'd seen Dell throw a hard, roundhouse curve that made college sluggers look like they were swinging with rented arms. But both the coach and Dell himself said nothing was wrong. Tony didn't believe it, and he kept going to Dell's games after other scouts had given up. Finally Dell returned to form, and he admitted to his coach that he'd been weak from a flu bug that had run through the campus, but he thought the team needed him, so he kept mum.

"There's more to his story than just that flu bug," Tony told me. "Something's fishy there, I just feel it."

"What do you mean?"

"There's no possible way Dell should have lasted until the twenty-eighth round. But anyway, the point is, we got him."

"That's great," I said. "Now you've got four players drafted. That's better than a lot of years recently, right?"

"Yes, it is. And they promised me number five today."

"Who's that?"

"My sleeper."

"What's that kid's name anyway?"

"When they draft him, I'll tell you. But I already have his plane ticket."

We asked the toll-booth clerk which way to go for the Holiday Inn. Which one, she asked.

Tony went white. "You mean there's two?"

"The closest one," I said.

"That'd be south on I-77, a mile."

"Can you see it from the road?" Tony said.

"Not really."

"Why do you think they'd build a Holiday Inn that you can't see from the road, for heaven's sake?"

The woman shrugged. "I guess you'd have to ask the Holiday Inn people."

"Well, how far is the other Holiday Inn?" I said.

"It's northbound on 77, just two miles."

Tony shook his head and drove away. "This might be trouble," he said. "We're on a tight schedule. I want to get to Ft. Wayne tomorrow and then down to Cincinnati to sign Current."

I looked at my watch. We were an hour early. I suggested that we wait in the restaurant. Tony bought a *USA Today*. He opened the paper to the sports section, read the scores from Maine, Reading, Clearwater, and Spartanburg, then handed the whole paper to me, took one sip of his coffee and gathered up his hat and sweater to wait in the vestibule. "You can stay here and finish," he said. "I scouted that spot out. I can see the road from there."

At about nine-thirty, I finished the paper and my fifth cup of coffee and joined Tony. The vestibule was maybe twenty-five feet square, and Tony was pacing about it in elliptical nervous paths, like an annoyed zoo tiger. As time wore on, he made me stay there, on point, while he checked at the desk to see if the entryway we'd staked out was the only way in. It was. Ohio cars have license plates in front, Pennsylvania cars don't, so I looked at the front bumper of every arriving car, truck, and van. Each time I could say, "No, Tony, that's not him, " I'd save the old scout a short trip from the door to the parking lot. Finally, he made me call the other Holiday Inn. "I'm with the Philadelphia Phillies," I said, which was true, in a sense, "and we're down here at the other Holiday Inn, and we're supposed to meet Indiana University's shortstop to sign him to a professional contract."

"Describe him," the desk clerk said.

I'd never seen Morandini, but I'd claimed to be with the Phillies, so I couldn't admit I had no idea what he looked like. "Well, is there anyone around there who looks like a shortstop with his mom? His name is Mickey Morandini and his mom is, um, Mrs. Morandini. Can you page them?"

Either Morandini wasn't there, or the desk clerk at the other Holiday Inn thought I was deranged, because the line went dead a few minutes later.

By ten, when the meeting was scheduled to start, I'd witnessed miles of pacing and a rant about why Holiday Inn would build two motels so close together, neither one of which you could see from the highway. He made me call the other hotel again. We haven't seen any shortstops here, the clerk said, but if we do, we'll sure send them right over.

Tony couldn't take this anymore and wandered out to the end of the driveway, leaning out into the road, waiting for his fifth-round draft choice.

At ten-thirty, a van with no front license plate pulled in. Tony waved, called to me to bring his briefcase, then race-walked to the front door. Out of the driver's seat, dressed in a white Pony warm-up suit and looking irked and suspicious, came Mickey Morandini, a slender young man with the loose-limbed shuffle of a gym rat and spiky blond hair the same color and length as his mustache. His mother got out of the passenger seat, patting her hair and hoisting her purse to her shoulder. They'd gone to the wrong Holiday Inn, I just knew it.

Tony shook their hands, apologized for the poor directions and rented a room on the top floor. He never paid more than forty dollars a night for his own lodging, but he didn't flinch at dropping seventy-five dollars for an hour in the motel's nicest meeting room. This was a young man's first moment in pro ball, and things needed to be done first-class.

On the way up, Mrs. Morandini giggled. "Oh well," she said. "Maybe it was our fault. We really weren't lost for all that long."

But Mickey stood there, his lips pursed, sullen, looking at his feet.

The room held a rectangular oak table, wing chairs, a soft bed, and two side tables dressed in harvest-gold skirts. Tony invited Mickey and his mother to take a seat, then he spread out the contracts and papers in neat piles. "We could use an outfielder like you," Tony said. "A ballplayer with a good glove and excellent speed who can get on base and disrupt the pitchers. Now, I know you played shortstop in college, but I projected you as an outfielder, probably left, and that's where we drafted you. But when you get down there to spring training, they can play you wherever they want."

Tony doled out the rest of his basic presentation: the virtues of Veterans Stadium, the Clearwater minor league complex, the minicamp, the Phillies minor league chain in general, and the Batavia Clippers in particular. Throughout, Mrs. Morandini nodded and muttered, but Mickey slumped in his chair, stone faced, pushed back from the table, acknowledging Tony with a few slight nods. He wore a T-shirt touting Indiana University's 1987 NCAA basketball championship, and around his neck was a gold chain with a jeweled pendant, #5, his uniform number. For the most part, Mickey kept his hands folded, but three or four times his left hand darted to his throat to touch the #5.

"Now," Tony said, "since you were selected to work out for the Olympic team—well, it's an honor, and you want to try it, and you're interested in it, and you're welcome to do it. When you're ready to report to our ballclub, I'll tell you who to call, and they'll make arrangements for you to fly in to wherever they want to send you."

I had expected Tony's speech about how the Olympics were just a rah-rah thing, only a demonstration sport, which could very possibly jeopardize the big-league future of a twenty-two-year-old shortstop trying to learn to play left field. But Tony had mentioned this to Mickey on the phone, and Tony Lucadello hard-sells no one.

Tony opened the three copies of the contract, handing one to Mickey and one to Mrs. Morandini. He read off the terms slowly, twice through: the maximum $700-a-month salary, the incentive bonus plan, the $25,000 bonus and the delivery of that bonus. "The terms of the contract, all that preprinted part, those are drawn up by the National Association, which is to protect you, and every ball player signs the same thing. You couldn't change that if you had a thousand and one lawyers," Tony said, smiling, and Mrs. Morandini giggled. Mickey pushed his chair a few more inches away from the table.

"Now, do you have any questions?"

Mickey and his mother exchanged a quick glance.

"Um, is twenty-five thousand the highest you can give him?"

"Yes." Tony skipped not a beat. "Yes. I only make one offer. That's just the way I operate. You're free to do what you think is best."

Mickey reached to his throat and tapped his #5.

Mrs. Morandini looked across the table straight into Tony's eyes. "I thought he'd be worth a little bit more than that."

"Well, he's only gettin' seven thousand less than what Mike Schmidt got."

"You signed Mike Schmidt, right?" Mickey said.

"Yes, him and forty-eight others. Mike signed for that, and he was drafted number two." Tony tossed his copy of the contract on the table, poured himself a glass of water, and sat back in his chair. "Now if you're interested, well, I'd be glad to sign you, and I want your mother to sign the contract, too. What do you think?"

I had been worried that Mickey would turn the offer down, but now he thought of himself in the outfield, like his boyhood heroes Al Oliver and Roberto Clemente, playing in front of fifty thousand fellow Pennsylvanians, with a big burgundy number 5 stretching across his back, and his face broke into a smile and he slapped his hands on the edge of the table. "Great!"

"Is this what you really want?" said his mother.

"All my life."

Mrs. Morandini laughed. "Okay."

And so Mickey signed the contract, left-handed, which caught Tony a little off guard, since players who bat left and throw right tend to sign autographs right-handed.

In the Holiday Inn restaurant, Tony bought lunch for Mickey and his mother. Mickey was more animated now, relieved of the burden of worrying about money and juiced about his future as an American Olympian and, just maybe, a major league ball player. He had come to the meeting intending to sign only if the offer was at least $40,000. "When I was back in Little League, I used to dream about stuff like this. I still have a long way to go, a lot to accomplish, but I've earned myself the chance."

At the salad bar, Mrs. Morandini and I turned to watch Tony stand up and show Mickey something about his swing.

"He really signed forty-nine big leaguers?" she said.

"Going on fifty," I said.

"Maybe Mickey can be fifty."

"Maybe. But at the rate Tony's going, Mickey may be number sixty."

"I remember when Mickey tried out for Little League," she said. "I was so scared that he wasn't going to make it, you know, afraid he wasn't good enough. All these parents were sittin' there, and I kept saying, 'Do you think he'll make it?' And here he was the first pick in the draft. And I kept telling him, 'Don't forget, Mickey, you're just a new player, you're not gonna play every day.' He has not sat out one game yet. Everywhere he's gone, he's played."

But that streak would soon end for Mickey Morandini. He made the Olympic team all right—even as the Phillies' first-round choice, the pitcher from Baylor, was cut—but Mickey played less than any other player, and as the exhibition games of summer led up to the Olympic games of autumn, he played even less frequently. In the meantime, Tom Marsh became the starting left fielder at Batavia. By October, Marsh had spent a month in the Instructional League—reporting to the ballpark at 9:00 A.M., working out for three hours, eating lunch with familiar teammates, and playing games against the best prospects from other teams—when Morandini reported there, a little rusty, but with a gold medal on the mantel back in Leechburg.

We got up just as early the next day, this time to drive to Ft. Wayne. "They drafted my sleeper in the forty-fourth round. His name is Mike Dafforn. I wanted to sign him over at the Hart Motel, but the mother insisted that we come over to the house." Yesterday, when Tony returned from Cleveland, he had called his office to tell them he'd already signed Marsh and Morandini. Well, they said, that's good, because we have two more for you to go sign, Dafforn and this right fielder for the University of Cincinnati, Joe Tenhunfeld. Will do, Tony said. I plan to have everyone signed by Sunday.

Sure, they said, humoring him, that'd be fine.

Even first-round draft choices often pass up contracts for another year or two of school. But here was a seventy-five-year-old man saying he'd be able to bop all over his territory and have all six of his draftees under contract within two days of the end of the draft.

"I like to sign 'em as fast as I can," Tony told me. We were headed south on I-75. Ohio had just raised its speed limit on interstate highways to sixty-five, and Tony set the Caprice's cruise control a jaunty two miles above the limit. "The longer they play pro ball this summer, the better chance they have to move up next year. But every signing is different. Some of them go smooth, some go rough. And the thing is, you never know what to expect."

"How many ball players have you signed?"

"I have no idea," he said, laughing. "It must be into the hundreds. I only keep track of the big leaguers, and I've signed forty-nine of those."

"I know."

"Did I ever tell you about the time I signed Freddy Andrews? He played two years for us in the big leagues, back in the midseventies."

I flipped down the sun shade and told him no, he sure hadn't.

Back in the tumult of the late sixties, Tony said, Fred Andrews lived with his mother in Chicago, on Forty-eighth Street, maybe the most dangerous place on the South Side. Two gangs ran the neighborhood—one north of Forty-eighth Street, the other south—and when a boy reached about fifteen, the gangs would recruit him, threatening his family to make him join. Fred had a relative who coached baseball at Princeton High School in Cincinnati, and the coach got Fred out of there, right before his junior year.

Freddy Andrews became a gifted second baseman, and Tony convinced the Phillies to draft him ninth. Tony wanted to sign him right after graduation, but he needed to get Fred's mother to sign, too, so Fred went home and Tony flew to Chicago the next night.

Tony called from the hotel to see if Fred and his mother would come there. "No," Fred said, "I'm sorry. My mom works at a hospital nearby, and she doesn't get home until seven. At that time of day, we don't have any way to get from here to there."

"Fine," Tony said. "I can just come to your apartment."

That evening Tony went downstairs to hail a cab. When the first cab stopped, Tony made the mistake of saying "4848 South State Street" before he got in, and the white driver waved his hand and screeched away. Tony got in the next cab, slammed the door, and *then* gave the address. The driver, who was black, just sat there.

"Well, c'mon," Tony said. "Didn't you hear what I said?"

"Yeah, I heard you. You don't want to go there."

"You're going to have to take me, or I'll turn you in and you'll lose your hack license."

"All right." He put the cab in gear. "But we're gonna have some rules. When we get close to 4848 South State Street, you pay me. And when I tell you to lay down in that backseat, you lay down."

At about Thirty-eighth Street, the cabbie told Tony to pay. "Now lay down on the floor," the cabbie said, "and don't even think about moving until I say so. Don't you know this is the worst neighborhood in this whole city? I haven't seen a white man down here for years. Believe me, I wouldn't go myself if I didn't need this job. If I stopped this cab, they might tear me out of here, beat me up, take all my money, and when they see you in the back there . . . Anyway, when I slam on the brakes, you run right to that front door."

Tony jumped out, ran to the front door, and there was

Freddy Andrews, waiting. They went upstairs, and Mrs. Andrews told Tony about the gang violence in the neighborhood. "No one goes out after dark," she said.

"The signing itself was one of the easiest I ever had," Tony told me, exiting I-75 and heading west, toward Ft. Wayne, on U.S. 30. "That young man wanted to get out of that neighborhood, and we were giving him enough money to do it."

At about nine-thirty, with all the papers signed, Tony gave Fred a plane ticket and a pep talk and then asked to use the phone to call a cab. Mrs. Andrews shook her head. Forget it. No cab'll come down here at night. But Tony was helping her boy, so she'd try to think of something. She started calling neighbors. After a few calls, she managed to convince a friend in the next building, a man who owned his own car, to drive Tony back downtown for twenty dollars. "He's parked out in the alley," she said. "Freddy will hold the door open for you and you run out there, dive into the backseat, and cover yourself up with a piece of canvas he's got back there."

"My heart didn't slow down until the next week," Tony told me. "But it was all worth it. Fred played in the big leagues, and he even named his first son after me: Tony Andrews. Hey—what's that?"

Behind us, a gray state patrol cruiser turned on its lights and, for a second, flicked on its siren. Tony pulled to the shoulder.

The trooper told Tony he'd been clocked going seventy. "Oh," Tony said. "Well, I'm very sorry, officer. But with the speed limit sixty-five now—"

"That's just on the interstates," the trooper said, "not on just any four-lane highway." He explained the state patrol's ticketing policy in the tone of a stern geometry teacher who acknowledges that you've done your homework but insists that, though it pains him to do so, he's going to have to give you an F on the work—and yes, that grade will be attached to your permanent record.

"Well, it's just so confusing," Tony said. "But I understand. You have to do your job, just like I have to do mine." He waited a beat, while the trooper studied Tony's license and registration. "I'm a major league baseball scout for the Philadelphia Phillies."

The cop, unimpressed, told Tony he would either have to pay the forty-dollar fine right now or agree to appear in court next month. Tony handed over his Visa card, and the cop ran it through the cruncher on his front seat. Tony pulled away and we never got above fifty the rest of the way to Ft. Wayne.

"You know, in all the time I've been scouting, all the miles I've driven, I've never gotten a speeding ticket. I've only been pulled over a couple other times, but they'd find out I'm a big-league scout, and they'd just ask for an autographed ball and then warn me. This guy here must be a football fan."

"One ticket per 2.3 million miles driven," I said. "Not a bad record."

"No, it's not, but it really bothers me. If I can't drive this car, maybe it's time to quit."

We stopped to pick up Norm Kramer, who was as jumpy and excited as Tony. The Dafforns lived in a subdivision of middle-sized houses on middle-sized lots. A yard sale on the block clogged the narrow streets with cars and people and leashed schnauzers. We crept past to the only driveway not filled with card tables, broken Barbies, and 1965 issues of Look magazine. "Man, I put a lot of work into this kid," Norm said. "I never thought, in my wildest dreams, I'd ever help sign a player in my own zip code."

On the brown garage door of the Dafforns' stucco ranch-style were two paper banners, each several feet long and produced on a dot-matrix printer. One read, CONGRATULATIONS

MIKE!!! WE'RE PROUD OF YOU!!! The other had a little drawing of a bat, ball and glove on each end and read, PHILLIES HERE I COME.

"Well, Tony," Norm said, pointing at the banners. "This doesn't look like a tough signing."

"Probably not," Tony said. "He's just happy to get the chance. But we'll see. Let's not talk about it, okay?"

Mrs. Dafforn greeted us at the door. "It's just been killing us, keeping all this a secret," she said, beaming and hugging Tony, which made the little old shortstop blush.

Tony nodded. "That was the way it had to be."

"I just thank the Lord that you came into Mike's life," she said, ushering us into the kitchen. "I'm telling you: it's just like 'Highway to Heaven.' "

Mike Dafforn met us near the microwave, smiling and nodding and shaking hands. He was affably shy, answering any question with a small shrug, a tiny, awkward laugh, and a reply like "I guess" or "Okay."

Mrs. Dafforn took Tony's narrow-brimmed straw hat and seated us at her round kitchen table, which was covered with a white lace tablecloth and bathed in the promise of June sunlight. Mr. Dafforn, a sullen-looking man with a thick walrusy mustache, sat next to his wife.

Tony's methodical spiel was similar in organization to the one he'd given Marsh and Morandini, but to Dafforn, who'd never lived away from home, Tony emphasized the real-world items: the insurance policy, the split of the bonus "to help with your taxes," the measly, bush-league per diem. Mike tried to approach this with the gravity he supposed appropriate to a grown-up decision, but the flicker of a grin that danced across his face every minute or so betrayed him.

Mrs. Dafforn followed along, giddy, unlikely to question a contract proffered by an old man whom she perceived as an angel from the happy-ending world of family-hour TV. Mr. Dafforn, though, locked his brow into a frown. He kept putting on and removing a pair of reading glasses, examining a clause or two of the contract and then tossing the glasses on the table and staring up at the detailing in the brown stained-glass light fixture.

Mike would be signed to Martinsville, Virginia, in the Appalachian League, the lowest rung in pro ball. His bonus was small. Tony finished explaining everything, tossed Mike's plane ticket to Florida onto the lace tablecloth, and asked if anyone had any questions.

Mrs. Dafforn looked up, in zeal and adoration. "Not a one I can think of. How about you, Dad?"

Mr. Dafforn put on his reading glasses and glanced once again at the contract. "Well, what does Mike think?"

Mike shrugged and laughed, just a little. "Naw. I can't think of anything. Except, uh"—he held out his pitching hand—"who has a good pen?"

He signed all three copies of the contract, and Mrs. Dafforn handed me her camera to record the event. Mr. Dafforn signed them, too, still looking a little unhappy—to me, anyway. Maybe I missed something; the strong, silent types always confuse the hell out of me. "Write slowly, Dad," his wife said. "Take your time, because we'll never get the chance to sign anything like this again."

Mr. Dafforn pursed his lips and moved his hand as slowly as a diligent second-grader in a penmanship competition.

Once all the paperwork was signed, Tony stood up and welcomed Mike Dafforn to the Phillies. Mrs. Dafforn applauded and then hugged Tony and Norm Kramer. "I've got something for you," Tony said. "Wait right here."

"Boy, after this cloak-and-dagger stuff," Norm said, "it's going to be hard to go back to plain old scouting. Maybe I ought to apply to work for the CIA." He put his arm around Mike. "Did I tell you that you're the first player I ever signed in my own zip code?"

Tony came back from the car with two wooden bats, one

Phillies cap, and an official National League baseball. He gave
one bat to Mike. "They have the designated hitter in that
league," he said. "But you'll still take BP, because when you
get to the big leagues, you'll have to hit."

Mr. Dafforn's frown was gone now.

"Just like I promised," Tony said, handing him the cap
and the ball and the Louisville Slugger. "You kept up your
end of the bargain by keeping everything a secret."

Mr. Dafforn pulled the hat forward on his head from the
back to the front so that the bill came down too far over his
eyes. Mrs. Dafforn took the pen that Mike had used to sign the
contract, dated the baseball, and asked Tony and Norm and
Mike to sign it. She hugged each of them. Tony warned Mike
about getting his head and shoulders ahead of his pitching
arm in his windup, and Mike said he wouldn't, that throwing
up against a wall had cured him of that. Tony gave the Sleeper
a business card. "Anytime you need anything, you understand."

Mike shrugged and laughed just a little. "Okay."

"Call collect. Anytime, day or night. You promise?"

"Yeah."

Mr. Dafforn stood behind us near the Mr. Coffee, running
his hands along the white ash of the bat. He sniffed it. He
grabbed it by the handle, pulling it close to his chest, waving
it in safe and tiny circles.

Mrs. Dafforn offered us lunch.

"No," Tony told her, "we'd love to stay for lunch, but we
have another player to sign today, and we're in a hurry. Maybe
another time." Again everyone shook hands, and Mrs. Dafforn
hugged Tony.

"You go down there to Florida," Tony said to Mike, "and
you really impress 'em. Throw strikes. Play with enthusiasm."

We got into Tony's Caprice. Mike put his arm around his
mother, and they waved. In the driveway, under the PHILLIES
HERE I COME banner, Mr. Dafforn, a father of a pro ball player,

swung his new bat so hard his cap fell off. He shrugged and then, smiling, bent to pick it up.

In a conference room at the Warsaw, Indiana, Holiday Inn, Tony learned why Tim Dell had lasted until the twenty-eighth round. Team Canada—low on six-five pitchers who might be the next Fergie Jenkins—was reluctant to see Dell turn pro before Seoul. Dell thought he had been mishandled by the Canadian manager the year before and wanted out, though he had enjoyed working with their pitching coach, Fergie Jenkins himself. When Jenkins and the manager had a falling out and Jenkins left to coach for the Texas Rangers, Dell told Team Canada he was turning pro. Still, they kept him on the roster. "The Canadian Olympic coach told me he was going to write to every team in the majors and tell them I wouldn't sign this year," said Dell, a rangy, honor-roll student with huge hands and brown lizard-skin cowboy boots. "I'm glad to be going with the Phillies, and with you, Tony, but when I heard the twenty-eighth round, I was just sick. I had guys from six or seven teams tell me they'd take me in the first five rounds."

Tony nodded. He had been one of those scouts, and he would have loved to give Dell the kind of bonus a third-round pick would get, the kind of bonus he thought Dell deserved. But the Olympic snafu explained everything. First, teams that place undue pressure on players to bypass the Olympics can be sued for tampering. More importantly, each team has only twenty work visas to use for foreign players; if Dell signed and didn't play this year, the team that wasted a visa on him might have to release another player.

"If they make me play for Team Canada," Tim said, "I'm just gonna go up there and throw underhanded until they cut me."

"This coach has done things that just aren't right," said Tom Roy, Dell's pitching coach, who'd come to the meeting as a proxy for the boy's parents. "Tim received a letter last month, an official offer to join Team Canada, and they said if he didn't send it back in three weeks, they'd assume he wasn't coming. Timmy never sent it back and yet they still have him on their roster. He told them on the phone he wasn't playing, and I told them he wasn't playing, and yet they won't give him his release." Roy had once been a commission scout for Tony. He quit somewhat reluctantly a few years ago when he expanded the Christian ministry he runs—a ministry which includes baseball clinics organized by Tom and coached by major league players, who also share stories about their faith in Christ. It was at one of those camps, in Oliver, British Columbia, that Roy discovered Tim Dell.

Roy asked thorny questions about the contract and the Olympics and the amount of the bonus and Tim Dell's future, and Tim listened, hands folded in his lap, rapt and confident, as if he were being defended in a misdemeanor trial by a beloved and accomplished older brother. Tony called his boss, Jack Pastore, to ask about a few of the more iffy questions. "This Olympics has me turned inside out," Tony said to Pastore. "Let me ask you this. Can we put in his contract that he's guaranteed to go to the Instructional League?"

Tim looked at Tom Roy and arched his eyebrows. A good autumn in the Instructional League could be worth more than money, since the attention of higher-ups there might accelerate his climb toward the majors.

"I appreciate that, Jack. He won't disappoint you." He hung up. "Well, I got him to agree to it. I've never promised that to a player before in my life, but I'm promising it to you, Tim."

"This is going to be Tim's decision," said Tom Roy, "but I have to know one thing, not for money's sake but for sanity's sake. Do you really think Timmy's a twenty-eighth-round draft choice?"

"You can't worry about that," Tony said. "I think he can

play in the major leagues. Not just play, but be a star there. That's all that matters."

Tim and Tom went out into the hall and Norm Kramer and I speculated about what Tim would decide. Tony forbid us to talk about it, and so we took turns pacing around the room. The sun began to set and, in the pale pink light of dusk, a striped hot-air balloon drifted past our window. Tony stood, watching it fly. "Why deprive a young man from going into professional ball if that's what he wants? He's already served two years for the Olympics. If it was me . . . If he says he's gonna sue 'em for depriving him of his rights when he already told 'em he wasn't gonna play, well, that'd shake 'em up."

"Yep," Norm and I agreed.

"Even if he signs," Tony said, "he can't report until that daggone Olympics gives him his release. No matter what he does, I'm gonna have to go down to Cincinnati tomorrow and try to sign Current and Tenhunfeld, and then I'll have to drop everything and hightail it up here, in case they let him go, so I can get him on the first plane down to that minicamp."

We waited in silence almost another half hour, and I was sure Dell would come back and say he needed more time to sort all this out. But there was a knock on the door; I opened it and Dell breezed past me. "Let's do it!" he said. "Who has a pen?"

In southwestern Ohio, in a dusty ballpark with no bleachers, chimneys of nearby factories lining the horizon, Tony Lucadello unfolded his lawn chair near the home team's dugout to watch the Trenton Auto Parts team take on visiting Westerville. "That's my catcher there," he whispered. "Number fourteen. Bats left. Throws right. If other scouts would have seen him when I did, I honestly believe he'd have gone in the first round."

We had just come from a Days Inn near the interstate,

where Tony had signed Joe Tenhunfeld, a soft-spoken art major and left fielder with the biggest hands I'd ever seen. He was a longshot whose own college coach had dismissed his chances in pro ball. But Tony liked Tenhunfeld's arm and loved his flashes of bat power. Halfway through going over the contract, even before he reached the page with the amount of the bonus on it, Tony said, "Now, I make only one offer, and then you can take it or leave it," and Tenhunfeld blurted, "I'll take it." Easy signing.

After his Trenton team finished infield, Current had a buddy toss him a couple dozen plastic golf balls. "That's made a difference for him," Tony whispered. "He's still a raw player, but remember, he's just seventeen."

The sandlot game began. The sparse crowd spread itself out on blankets behind the backstop. Current came up in the first inning. Maturity seemed to have crept upward on him: he had huge, defined calves and thighs, manly biceps, and taut forearms, but he still had a boy's rounded shoulders and blank, untroubled face. He popped out to left. "I'd like to see him stop hittin' the ball to the opposite field," Tony said. "With his strength and size, he's gotta pull that ball."

A few feet away, half a dozen paunchy, shirtless middle-aged men whispered among themselves and occasionally pointed at Matt and at Tony.

At a little after three o'clock. Matt's father, Ron Current, arrived at the ballpark from the factory where he worked. He sat in the grass next to Tony's lawn chair, and they chatted about Matt's future, particularly how likely the boy might be to turn down his football scholarship at Western Kentucky. Tony wouldn't tell him the amount of the bonus. "That'll have to wait until after the game," he said. "I'll tell you the whole setup then."

Ron Current accepted that. Ultimately, the decision would be Matt's, he said, in the sort of midwestern accent that makes just about every available vowel into a schwa. "Myself, baseball's always been my life," he said. *Musulf, basebull's alwuz been m'life.* "I coached Babe Ruth ball for a long time, and I've always been a big fan, especially of the Cincinnati Reds." *Cincinnatuh.*

Matt Current first impressed me in the top of the fourth, when, from one knee, he snapped a pickoff throw to third base, catching Westerville's fastest runner in a rundown and, eventually, tagging him out. In the bottom of the fourth, he lined a single, but still to left field, and in the sixth, he hit a Texas Leaguer, again to left.

"He's never pulled the ball," Ron Current said.

"He will," Tony said. "Believe me."

The shirtless men began to elbow one another, some kind of tribal, southwestern Ohio ritual for choosing a spokesman. Finally, the most sunburned of the men approached Tony. "Hey," he said. "Are you a scout?"

"Yes, I am." Tony stood up, introduced himself, and shook the man's hand.

The sunburned man looked at me. I was dressed in a polo shirt, khaki shorts, and topsiders. "You're a lawyer, right?"

"Um, no," I said, almost dumbstruck. "I'm a writer."

The man shrugged and stuck out his lower lip. *Well, at least he's not a lawyer.* He returned to Tony. "So you're the one what drafted the Current boy, eh? Yeah, I read about that in the Middletown paper. You're not from the Reds, are you?"

"The Phillies."

"Damn. Lost my bet. Too bad it's not the Reds. They need somethin'."

Tony laughed. "Well, he hasn't signed nothin' yet, so we'll see." Under his breath, to me and to Mr. Current, Tony muttered, "Fans."

Tony couldn't stand to see Matt hit another opposite-field single, and he walked near the fence and motioned the boy over from the on-deck circle. "When you swing," Tony said, "pivot your weight off your rear foot."

Matt Current pulled the first pitch, a screaming grounder into the gap between first and second.

"What'd I tell you?" Tony said to Ron Current. "See you at the motel."

By the time everyone squeezed into Tony's room at the Days Inn, I had to sit on the bathroom countertop. On chairs, tables, and the edges of the bed were Matt, his parents, his girl friend, his younger brother, Hugh Higdon—Tony's part-time scout for Cincinnati—and Higdon's son. Tony sat at a desk chair in the middle of the room and made his pitch.

The presentation was Tony at his most methodical. Matt, after all, was only seventeen. Imagine having your seventeen-year-old son turn down a college scholarship to play baseball for strangers, to live in backwater towns and try to get by on a $700-a-month salary.

When I began traveling with Tony, I thought any decent student would be better off going to college. But Tony changed my mind. If you get enough money to pay for at least three-quarters of a college education, and if you love baseball, I don't think there's a decision to make. You sign. You'll have better instruction and you'll get more years to prove yourself. Put your bonus in a bank and let it collect interest. Even if you have a scholarship, you could be out of luck if you're injured. In pro ball, you have that bonus up front. When baseball is over, you go to college. This, for just about everyone, would make sense. I've taught college classes for seven years and can tell you that the republic's most motivated eighteen-year-old student would be hard-pressed to match the thirst for knowledge of its least motivated thirty-year-old.

But something was bothering Matt Current. At the ball-park, Ron Current said that the Western Kentucky coach told Matt that his scholarship was worth thirty thousand dollars, and that if he accepted less, he was selling himself short.

Tony's offer, when he finally got to the contract itself, was only twenty-two thousand.

Matt kept glancing at his girl friend, and I wondered if he was loath to sign because it would take him so far away from her.

Tony admitted the bonus was low, but explained it was all he could get his office to authorize. "Now I have one more thing to offer you," Tony said, "but first I have to tell you a story. Yesterday, I got a speeding ticket. I didn't know I was speeding, but I was, and I paid it with my own credit card. Well, the more I thought about that ticket, the more it started to eat at me, really it did. I've been with the Phillies for thirty years and never been arrested once. Now, my first thought was to ask them to pick up that tab, to let me put it on my expenses. But I thought of something else. This is what I got my office to authorize, which is worth much more to me than the money to pay that fine: you are going—if you sign—to the Instructional League automatically. Now, you can't beat that. We're giving you everything in God's world to see that you get a good start in baseball. Now it's up to you."

Matt sat at the TV table, his hands gripping the edges, eyes fixed on the shag carpet except when he glanced at his girl friend. He worried that the money wasn't enough. He worried that he'd miss football. He worried that college might be a better choice. And well, yeah, there was that other thing.

Finally, Matt, his girl friend and his parents went into the parking lot. After a few minutes, the girl friend and Mrs. Current returned. Ron Current came in next. No one spoke. Matt knocked and Tony opened the door.

"Well?"

"I'm gonna take it."

His parents applauded. Tony slapped him on the back and directed him to the table to sign the contracts. "I told him," the girl friend said "not to do anything on my account. If things don't work out for him, and he did it for me, I

couldn't live with that. I want him to do what's best for him."
I looked at her. She was seventeen, too, headed for Indiana
University in the fall. She'll do well.

With the contracts signed, everyone shook hands. Tony
welcomed Matt to the Phillies, and we all filed into the
parking lot. "I didn't know what he was going to do," said
Matt's mom. "But, Tony, you've been so good to Matt, to us
all." She hugged him. They drove away, tooting the horn.

Tony and I watched them driving away, leaning against
the trunk of his car. He took a deep breath and let it out slowly.
"Oh, boy."

"Big week," I said. "These signings are hard work."

The daylight slid from the warm sky as if someone had
pulled a plug. I could hear the trucks roaring down I-75. On
the horizon, duffers at a driving range blasted balls our way.

"Yes, but these were easy. The draft's been over for two
days, and I already have all six of my ballplayers signed. My
hardest signing was years ago. I had to run a tryout camp up
in Janesville, Wisconsin, with around sixty or seventy kids,
and the kid that impressed me was a sixteen-year-old by the
name of Bob Hanney. This was before the draft, and other
teams knew about him, but I'd gotten the inside track.

"About three or four clubs made him offers. When my
chance came, I presented my offer: five-hundred-dollar bonus,
that was it. Like the Drotts, the family was shocked, and they
told me they couldn't sign for that. I told them I was sorry, but
that if they thought that he ought to sign with another team
for more money, then I wouldn't stand in their way.

"I packed up my things and started to leave. The father
and the boy walked with me to my car. I said good-bye, but all
at once the father said to me. 'Tony, do you know what kind
of business I'm in?'

" 'No, I don't.'

" 'The pancake-mix business. I made up a recipe that
makes the greatest pancakes in the world. But I'm just gettin'

off the ground. I'm well known here in Wisconsin and a little bit down in northern Illinois. I sell a lot of it to restaurants. Why don't you come back and take a look at my shop?'

"So we went around behind the house, into this shed, and he showed me all these cases of pancake mix, twelve boxes to the carton, twelve cartons to the case. I asked him what he charged for a box, a carton and a case, and I found out it was more than the other pancake mixes sold for, the famous ones. I didn't say nothin', and we went back out to my car.

"I opened the door, and the father stopped me. 'Tony,' he says, 'you know I want you to sign our boy. I'll tell you what. I'll make a deal with you. If you'll agree to sell a hundred cases of my Hanney's Pancake Mix in the state of Ohio, where I'm not known at all, where you can get some new business for me, why, you can sign my boy on your terms.'

"I was a very confident young man, and I accepted. I had to hit the road for a couple weeks, so I called my wife and told her he was shipping those cases to the house and to just stack 'em in the garage. She was pretty upset because she thought we were gonna have to pay for 'em, which we were if I didn't sell any.

"When I got home, there were boxes of pancake mix everywhere: it didn't all fit in the garage, so they stacked it in the hallway, in the living room, even in our bedroom. I tried to calm my wife down, and I told her I'd take a couple cases over to this small store where we traded. 'I'll do it now,' I says, 'just to show you how easy it is.'

"The grocer was a friend of mine, and he listened to what I had to say, and then he took me over to the shelves and said, 'Tony, I can't handle that. I don't have space for any more brands of pancake mix.'

"So I put the cases back in the car and went home. My wife said, 'See, you can't sell it,' but I told her I had another idea. 'Get on the phone,' I said, 'and call everyone you know in Fostoria, and tell them to please call the grocery store and ask 'em if they sell Hanney's Pancake Mix. The grocer'll say no, and then have 'em say, "Oh, that's too bad," and hang up.'

"The next day I went back to the store, and the grocer called me over and asked me the name of that pancake mix I'd tried to sell him. I told him: Hanney's Pancake Mix.

" 'We've had twenty calls for it! I'll buy those two cases from you.'

"I did that with every other grocery store in town. From scouting I had friends in almost every town in Ohio, and I had them all do the same thing. By the end of the summer I'd sold my hundred cases.

"Last year, I told that story to a couple friends at a ball game down in Lancaster, Ohio, and some guy in the bleachers, a couple rows back, jumped up and hollered, 'I remember you. I bought two cases from you, and I remember it well because I never sold a box of it.' "

It was dark now. Tony Lucadello had fourteen players under contract to the Philadelphia Phillies.

"I never heard of Bob Hanney," I said.

"That's because he hurt his arm and never made it," Tony said, "but that was the hardest work I ever had to do to sign a ball player. Still, like I said, like you've seen, every signing's different."

Tony went back inside the Days Inn and made a few phone calls. Within an hour, he had lined up a month's worth of games to see. The '88s were signed. Time to find a few '89s. His draft list would be in the mail to Philadelphia in only 339 days.

10

The Batavia Clippers

When I was growing up, the radio station every happening seventh-grader listened to was CKLW, a Top Forty AM boomer out of Windsor, Ontario, on which the fast-talking deejays did hokey characters, the playlist was so small the song cycle repeated itself every two hours, and the airtime devoted to Canadian artists (as required by law) sent me to college thinking that the Guess Who were as big as the Beatles.

This is the station Tony listened to in his car. The format has changed to popular music from the thirties and forties, and when he was alone, Tony would turn the sound up medium high, brooding through all-day salutes to Rosemary Clooney about how to improve the game of baseball.

He had friends at every crossroads in the Midwest, but Tony still spent most of his life alone, in empty ballparks, looking for lost coins and waiting for a game; in tiny motel rooms, filing reports and planning for tomorrow's game; in his leased car, thinking. Once in a while, he'd come upon something he couldn't bear to forget, and pulling the car into a rest area or onto the shoulder, he'd take out the notepad on which he calculated his daily mileage, snatch a ballpoint pen from the eyeglasses case on the dashboard, and scrawl out epipha-nies. "Ninety-four percent of today's young players do not grip the bat in the proper spot with their bottom hand," he wrote one day, his engine running and the wind of passing tractor trailers shaking the car. "Nearly all young players grip the bat down on the knob and don't hit the ball. This simple test will tell a player where to place his bottom hand on the bat: hold the bat on the handle an arm's length in front of you with the bottom hand. If the bat wavers and begins to drop, you are not gripping the bat at the proper spot."

I had gone home for a couple days to attend to the usual things travelers neglect and to remind my wife what I looked like. Tony had gone back to Indiana to help Tim Dell extricate himself from the Olympics and to watch games in Mickey Mantle and Stan Musial leagues: games with players for the '89 draft, and the '90, and the '91. After a few days home, I called Virginia Lucadello, who has spent a half century field-ing Tony's calls and giving out the number of some little motel somewhere. Then I called Tony to set up a place to meet him and resume our travels.

"Oh, so you still want to go through with the book, huh?" he said, deadpan. "I thought you might have gone home and told your wife you were tired of an old man like me. You know, that there just wasn't enough to interest you and all that jazz."

But he took out a legal pad and read me his schedule for the next week. Dell had finally reported, Tony said, and so now he was free to get into central Ohio. "If it's as dry there as it is here," he said, "then that's not ideal circumstances to see ball players. But I have to cover my territory. And all the other scouts have the same problem."

We chatted for a while, and I was about ready to hang up when Tony said, "Hey, how far is Batavia, New York, from you? You're out east there. It can't be too far."

Fairfax, Virginia, isn't exactly near upstate New York, I told him.

"Oh. Well. You know I've got six players up there. Marsh, Dell, Viggiano, Tracy, Elam and Tenhunfeld."

"Six, huh?"

"I've always made it a policy not to bother the skippers of those minor league clubs, you know. They have their own job to do. Besides, if you bug 'em too much about a kid, it may come back to hurt the kid. I don't want 'em to play favorites with my kids. I just want 'em to get a fair shot."

"Don't they usually get a fair shot," I asked. "I mean, with your reputation and all."

Tony was silent for a long time. "Well," he said, "it depends."

"On what?"

"We can talk about it in person. Anyway, what I was thinking—maybe you can help me figure this out—what I was thinking was this: I wonder how I can get a scouting report on those six players? Their season starts today."

I'm slow. I admit it.

"Oh, hey, how about if I go up to Batavia? You've trained me as a scout some. Now I can go see if I've learned anything."

"You'd do that for me?" Tony laughed. "That would be wonderful."

The next day I drove the seven hours to Geneva, New York, at the north tip of Seneca Lake, where the Batavia Clippers were to play the Geneva Cubs. I arrived at the ballpark before anyone but the grounds crew. I looked for money, searching the parking lot, around the concession stand and underneath the stands. I didn't find anything. As the players trickled onto the field—in hand-me-down jerseys from the Chicago Cubs and Philadelphia Phillies—I stretched out on the warped, sun-warmed bleachers, watching BP and remembering to scout young ball players below the waist.

The sun settled near the top of the pine woods just beyond the outfield walls of McDonough Park. I climbed a steep staircase to the red aluminum press box, which dangled over the few enclosed bleachers like the paddock at a rural racetrack. Ken Shepard, the twenty-three-year-old general manager of the Geneva Cubs, handed a slip of paper to the local radio guy moonlighting at the PA, who announced the name of one lucky fan, tonight's participant in the Geneva Cubs Grocery Grab. Behind home plate were parallel rows of canned fruits and vegetables, boxed pasta and detergents, jars of jellies and sauces, rolls of film and paper towels, bags of snack foods, and match-light charcoal. Tonight's Lucky Fan was a smiling and overweight fiftyish guy in a T-shirt and a mesh ball cap. Shepard rolled a grocery cart into the on-deck circle. The PA guy explained the rules: the cart stays put and, for one minute, Tonight's Lucky Fan grabs groceries, keeping whatever he can dump in the cart.

In the bullpen, Batavia's starting pitcher, Matt Viggiano, a freckled nineteen-year-old signed out of the Detroit sandlots by Tony Lucadello, stopped his warm-up tosses to watch. The grounds crew—a shirtless guy wetting down the infield dirt—turned to face the plate.

"On your mark," the PA guy said, and the crowd joined in for "Get set" and "Go!" The hefty man moved his arms as if running, but below the waist, he merely hurried to the groceries. The crowd chanted "Grab, grab, grab," and Tonight's Lucky Fan loaded his arms with as many boxes and bags and cans as he could, chugging back to the cart and breathing hard.

"Fifteen seconds," said the PA guy, and Tonight's Lucky Fan panicked. He snatched up a box of spaghetti, then, stooping for some potato chips, dropped the spaghetti. When he reached for the spaghetti, he dropped the chips. Tonight's

Lucky Fan then knelt, reaching for toilet paper with one hand, the spaghetti and the chips with the other. He stood up and hurried to the cart. "Six, five," counted the crowd, "four, three . . ." His pumping arms grasped the spaghetti and chips too tightly, and three steps from the cart, the boxes exploded, setting in flight a shower of crushed chips and splayed rays of rotating dry spaghetti. "Awww!" said the crowd.

The grounds crew shook his head, coiling up his hose, dismayed that he now had to pick up spilled food behind the plate, which was probably not in his job description. But Shepard—a slight but jockish guy whose tenth college reunion is in the future—pitched in to help, scooping up the unclaimed groceries and then getting down on his knees to gather the ill-fated starches. Laughing and loose, Viggiano jogged to the dugout. The PA guy popped a cassette of the national anthem into a small tape recorder, holding his mike to its speaker.

There were two and a half Lucadello signees in the starting lineup: Viggiano on the mound, Tenhunfeld in right, and in left, Fred Felton—the fleet Wright State outfielder who'd seen me humiliate myself with the plastic golf ball drill in his dorm last spring.

Viggiano was listed on the roster as a six-footer. Right. When Tony signed his six players this year, he had me help them fill out publicity forms. When we reached the height blank, they'd say their height, and Tony would tell me to add an inch. For their weight, I'd add ten pounds. In Matt's case, being identified as a six-footer was vital; few big-league right-handers are smaller.

He started out strong, getting the first three batters out—a guy named Skip Eggleston, an eighteen-year-old from the San Pedro de Macoris shortstop factory, and University of Michigan third baseman Billy St. Peter—one, two, three. He looked sharp, throwing strikes, changing speeds, fooling the hitters. Then again, he should have looked good. The New York–Penn is a high rookie league, so it plays a short season, primarily with just-drafted collegians. But younger players like Viggiano, unable to catch on with the lowest-rung Class A club—in the Phillies' case, Spartanburg—keep playing games in Florida in what's called extended spring training. Though most of the players Viggiano faced were two or three years older, they were new to pro ball. He, on the other hand, had not only a season of pro ball behind him but also seventy-five innings in extended spring training against players from the Tigers, Reds and Cardinals systems.

So Viggiano—well conditioned, in a groove and aided by the setting sun that shone, hot and unmerciful, in the hitters' eyes until the seventh inning—took advantage of the hitters' rusty timing and sailed through the Geneva Cubs lineup. In the third inning, he got the only run he needed when the evangelistic Felton doubled off the Grace Baptist Church sign in right-center, stole third and scored on a wild pitch. Otherwise, Tony's boys didn't help Matt out much. In Felton's other three at-bats, he struck out twice and popped up. Tenhunfeld struck out twice and popped up twice, in addition to making a wild and embarrassing rainbow throw in the sixth inning that put Viggiano in a jam. But Viggiano worked out of it and wound up with a complete-game, four-hit shutout.

"Player of the game?" Shepard asked in the press box as the players, by rote, filed onto the field to shake hands.

"Gotta be Viggiano," I said, too loud and too fast. I must have sounded like a blood relative or, at least, an athletic booster from Viggiano's Warren, Michigan, high school.

"It has to be a Cub," Shepard said.

There wasn't much to choose from there, and I kept out of it. Shepard and the PA guy tried to remember if any of the three people who got hits had made any good defensive plays. The Geneva Cubs would, over the course of the season, prove to be the worst team in the league, and later that summer, I often thought of Shepard and the PA guy resuming this debate during home games for a team that sometimes went weeks between wins. During the Cubs' longest losing streak, Shepard, on a whim, said he'd sleep in the press box until the team won a game. He spent the next twenty-two nights on an army cot, dangling above darkened McDonough Field, getting phone calls from wacky morning-zoo radio shows all over America and wondering if this was how Branch Rickey started.

In the morning, I called Tony at the Knights Inn in Richmond, Indiana, with my report. "I don't count Felton," Tony reminded me. "I didn't sign him. Now, what about Marsh? Did they play him?"

"No."

"What can they be thinking! You mean to tell me they played Fred ahead of Marsh?"

"Yeah. They played Marsh on opening day and he got three hits, but the manager said he was too hyped up and so he sat Marsh down and told him to try to get a little composure."

"Composure! For heaven's sake. Now I've heard everything. You mean to tell me they're benching ball players now for being too aggressive? You see what I mean about our game? You see what's happening? Fred's a good young man, and I certainly wish him all the best, but he's not one-tenth the ball player Marsh is. Marsh is a *prospect*; can't they see that? Marsh is a hundred times better than Fred, but they're not going to see that if they let him just sit there. Why don't they treat my ball players better than this?"

"I don't know. I'll ask."

"Well, they have their job to do, and I'm not trying to interfere. They don't interfere with me. If you ask 'em, be real diplomatic-like. I don't want them to think you're criticizing them. They might take it out on my ball players. Hey, by the way, I found another sleeper, over in Seymour, Indiana."

"For next year?"
"For this year."

No one in sports is as untroubled and relaxed as a starting pitcher the day after a shutout. Basking in the afterglow of last night's work, he faces a day in which little will be asked of him save a series of shy smiles as fans, teammates and reporters walk up and say, "Nice game." While the other Batavia Clippers took BP and infield, Matt Viggiano and I sat in the bleachers at Batavia's Dwyer Stadium. The ramshackle wooden blue ballpark, almost fifty years old and looking it, was one of the country's first WPA projects—supposedly built after a phone call from Batavia's Mayor Mahoney to America's President Roosevelt. "I'd like to take BP," Matt said. "But last time I did, I got fined five dollars. Me and another pitcher came out early and we were hittin' without the coach watchin', and I hit one out. They fined me because they lost a ball." He shrugged. "It was worth five bucks."

Viggiano had been drafted as a pitcher-catcher-outfielder but was converted to pitcher in spring training. He was pained to see the New York–Penn League put in the designated hitter rule this year. "I'll get used to it," he said. "I'll get my cuts up in the big leagues. I want to play in the big leagues. It don't matter which team, but I prefer the Phillies, 'cause it's my favorite team, even before I got drafted."

"How does a kid from outside Detroit come to root for the Phillies?"

"I played on a team in the Little League World Series that had Phillies uniforms. Plus I always liked Mike Schmidt."

In the outfield Tom Marsh was chasing down flies with a group of outfielders. The other ball players had their Darryl Strawberry–model nonchalance down, but Marsh bounced up and down in between his turns like a windup toy with endurance and a good arm.

"Tony's just like a part of my family," Matt told me. "He's always there for you, for all the guys. We know who we are, the guys who Tony signed."

"Do you have a secret handshake or something?"

"Nah, but we look out for each other. When a new guy joins the team and we hear he's been signed by Tony, we seek him out. We know that if he's the kind of player Tony would sign, then he's probably a great ball player and a great guy. If one of his players don't have a good year, they're gonna come around. We all have something in us that impressed Tony, and we don't want to let him down."

We talked until the Clippers yielded the field to the visiting Geneva Cubs. Marsh, who'd hit a dead-center-field homer in BP, stopped to say hello, and I remembered to ask the Clippers manager, Don McCormack, why Marsh wasn't playing. Everybody deserves a look in these first few games, he said, but you can only play ten guys at once. "Marsh'll get back in tomorrow, probably."

Closer to game time I risked the climb to the stadium roof. The wire backstop had scores of gaps big enough for foul balls to rocket through, and the press box was more like a poorly maintained backyard treehouse with electricity, by which I mean no criticism. I'd hate to see the minor leagues, newly hip, follow the chain-restaurant mentality of the big leagues straight into aesthetic hell and interchangeable oblivion. This was the electronic scoreboard's first year at Dwyer Stadium. In the past, junior high kids would sprint out to hang numbers on the old scoreboard in right-center when the ball was dead. The Batavians seemed pleased to have raised the money for the new, bland electronic rectangle, but I was sorry to have missed the old scoreboard—still faintly visible under a single coat of white paint—and I was pleased when the new one began to malfunction in the third inning.

Batavia started Rick Trlicek, from LaGrange, Texas, last year's fourth-round draft choice, who'd had a 4.10 ERA the season before at Utica. The highest player the Phillies drafted for Tony in 1987 was outfielder Mark Cobb, sixteenth, who was playing at Class A Clearwater, two rungs up the ladder from Batavia, and already rated among the Phillies top-ten minor league prospects.

For four innings, Trlicek was just wild enough to spook the hitters, just controlled enough to keep the runners he walked from scoring. But he began the fifth with two walks, then got behind the count to the next hitter, and Tim Dell began warming up in the bullpen. Dell had always been a starter, and he had the varied stuff and physical stamina to stay a starter, but by the time he joined the team, McCormack had his rotation set.

Trlicek gave up a sacrifice fly, another walk, and a three-run double to St. Peter before getting out of the inning on a hard-hit ball that died in the thatchy infield grass of Dwyer Field.

These players from Texas, I could almost hear Tony wail, *where are they?* Tony was right; about half of the Batavia Clippers came from the Sun Belt, and only one, outfielder Leroy Ventress, looked like a prospect to me. The regular first baseman was a poor-fielding, six-foot, 250-pound kid from a Texas junior college. He had power and would go on to lead the team in homers. Big deal. That's just rookie league ball. The weight will catch up with him, and even if he loses it, he's too short to be a major league first baseman. We had a contest in the press box to coin a nickname for him. For several innings, the best anyone could do was "The Sultan of Suet." I won a hotdog with "Brian 'Eat-Eat' Cummings."

I asked Wayne Fuller, the Clippers' PA guy and a booster of Batavia baseball for years, how many players from a typical New York–Penn League team would go on to play in the majors. "In a good year, two or three," he said. "In a bad year none. Probably averages about one a year."

Think of that. This is a high rookie league—there's a rung

below this—and each year perhaps one of the thirty-some players who see action for each New York–Penn League team will draw a big-league paycheck. Tony, who signs about six players a year, averages better all by himself.

In the top of the sixth, Tim Dell came to the mound for his warm-up tosses. He gave up a single to the first batter, then set the next three batters down on routine grounders. He threw a big overhand curve, a lively fastball, and a deceptive, sinking change-up. In the seventh, trying to paint the corners of the plate, he ran into a little control problem, missing on pitches so narrowly that the crowd began to "ooh" and ride the ump. He gave up a run but then got out of the inning and his first jittery professional outing. McCormack pulled him after that, but Dell would go on, that season, to be Batavia's most effective pitcher—even miscast as a reliever—with a 1.21 ERA, 43 strikeouts, and only 13 walks. His lone start was a complete-game shutout.

Replacing Dell was Rick Tracy, another Tony Lucadello find. Tracy's from Bowling Green, only minutes from Fostoria, and Tony had seen him for the first time in a Little League game. During his senior year, Rick came to know Tony, who was interested in the young pitcher but who respected his wish to play college football. Recruited as a quarterback by hometown Bowling Green State University, Tracy lost the starting job to another freshman and wondered if he wanted to ride the bench for the next four years. Sick of football and floundering in the classroom, Tracy called the old scout and asked if he knew of a decent junior college baseball program. Instead, Tony took him out to throw a baseball against a wall. Weeks later, Tony signed Rick Tracy to his first professional contract.

Tracy stood to the side of the mound, keeping loose with soft, arcing throws to the catcher while Clippers officials dragged onto the field a big plywood cutout of an obese bear with a hole in its belly. "Time," the announcer said, "for the

Big Daddy's Ale House Target Throw." Three lucky fans chosen at random stand on home plate and throw a baseball at
the hole in Big Daddy. The prize money for a winning toss
had started at twenty-five dollars on opening day and was now
up to thirty dollars. Two kids thudded their throws off the
plywood and a middle-aged guy sailed a throw clean over
second base. The crowd said "aww" and Tracy waited for the
grounds crew to drag Big Daddy to the sidelines. He came to
the mound, the score tied 5–5.

He pitched two shutout innings, but then, in the tenth,
hung a curveball and gave up a go-ahead solo homer. *Just
think about the wall*, he thought, closing his eyes and breathing deep. *Just throw it up against that little square.* He set
down the next two batters on feeble tappers to second, then
got bailed out by a run in the bottom of the tenth. Coming to
the mound in the eleventh, he mowed down the top of the
order, one two three. Ventress hit a double in the bottom of
the inning to make Rick Tracy the winning pitcher.

After the game, I stopped to talk to him. "A book about
Tony, huh? You know, my dad knows a couple guys in this
little town, and every year they have a steak-and-beer thing."
Tracy smiled. "They had Tony come speak there last year, and
they said he was the best speaker they ever had. They got his
picture framed and signed and hung up on the wall now. They
paid him four hundred dollars, he donated the whole thing to
the town's baseball program. Hey, did he ever tell you that
onion juice story?"

I called Tony and told him about Dell and Tracy. "They
both looked great to me," I said. "Dell didn't have his best
stuff, but he was still probably the more impressive of the two,
if you look at the kind of tools he has and then project him
against tougher competition."

Tony roared. "Hey, I've got you trained good. I've got you talkin' like a scout now."

"Thanks."

"If you lived in my territory, I'd make you a contract scout."

"Aw, come on."

"I would. If I trained you, you could do it. Hey, how about Marsh? Did they play Marsh?"

"No."

"Aw, for heaven's sake."

"He's supposed to start tonight."

The next day, the longest day of the year, I had lunch with Tom Marsh. He couldn't remember if he'd ever ridden the bench before, and his two days out of the lineup were eating at him. Adjustment to minor league ball had been rougher than Marsh expected. He still hadn't received the first half of his meager bonus and had been forced to borrow money from his parents for his clubhouse and laundry dues. He missed his girl friend. He hated the community college dorm where the players were housed. The prefab cement building, in the middle of a vast and incessantly wind-blasted field, was a two-mile walk from the ballpark. Not even all the coaches had cars, and Marsh had to call a cab just to go buy groceries. The long walk would wear you out before a game, he said, but luckily Batavians were starting to recognize the ball players and gave them lifts to the park. He even missed pitching. "I could get hitters in this league out," he said, closing his eyes, picturing raw and jittery hitters unfamiliar with wooden bats. But what really bugged him was riding the pine. "Mac says I'm too hyped up," Marsh said, drumming his fingers on the table and looking around for a waitress. "Maybe he's right, but that's just the only way I know how to play. In college, you'd just get out of classes and go play ball. Here, it's just playing ball. Which is great if you're one of the ones playing."

He ate his pecan pie, and I grabbed the check.

"You know, I'm glad Tony told me not to pay attention to what the other guys got paid for their bonus. All the guys talk about it, and most of 'em are braggin'. I can't believe it. I mean, fifty, sixty, seventy thousand for guys that— Well, for guys, you know, who probably aren't going to make it."

"Maybe they're just lying."

"Maybe. I don't tell anyone what I got. The real money's in the big leagues, I know that. But I look around and—this may sound bad—but I look around and I don't see anyone any better than me."

That night, at home against the St. Catherines Blue Jays and one of the best pitchers in the league, the Batavia Clippers were shut out, 4–0. Marsh, batting eighth, went 0 for 3. But his first two at-bats were warning-track fly balls, including a broken-bat blast to center: an aluminum-bat homer, a wooden-bat out. He made a diving catch in the seventh and a good throw that narrowly missed doubling up the runner at second. By game's end, the sun still clung to the horizon, and Batavia had a new starting left fielder.

Marsh would prove to be the team's best hitter and its steadiest defensive outfielder. That winter—when most of the guys who said they'd received signing bonuses big enough to pay cash for a Jag rode home in their parents' Fords—Tom Marsh caught a jet to the Instructional League.

11

Brown
Diamonds

"Pool-table green," I said.

Don Shaw shook his head. A soft-spoken high-school English teacher, Shaw worked part-time for Tony, scouring central Ohio for ball players. "It's not that dark. Maybe parrot green."

"Not that yellowish."

We were in the bleachers of Cooper Stadium, in Columbus, Ohio, home of the Yankees' AAA team. This Tuesday morning, the stadium was also home to the Columbus Jammers Invitational. The Jammers played what would have been called "sandlot ball" a few years ago: amateur baseball for players seventeen and older. The prosaic "unlimited age baseball" has replaced the earlier name. The change is appropriate, as teams desert their sandlot infields for places like Cooper Stadium, with its synthetic surface.

"Toothpaste-gel green."

"No," Don Shaw said. "It's not that blue."

This was the greenest ballpark I'd seen for a month, even if it was a green not found in nature. Actually, that summer in the American Midwest, the only greens found in nature were pine trees. Even golf greens had gone brown and patchy. There hadn't been a rainstorm in Tony's territory since April. Late June saw an unprecedented run of 100-degree days, and the beanfields along I-71 on the way from Batavia to Columbus were more dirt than crops. Scouts that summer made a science of finding shade, and their small talk turned easily from the speed of a shortstop to the weather. No scout, not even Tony and others his age, could remember a year like this, a year where most hadn't missed a single game because of rain.

"How about Palmolive green?" Shaw said.

"Not quite that dark," I said. "But we're on the right track."

The temperature hit 100 about midmorning. We'd been all over the bleachers, following the whims of the shade, and dodging running water as workers hosed down the cement floor of the grandstand. The concession stand—a woman selling canned sodas out of two plastic chests—ran dry by noon. A few years before, Shaw had first brought Tony here to see Mark Cobb, who was now hitting .300 at Class A Spartanburg and who had since become the Phillies' best outfield prospect. But this year's talent was thin; Shaw was following only a few players. To judge from Tony's reactions, the old scout had seen nothing at all. I tried to help him out by getting lineups from the coaches. The heat shimmered in curtains from the ground and made me feel like I was walking barefoot across blacktop.

"Not quite watermelon green," Shaw said. "This is my boy, there on first, number 99. He usually plays short, but he's pitching tomorrow."

This was our third game of the day. If there hadn't been a player on Shaw's follow list, Tony would have left. But we stayed, watching a kid play out of position, brooding over the color of the turf, chatting about the wall Shaw was going to build in his toddler grandson's backyard. Tony walked up the first-base line to stretch his legs. He wore a short-sleeved white shirt and his blue hat and—even in this heat—a red tie.

Late in the game, number 99 came in to pitch. "I'd rather the kid start than relieve," Shaw said, looking for Tony, who had walked to the right-field end of the grandstand and seemed to be staring into space. "But this way, at least, Tony gets to see him throw."

Number 99 had control problems but threw hard. A pack of scouts nearby had removed their radar guns from their cases and begun to scribble notes on their clipboards.

"Not much movement on the kid's fastball," I ventured.

Shaw nodded. "Not today, you're right. I've seen him throw better. He needs the kind of warm-up a starter gets." Shaw looked down the line at his boss. The old scout had taken a seat and folded his hands in his lap. He scarcely seemed to be watching.

"You know what?" Shaw said. "It reminds me most of the syrup they pour onto lime sno-cones."

"Touché." I tipped my cap.

At the end of the inning, Tony returned. "Ready to go?"

"If you are," Shaw said. "I've seen the kid enough before."

"Uh-huh." Tony looked at his watch. "Well, let's go, okay? Do you know any place around here that serves a fruit plate?"

Don Shaw gathered his lineup cards, and he and Tony said good-bye to the scouts and college coaches who remained. Underneath the stadium, Tony pulled Shaw aside. "I didn't want to say anything in front of everybody," Tony said. "The kid's got a problem with his left knee. It's too stiff. You can't see it right from where you were sitting." He shook his head. "Don't waste any more time on him," Tony whispered. "He's no prospect."

"I'm glad to get out of the cities," Tony said, on our way from Columbus to Piqua. "I've seen the top kids, and I can leave them to my part-time men. I need to get into the backcountry." He said this with the same decided tone a man would use to say he needed a drink.

We checked into the Piqua L & K Motel around noon and made it to Piqua's Jim Hardman Field by one. No first-time visitor could have found his way down the meandering side streets without stopping at the Mini-Mart for directions.

A barrel-chested man with a garden hose staggered across the infield in the windless heat, waging a losing battle with the parched ground. Fairborn Legion Post 526 would be here in six hours to play Piqua Post 184. Tony came six hours early, to see a relief pitcher from Fairborn and to meet the new Piqua coach. The players were still scattered across various central-Ohio burger joints and municipal swimming pools and tool-and-die shops, working summer jobs, minds less on that night's baseball game than on earning enough money to buy that used Mercury over at Townline Auto Sales.

The man with the hose turned out to be the new head coach at a tiny community college nearby. He kept watering as he talked; the spray dried almost instantly as it hit the dirt. Tony gave him a business card and begged him to send next year's schedule, and the man wagged his head and said, "You bet I will." The guy couldn't have known that the old man in the coat and tie was the most successful baseball scout in history. Here he was—a rookie coach at a school that had never produced a major leaguer—talking to a pro scout. That schedule would arrive in Fostoria, Ohio, the day after it was typed.

"Now what you just saw there was the key to my success," Tony whispered as we looked for coins under the bleachers. "That young man may never have a ball player for me. But I still have to treat him with respect, see. First of all, it's hard for a young man like that, with a family and all, to break into coaching. It don't pay well; they're doing it for the love of the game, and without men like that, there'd be no ball players for me to see. So that's first." Then Tony turned to me and smiled, eyes dancing. "But then there's this: you never know how someone, someday might help you. He *might* have a player for me. He might *see* a player for me, then. As along as I treat him with respect *now* when he's at this level, where he don't see a lot of scouts, then whenever he's in a position to help me, why, he'll do it." Tony slapped me on the back. "That's how I find ball players that drive the other scouts nuts, players nobody knew about who go on to succeed in pro ball. I couldn't do it without the help of my friends: old friends and new friends. Hey, look at that!"

He stooped over and blew the dust from a quarter.

"Now *that* made my day."

We sat down in the bleachers, and Tony prodded me about my trip to Batavia. He asked me how the community supported the team, how the players' rooms looked, what the manager thought of each player, what I thought of each player, how happy the players seemed, how they were doing for money, how much the players thought throwing a ball against a wall had helped them.

Then he began to repeat himself, savoring my answers, like a father who sits down at a coffee shop next to someone who compliments his kid's performance in the school play. So you liked the sword-fight scene? the father says, afraid the subject will change. You can tell me the truth: did you really think the kid has a lovely singing voice?

"Well, maybe they're starting to treat my ball players better," Tony concluded.

"What do you mean," I asked. "How have they been mistreating your players?"

He just shrugged. "Well, we'll just see, okay?" And he cut the conversation off, in a hurry to make a few phone calls, eat dinner, and avoid the rush-hour traffic in a town of twenty thousand so we'd get back here in time for batting practice. After all, we only had five hours.

* * *

We returned to Jim Hardman Field before the players arrived. Tony introduced himself to the new Piqua coach and gave the man his business card. The Piqua shortstop was going to Indiana University on a partial scholarship. Tony nodded. He knew that. Nice young man; no prospect. "Who else have you got," he asked. "Who else have you seen?"

We sat in the bleachers next to Jim Hardman, he of the field, Mr. Amateur Baseball in Piqua, Ohio. There is a Jim Hardman in most every small town in Tony's territory, and every Jim Hardman has a couple of Tony Lucadello's business cards. Retired from coaching, Hardman still comes to about half the games, and this night he had brought his wife and his six-year-old granddaughter, who was visiting from the Virgin Islands.

In the third inning, Miami coach Jon Pavlisko stopped by, on his way home from a scouting trip in Michigan, shaking his head about Tony's signing Todd Elam during spring training. Elam had dropped out of Miami, a towering but raw pitcher with shaky grades. Pavlisko figured baseball was over for him. The night before, though, Elam had been the winning pitcher at Batavia. "Well, Jon, I'll tell you," Tony said, looking toward the Fairborn bullpen, hoping the player he was there to see would begin to warm up. "It's the wall. I had him throw up against that wall. You should get a copy of the film, you know."

Pavlisko, who'd seemed a little reserved about the idea last autumn in Oxford, nodded. "I'd sure like to do that."

"Well, I have a copy in the trunk," Tony said. "I'll lend it to you."

The lights came on and Tony shook his head. Usually, we left ballparks before the lights came on, but sometimes we had no choice. Tony hates scouting at night. Players look quicker under the lights. Arms look better. Swings look faster. But it's an illusion, he told me.

Tony's reliever entered the game in the top of the sixth. The skinny, short-arming right-hander had been recommended to him by an old friend. The boy threw like a catcher. He walked a run in. Tony, ready to go, sent me to his car for the videotape. When I returned, Tony was on the edge of his seat, eager to leave without being seen and hurting the feelings of any coach or player or parent. But Mrs. Hardman detained him. "Can you sing your song for Mr. Lucadello," she asked her granddaughter.

Tony smiled, indulgently, and handed the videotape to Jon Pavlisko.

"C'mon, honey," coaxed Mrs. Hardman.

"Tay-AKE, meouttotheballgame," she shrieked, singing the song as fast as a six-year-old can.

Tony's face broke into a real smile. "That's just fantastic," he said when she finished, tousling her hair and shaking hands with Hardman and Pavlisko. "You go home down to the islands there and you teach all your little friends that song, okay?"

The girl nodded and again lit into song. Tony and I slipped away, taking a route behind the concession stand that shielded us from the view of the coaches and players. Behind us, the little girl's shrill voice rose above the din of the crowd: "I don't care if I NE-VER get back!"

Tony knew of a cafeteria in town that featured a fruit cup, wheat toast and Sanka on its breakfast buffet, so we stayed at the Piqua L & K the next two days and commuted twenty miles north to a Legion tournament in Sidney.

"So tell me about your sleeper," I said, driving up I-75, dew still on the Caprice.

"Which one?" Tony said.

"You have *two*?"

"Yep. I do now."

"Two for this year?"

"Well, if everything works out, I'll sign 'em this year to a 1989 contract, and they'll report to Florida next spring."

"So who are they?"

Tony looked out the side window at the cracked gray dirt and ruined crops. "I don't think I better say yet."

I tried to assure him his secrets were safe with me, that even if they *weren't* safe, nothing I'd write would be published until more than a year later.

"Naw," Tony said. "I hadn't better say. I've got 'em throwin' balls off their garages at home. If they stick to that, they'll improve some, and once they do that, I'll tell you. Okay?" He smiled and pointed out the Sidney exit. "You wouldn't want to jinx the old scout, would you?"

The infield at Sidney's Custenborder Field had been watered every third day during the drought. In any normal Ohio summer, the infield grass would have been considered brown and dead. This year, though, the outfield grass—and all the other grass in Sidney—was the color of peanut shells and crunched when you walked on it. The infield grass, by comparison, seemed positively verdant.

Tony again started his scouting day by striking up a conversation with a Parks Department employee, who this time turned out to be a much-traveled veteran umpire with opinions on all the best prospects in west north-central Ohio. He had known the local star, Froning, a big right-handed senior, for years. Knew the family. Knew the grandparents, even. The maintenance director–ump provided Tony with a character sketch and an oral transcript of the boy's grades that could have placed the kid in any Jesuit college in the Midwest.

Froning was one of the first players to arrive. Tony, in

planning his schedule, had called the Sidney coach to see when Froning was most likely to pitch. The coach had subsequently fiddled with his rotation and Tony learned Froning wouldn't appear in this tournament at all.

Unfazed, Tony shook hands with the boy, and they sat down together in the cool shade of the home dugout. Not seeing Froning pitch wouldn't make much difference. Tony had seen him four times now and knew all he really needed to know: keep an eye on this kid. Anything Froning might have done that day, short of snorting cocaine off the pitching rubber, would have been irrelevant. Tony knew he'd decide whether Froning was ready for pro ball during the high school season next spring. But scouting is not—in the infamous words of Cincinnati Reds owner Marge Schott—just sitting around and watching ball games. Tony pressed a business card into Froning's palm, then produced a carbonless form from the breast pocket of his white shirt and told the boy he needed to get "all the dope on you." Tony made idle chatter about Sidney's season while getting down on paper Froning's address and phone number and vital statistics and parents' names. Though he'd already secured this information from the coach, Tony filled out the form then to demonstrate his interest. Froning was undecided about college. "That's fine," Tony said. "I wouldn't want you to do anything you hadn't thought through, or that your parents didn't approve of." Patiently, Tony explained all the boy's options: junior college, college, and pro. The boy listened, beaming. Tony gave him another card, a spare, then shook hands, wished him luck and asked him to promise not to tell any scouts about this little chat. "If they knew I was interested in you," he said, "it'd kill me."

Tony and I sat down in the bleachers, and Tony fixed his eyes below the waists of the players loosening up. He sent me to get lineups from the Sidney and the Marietta coaches.

"With that briefcase there," he said, "people think you're a scout. If they ask you, tell 'em you're with the Yankees."

"Why the Yankees?"

" 'Cause they change their people around so much, no-body'll know the difference."

When I got back, I asked Tony if he'd seen anyone he liked.

"Number 20 for Marietta, the shortstop, where's he bat?"

"Third."

"Even against a right-hander, huh?"

"Switch-hitter," I said. "The coach told me he was the best kid he had."

Tony laughed. "You see, that's why I don't get lineups anymore. I finally talked my office out of it. For forty-five years, they made me do it. But it's a waste of time for me. Sometimes the coaches brag up their pets and ignore other good players, which is how the two sleepers I have now became sleepers. Most of the time, though, they tell you about the obvious players. I like to pick 'em out myself, and then if I need the dope on the boy, I ask the coaches. Take this number 20. Listen: whenever a six-foot-tall, switch-hitting shortstop bats third or cleanup, you better look at him."

Number 20, it turned out, was by far the best player on the field, although the dim, low-rent-carnival wattage of the outfield lights made everyone a dangerous hitter. "There's one thing that bugs me," Tony said. "See if you can pick it out."

"At bat or in the field?"

"In the field."

Honestly: he looked good to me. He hadn't made an error all game. "Well, it's not his arm."

Tony scowled. "Heavens, no."

"How about the way he positions his feet?" I didn't know what I meant by this, but it sounded like something Tony might say.

"No, no. Notice how close he plays to the bag. Doesn't that tell you something?"

I stammered out a few asinine guesses.

Tony finally put me out of my misery. "He's afraid to play too far off the bag. Whenever an infielder plays too close, you know he doesn't have the confidence that he's going to get there fast enough. I project him as an outfielder."

Tony scouted the crowd and noticed a woman in the bleachers, near his lawn chair, who howled number 20's name during each of his at-bats. "The mother," he whispered to me. He pulled another carbonless form from his breast pocket. "I need all the dope on your boy," he said to her. "I'm a scout for the Philadelphia Phillies."

Near the end of the game, a half-dozen guys from the Pemberville American Legion team stopped by Custenborder Field to size up Marion, the team they would face the next day. They were horsing around with some plastic Uzi-replica squirt guns. One of the boys was Aaron Hampton, whose new, unmortared, cement-block wall we'd seen last fall in Fostoria. This spring, thanks to the wall and to the plastic golf ball drill, Aaron, a .103 hitter as a freshman, had become Fostoria High's starting shortstop as a sophomore and raised his batting average to .373. The wall helped his foot speed, readied him for bad hops, and allowed him to make plays on balls that, the year before, he'd have watched bound into the outfield. Because Fostoria didn't have a Legion team, Aaron joined Pemberville's.

"What are you doing with that?" Tony pointed at the ersatz Uzi. "Why aren't you carrying a bat or a glove? Don't you want to be a ball player?"

Aaron laughed, handed the squirt gun to one of his pals and sat down next to Tony. "Yeah."

"At least you weren't throwin' a football around. I'm afraid you're gonna give up baseball for football."

"Noooo." Rhymes with "zoo."

"Well, I have something to tell you."

"Okay." Aaron looked up at Tony like a boy waiting for his grandfather to dispense a Christmas present.

"Get your body in front of the ball. Only make the play beside you when you can't make it any other way. Don't try to be one of these Fancy Dans. We've got too many of them in baseball already."

Aaron frowned. "When did you see me do that?"

"I've seen you a few times when you didn't know I was there. And I have spies."

Aaron was one of Tony's hometown projects. He'd been one of the kids featured in the *Coaching Clinic* videotape. That winter, Tony had taken Aaron to bat against Rick Tracy, and this spring, Tony had deputized some local baseball fans to watch each of Aaron's games and report back. But the Phillies had recently released one of Tony's other hometown projects, Aaron's cousin Rodney, because he was just plain lazy. "I haven't talked to him about it yet," Aaron said. "This winter, Rick Tracy and me, we'd call him up to go work out, but he wasn't around much. I mean, if you get cut 'cause you can't play, that's one thing, but because you're lazy . . ." Aaron shook his head. "That's something you can correct. A lot of people think he's my brother. If Tony does sign me, they'll remember Rodney and I might go down there a little behind people because they'll think I'm like Rodney. I know I'll have to work harder than the next guy. Which is fine with me, 'cause in the long run, it'll make me the better player."

I was disarmed to hear this from a boy barely fifteen. But Tony expected it. He folded his lawn chair, and Aaron Hampton offered to carry it, and the two Fostorians walked away from the gloaming of Custenborder Field, into the hot dry night, arms around each other, weighing plans for college.

* * *

The next day shattered heat records all over the Midwest. A bank in Sidney registered 100 degrees by ten. Of the three players Tony wanted to see in the tournament that morning, one had a sore arm, one had made an eleventh-hour college commitment, and the third—Aaron Hampton—was used as a DH. What Tony expected to be a productive tournament had gone bust, though he did persuade a curious grandfather, who recognized Tony from an article in *Baseball Digest*, to build a wall in his grandkids' backyard. By noon, we'd seen parts of three games, but Tony had taken to heart that long-ago advice from Branch Rickey: "If there's nothing there, go." After a brief stop for the McDonald's salad that had become Tony's ritual lunch, we headed up I-75 to Bowling Green for a Great Lakes Summer Collegiate League game.

Collegiate summer leagues are a fairly new phenomenon, with the exception of the venerable Cape Cod League, on which all the others are modeled. Basically, the leagues work as de facto amateur minor leagues. College coaches assemble teams of college all-stars, allowing the players to develop against top talent and, in theory, allowing scouts to see a given region's best college players in a concentrated area. The Great Lakes League has an added draw for scouts: it is the only collegiate league other than the Cape Cod to use wooden bats. If you want to hear the crack of the bat, sadly your only chance is pro ball and these two collegiate leagues. For scouts, this problem goes beyond aesthetics. Aluminum bats are forgiving tools; a ball that pings off the handle—a ball that would snap a wooden bat and become an easy grounder—often produces bloop singles. Aluminum-bat homers are often wooden-bat fly balls. Many players, when signed to their first pro contract, have never swung a wooden bat in their lives. Scouts must guess how well a kid will adjust. More often than you'd think, they guess wrong.

The Great Lakes League, in its second year, has some work to do. Many of the best midwestern players still go to Cape Cod for the summer, because the competition is the best in the country, because the teams draw well, because the part-time jobs league organizers find for the players are the most lucrative of any league, and because—well, come on—where would you rather spend your summer, Falmouth or Muncie?

Dr. Bobby Brown asked Tony to scout the league for him. So far, Tony told me, he liked what he'd seen. The level of competition was improving, the facilities were decent, the coaching seemed good, and the wooden bats were a big, big plus.

"What bothers me is this: they don't draw." He unfolded his lawn chair underneath the scant shade of a scraggly pine down the right-field line of Bowling Green State University's Warren E. Steller Field. "Look at this," he said, sweeping his hand toward the almost empty grandstand. "How many people would you say there are here?"

"Forty. Tops."

"That's about right. Now how many of those do you think aren't the families or the girl friends of the players?"

I shrugged. "Three."

Tony nodded. "If that. I'll be honest with you. I worry about what's going to happen to our game when you have crowds this small coming to see players this good. These are the two worst teams in this league, and yet still, there's probably ten players here who'll get to play some pro ball. But where are the people?"

In all fairness to the baseball fans of Bowling Green, Ohio, the conditions were less than ideal for that day's doubleheader between the Muncie Chiefs and the Bowling Green Breeze, the most aptly named team in all sports. The whole university sits on a vast flat prairie, with nothing—except the low, soulless cement lecture halls designed by the architectural firm of Shoebox, Cinderblock, and Redi-Mix—to deflect the blasts of

211

the westerly winds. Some enterprising and well-intentioned groundskeeper planted a ring of nursery conifers around the ballpark, but the incessant winds bent most of the poor things sideways, and what shade they provide is cast in peculiar twisted shapes unsuited to your basic K-Mart lawn chair. Mike Trbovich, part-time Dodgers scout—a tall man with a raspy voice, about Tony's age—sat down beside us. Trbovich had signed former BGSU pitcher Orel Hershiser. "It's worse in the spring," he said. "You take a thirty-degree day and you add these winds here, and we're talkin' Yukon."

"I don't know if it's worse than this," Tony said. "In all my years, I never saw a summer like this."

"True enough," said Trbovich. "I just heard on the radio it's a hundred and six."

"Unbelievable." Tony's hat blew off and flew a good thirty feet. I retrieved it for him. He wiped his brow with a handkerchief and put the hat back on.

The winds kicked up thick khaki clouds of dirt and blew the center-field flag perpendicular to the pole. Slow curveballs got smacked by updrafts and hurtled against the backstop. Soft bloop hits carried to the fence and routine pop-ups sailed most of the way to Oz. "I'd go now," Tony shouted above the ever-louder roar of the hot wind. "But I promised Dr. Brown I'd scout this league, and I think I should see at least part of the next game." He had marked up a scorecard, writing "NP" next to the names of all the players who were no prospect, "SA" next to the players he wanted to see again, a check mark next to players he was interested in. Except for three "SA"s and one check mark—a starting pitcher not scheduled to play—the card was covered with "NP"s.

I found it hard to breathe, and I wanted to go back to my air-conditioned motel room, soak in a tub of tepid water, and drink many cold beers.

Even with the scant crowd, the concession stand ran out of pop by the middle of the second game. A stray seat cushion flew from somewhere near the third-base dugout and stayed aloft, spinning and dipping, until it cleared the outfield fence. The wind pasted my filthy clothes to my sweat-soaked body. I kept asking Tony how much longer, like a kid in the back of a car crossing Kansas. The old scout's striped red tie blew back behind his head, like the scarf of a bomber pilot, but somehow he managed to keep his eyes and his mind on the game. By the time he said we could go, I was too drained even to show gratitude. I felt like I'd spent the last two hours inside a dryer vent.

12

The Passed Torch
of Dreams

Hours before the game, under the shade of an oak tree flanking Jackson, Michigan's, J. J. Best Field, Tony waited for Lincoln Schomer, Yale class of 1992. Just this year, the American Legion post in Jackson had withdrawn its support of the baseball team, and the interested players had gravitated to a loosely organized men's league, where every game was in danger of being forfeited for a shortage of players. It's doubtful any other major league scout has ever been here. The teams in the league don't even have uniforms; Jackson's team members wear their own green T-shirts. Hillsdale—Jackson's opponent—wears red T-shirts. There was no field-maintenance budget. J. J. Best Field hadn't seen a drop of water for more than two months. The grass had turned to straw.

Linc Schomer drove up in a Ford Bronco, parking next to Tony's Caprice in the lot the field shares with the Jackson Abrasive Plant. Inside the plant, an aluminum barn, is conducted the manufacture of an incessant whine that is indeed abrasive. Linc scanned the field, looking for the hat. He grabbed a gym bag from the backseat and jogged over to the oak tree.

"Get suited up," Tony said. "I want to show you something."

Linc nodded, putting on sanitary hose, pulling his baseball pants over his shorts, and lacing up his spikes. He was a tall, broad-shouldered, pigeon-toed kid with the coltish gait of a natural athlete. He had quarterbacked Jackson's Lumen Christi High School into the state playoffs, and though his senior season in baseball had been a disappointment, he planned to play baseball and football at Yale.

"Hold the bat for me," Tony said, "with your arms extended."

Linc obeyed. He gripped the bat near the knob, and as Tony watched, hands on hips, the bat trembled in the boy's hands.

"Well, now, you see, you don't hold it right. You don't have control over that bat. Here, now." He walked behind the boy, wrapping his short arms around him and sliding Linc's hands up the barrel of the bat. "Try that."

On the edge of the shade, Linc swung the bat, again and again. Tony sat back down in his lawn chair, studying the boy as an artist would a model. "Didn't you bring a batting glove?"

"Forgot 'em."

"You'll get blisters."

"I'll be okay."

"Well, all right. Now I have to show you one more thing." Tony wanted Linc, a lefty, to learn how to pivot off his left foot so that he could pull the ball. Tony stood and demonstrated. Linc, who clearly thought of Tony Lucadello as a third grandfather, watched in reverent silence, then began to swing the bat again. Even though he'd wanted very much to go to Yale, he also wanted to be drafted to play pro baseball. He probably wouldn't have signed, but he wanted the option. That hadn't worked out, and now he was bound for New Haven, resolute, determined to letter in both football and baseball, holding out the hope of getting drafted three or four years from now.

"Are you getting blisters?"

"A little."

"Well, stop it then. Save it for the game. I want you to pull one for me in the game."

Thirty-five years earlier, Tony had begun scouting Linc's father, Jack, a fireballing, six-five, right-handed pitcher. Tony watched Jack Schomer pitch all through high school, coming to know the family. He reassured Jack's mother, who'd leaned toward Jack's going to college, though with six boys in the house she didn't know where the money would come from. But she sensed that the little man in the coat and tie and hat was genuinely concerned about her son. Right out of high school, Jack Schomer signed with the Chicago Cubs, and as Tony insisted, he put his entire bonus in the bank. Tony Lucadello—who has signed two Cy Young winners—said that Jack Schomer may have been the best pitcher he ever signed.

Jack Schomer had two outstanding seasons, but at the end of the second, as he was heading home from Colorado, where he'd been making Western League hitters talk to themselves, the car Jack Schomer was riding in flipped over, and the promising young hurler was pinned underneath. End of career.

He took his bonus out of the bank, put himself through Michigan State University, and is now a partner with a big Ann Arbor law firm. As he raised his three sons, his old friend Tony Lucadello would pop into town, bearing balls and bats and Phillies hats. He convinced Jack to build a wall in the backyard. Tony went to the boys' games—sometimes managing to see all three play in one night—and though none were quite the prospect their father had been, Tony helped each get the attention of college coaches, first from Brown, then Notre Dame and now Yale.

I sat in the bleachers next to Jack Schomer and his wife,

Gail, while Tony set up his lawn chair next to Jack's parents. We were about half the crowd. Jack Schomer, now fifty, is tan and fit, a soft-spoken but intense man who looks like he could still throw a fastball that would make a radar gun go boom. Jack and Gail told me how much Tony had helped them in raising their sons, how much they appreciated having an auxiliary grandfather around to solve problems that only on the surface were about baseball talent.

"I really believe Tony represents a philosophy of life," Gail Schomer told me, her eyes on Linc, in the on-deck circle. "He's a man who works alone. He's kind and gentle to other people. He holds the brass ring in front of the boys and says, "This is yours, if you want it." He's lived a life that's fulfilled a single-minded purpose, without regard for his own personal comforts, and he's helped an untold number of people along the way."

On his way to the plate, Linc Schomer waved shyly at his grandparents and at Tony. He choked up on the bat and, on the first pitch, pivoted off his right foot and hit a triple off the center-field fence. Dad Schomer and Tony slapped each other on the back. Jack Schomer tapped me on the shoulder with his index finger. "As a lawyer with a major law firm, I can tell you this: there's quality advice and there's just advice. That man over there represents quality advice."

After the game, Jack and Gail persuaded Tony to come back to their house for a piece of cherry pie that he kept trying to tell them was off his diet. But when we got there, Tony relented. "Just a real, real small piece though. A sliver." We sat in the family room, surrounded by pictures—the three boys playing football, a huge, recent family picture, and a color mug shot of twenty-year-old Jack Schomer in a Chicago Cubs uniform. Jack and his parents sat with me around the kitchen table, reminiscing about their first meeting with Tony. Dad Schomer, who'd emigrated from Germany when he was seventeen, was still every bit the proud parent of a star athlete, and he boasted up Jack's pitching prowess enough to make his son blush.

Jack walked to the kitchen window. "Hey, look at this."

Tony had looked restless even when we were eating, and while we talked in the kitchen, he and Linc had slipped out the side door. I heard the dull slaps of wood against hollow plastic and knew what the old scout was up to. I pulled back the kitchen curtains and there, in the backyard, as darkness crept down upon Jackson, Michigan, was Tony Lucadello, seventy-five, on one knee, tossing a hundred plastic golf balls up to Linc Schomer, eighteen.

In late June, the Phillies fired their general manager, part of the long-rumored shake-up of a team going nowhere fast. Soon after, they fired their farm director and demoted their scouting director. The Philadelphia newspapers reported that other organizational changes were forthcoming, possibly including the firing of scouts.

"I don't hear the rumors, to be honest with you," Tony told me, pulling up to a full-service pump in Dowagiac, Michigan. "Livin' out east like you do, you probably know more than me."

We walked across the street to a corner grocery, bought two bottles of apple juice and sipped them on vinyl chairs inside the filling station.

"Are you worried?"

"At my age?" he scoffed. "Heavens no. If they want me out, I'll go. I have a career behind me. I'd like to stay, but . . ." He shrugged.

"Seems to me that one of the reasons the Phillies are struggling is that they're taking the word of the Scouting Bureau and the cross-checkers over the word of people like you."

"Maybe," Tony said. "What I *am* worried about is that

they'll make me fire my part-time men. This new GM is from the St. Louis Cardinals, and they don't believe in part-timers. Now with us in last place and not drawing the fans like we were, I'm afraid they're going to want us to cut back. If they do that, I'll tell 'em what they can do with this job." He got up and spiked his half-empty juice bottle in the metal trash can. "But then I'd be afraid those daggone coaches wouldn't treat my ball players right."

We stopped for lunch—two fast-food salads—and drove to the Dowagiac Rotary Field. Tony still seemed peeved. We got out and began circling the dirt parking lot, looking for money. "Let me tell you a story," he said. "We had a farm director a few years ago by the name of Howie Bedell, who hired all his own people to coach the minor league teams, and he started kickin' my players around. He'd been up to no good for a long time, playin' favorites and all that, when one year he released one of my players—a fine ball player, but they never played him enough to find out. Howie Bedell had been treating me like dirt for a long time. I was fed up, and I told my wife it was time to make a change."

Tony called the Phillies offices and tried to reach then-president Ruly Carpenter, but Carpenter was on vacation in North Carolina, shooting quail. Paul Owens, the GM, was in a meeting. "Have him call me," Tony said. "As soon as he can."

About an hour later, Owens called back. "I'm not going into any detail, Mr. Owens," Tony said. "I'm just going to tell you something. I don't like the way Howie Bedell's been treating me and my players. He don't play 'em, he bad-mouths 'em, and now he's releasin' 'em. I've decided that I have to do one of two things: give up this job and get a job somewhere else, or you can get rid of Howie Bedell." This was a Monday. "You have until Saturday, and my resignation will be in the mail Sunday morning."

Wednesday, Dallas Green, the Phillies manager, called Tony to say they'd fired Howie Bedell. Tony said he was sorry to have been the cause of that but felt he'd had no other choice.

Dallas Green said Tony wasn't the only reason. Green, Paul Owens, Ruly Carpenter, and Ruly's father, Robert Carpenter, who'd hired Tony away from the Cubs many years before, had met to talk about his protest. After Paul Owens explained that this was between Tony Lucadello and Howie Bedell, Robert Carpenter rose to his feet and said, "Bedell goes. Nobody fires Tony. My son can't fire him. I can't fire him. He's too loyal and too good a man for us to lose him."

Tony picked up something that looked like a penny. It was a stone. He cast it into the bushes. "Mr. Robert Carpenter is dead now, and Ruly Carpenter sold the team seven years ago. Mr. Owens is our acting farm director, but he's semi-retired. Dallas Green's gone, too."

The sky looked like rain.

"Do you want to meet that player," he asked.

"Which player?"

"Jeff Nate's his name. The one Howie Bedell released."

"Sure. When?"

"Now. He works about a mile from here."

John Nate Beverage, Inc., sits in a cold, cavernous aluminum barn on the north edge of Dowagiac. Plastic and neon signs touting every imaginable Anheuser-Busch product dot the walls of the warehouse. The cement floor is as smooth and clean as the ice behind a Zamboni machine. The offices were, as yet, half-furnished, with more Clydesdale statuettes than desks. While John Nate himself conducted a guided tour of his new facility for Tony, a man who's never even sipped an alcoholic beverage, Jeff Nate and I sat in his dad's office, talking baseball.

Jeff Nate, dark skinned and white toothed, dressed in chinos, a powder-blue UCLA cap, and a pressed, pinstriped

Oxford shirt with a Budweiser patch sewn on its breast, graduated from high school the same year I did, 1979. Now he helps his father with the family business, driving the beer trucks, making sales calls, "whatever needs to be done." He also coaches the boy's high-school baseball team in nearby St. Joseph, Michigan.

During his senior year, Jeff, a slugging shortstop with a strong but erratic arm, was taking infield when he noticed an old guy underneath the bleachers, looking for something. Tony gave his business card to the Dowagiac coach, who introduced the old scout to Jeff. After the game, the Nates invited Tony over for coffee. Tony saw almost all of Jeff's remaining games, and by draft time, Jeff's mother loved him and the whole family felt they'd known Tony for fifty years.

The Phillies drafted Jeff in the eighth round. Jeff and his parents had decided that if any other team drafted him, he'd go to college. Even with the Phillies, Jeff said, he was still leaning toward college. When Tony Lucadello came to sign him, Jeff remained ambivalent. But two hours later, he was a Phillie; two days later, he was playing baseball in Helena, Montana.

"I thought Tony's reputation would really help me get to the big leagues," Jeff said. "I mean, just about the first person who talked to me out there was Dallas Green. He was the farm director then, and he's pitching batting practice, and he calls out to me, 'Hey, you're a Lucadello product!' "

But Green wasn't around much the next year when, at Bend, Oregon, Jeff Nate rode the bench all year. He was only nineteen, younger and rawer than, say, Juan Samuel, the team's second baseman. He hadn't expected to star, or even to start; he just wanted to improve. Then he got wind that something was up, though he didn't know what at the time. But he heard whispers: *Don't play that kid.* The next thing he knew, he'd been given his unconditional release.

"The Phillies weren't drafting many players for Tony,"

Jeff said. "The year I signed, there was only one other guy, and they released him right after they did me. What happened was Tony complained to Howie Bedell, pointing out all the players they *had* drafted who weren't working out, and Howie Bedell took it out on us."

Jeff came home that winter, dazed and broken. A ball player released while still in the low minors has a black mark against him; the odds of making it to the big leagues become worse than those for the state lottery. Tony tried to help Jeff, cheering him up, telling him to get in shape, and finally putting in a good word with a friend in the Mets organization. Jeff had an uphill battle ahead, and though he played fairly well, the Mets traded him to the A's, where he finished out his career. "I got a call from a friend who was with Kansas City then," Jeff said. "And he invited me to spring training with them. But guess where Howie Bedell went when he got fired?"

"Kansas City?"

Jeff nodded. "So that was it for me. I was bitter the first time I was released, really bitter, and I'd've never got through it without Tony's help. Now I accept it. I believe things happen for a reason. Maybe if I'd've kept playing I'd've been in a plane crash. Who knows?"

He's spent the last four years coaching at St. Joseph, and the program he's molded has sent six players to major college programs, including one who broke Kirk Gibson's stolen base record at Michigan State and was drafted this year. "My shortstop, a kid named Brett Wyngarden, who'll be a senior this fall, is probably the best player to come out of this area in twenty years."

Jeff was talking about his goals—moving up in coaching, sending kids to the big leagues, coaching in pro ball, and maybe getting to the majors himself that way—when Tony knocked on the door and came in.

"We have to go," he said. "I want to get to the ballpark

early. Your dad was just telling me about a place here in town where I can get a nice fruit plate. But I first need to ask you something, Jeff. I was wondering if you might be interested in the assistant's job at Notre Dame University?"

Jeff's eyes widened, but he tried to play cool. "Yeah. I would. Definitely."

"Well, the job's open, you know." Tony pulled a business card from the pocket of his sports jacket and pressed it into Jeff's palm. "You do this. You go to the athletic director down there at Notre Dame University with that business card and tell him, 'If you want to know anything about me, about my ability to do this type of work, here's the man you ought to call, because he's one of the best scouts in the business.' That'll put you in solid. I've done this for a select few other coaches, men I wanted to see advance in this business, and it's always worked out, every time."

Jeff thanked Tony, and we left, ate and drove back to Rotary Field. A soft rain had begun to fall; it was the first time in months Tony faced a rainout. Tony saw a boy about twelve waiting in one of the dugouts, and he worried whether this was the correct field. The boy said yeah, this was where the American Legion team played, his stupid brother had dropped him off at the wrong place. Tony nodded, then asked to see the boy's baseball. The next thing I knew, Tony was standing on home plate, throwing grounders to the boy, barking instructions: "Spread your legs and get down on the ball." The Legion players began to arrive, so Tony stopped, took the boy aside, explained about practicing off a wall, then gave him a business card. When the boy saw the Philadelphia Phillies logo, his eyes popped and his jaw dropped. No cartoonist could have drawn a figure of starker astonishment.

The game between St. Joseph and Dowagiac was played in an ever harder rain, as though people had gone so long without seeing precipitation they were oblivious to it. Jeff Nate sat in Tony's car with us, antsy about how the Legion coach was using "his" players and touting the every gesture of Brett Wyngarden, who, to be fair, did look like a hell of a high school shortstop. But I kept thinking about that boy staggering home in the rain, both hands grasping Tony Lucadello's business card out in front of him like the Holy Grail.

Archbold, Ohio, population 3,500, always seemed to have inordinately good sports teams. I grew up fifteen miles away, in Bryan, Ohio—home of the Dum-Dum Sucker and, at about three times Archbold's size, the metropolis of extreme northwestern Ohio—and the Archbold Blue Streaks were always beating us in something. We consoled ourselves with sneers. What else is there to do in Archbold except play sports and come to Bryan to shop? Why, at the time, we had the only fast-food restaurants for an eighteen-mile radius! Pathetic.

Tony wanted to see a few innings of the American Legion game that night in Archbold, to see a kid on the visiting Oregon Clay team, a wounded-wing catcher who hit with power. He also wanted to get a glimpse of Archbold; he didn't think they had anything this year, but you never rule out those towns with good sports tradition.

Tony gassed up the Caprice at the Archbold Sohio. "There's another reason for this stop," he said. "There's someone I want to look up, someone I just got to thinking about."

"Who?"

He was looking through the Western Fulton County telephone directory, which was about the size of a thin, why-do-they-bother February issue of Esquire. "There's so many Grimes in here," Tony said. He tried two of the numbers but got no answer.

"Most of the factories around here don't get off until three," I said. "Maybe you can call back in a half hour. Now who's this guy?"

"Well, he's a pitcher I signed, about fifteen years ago. His name is Eddie Grime. Little left-handed pitcher, but boy could he throw. I signed him about the same time as Tom Underwood, who you know played almost ten years in the big leagues, and I rated them about equal in talent. But Eddie Grime just quit after two years, and I never found out why."

The name rang a bell. I was in high school with one pitcher, Steve Fireovid, who played briefly in the majors. Another major leaguer, Bruce Berenyi, went to high school just a few miles south of Bryan. But Eddie Grime rang a bell somehow. "What year did he sign?"

"It would have been . . . 1972, I guess. I signed him in his parents' kitchen, and I bought him a plane ticket from Toledo to Roanoke, Virginia, near our rookie league team in Pulaski. I saw him off at the airport, and I believe that's the last time I saw him."

Nineteen seventy-two. I would have been ten. Still no light bulbs.

The ballpark was a flat quartet of sandlot fields on the south edge of town, over the railroad tracks from the main drag of Route 2, near the new McDonald's. Tony wandered around the fields, asking park employees if they knew a man named Eddie Grime. Two teenaged girls said no. In the press box, a stocky boy smiled and said, yeah, sure he did. "He lives maybe two hundred yards from here. You can see the house."

Tony handed a business card to the boy. "Would you do a favor for an old man? Would you see if Eddie Grime is home, and if he is, would you give him this and tell him an old friend is looking for him?"

Minutes later, up drove a dark Chevy and out came Eddie Grime, his two boys in tow. He had close-cropped dark hair, heavy stubble, oily dirt on his hands. He saw Tony and beamed. "Boy, you haven't changed a bit!"

"Why, thank you," Tony said, shaking hands and introducing me. The guy did look familiar, but I couldn't place him.

"I bet I look different. I'm a working man now."

"Where are you working, Ed?" Tony asked.

"Over to Polycraft Injection Molding. I'm a plant manager."

"That's just great."

While the boys—Jordan, seven, and Philip, two—ran in circles on the dirt infield of one of the diamonds, Tony and Eddie sat in the bleachers, reminiscing about Eddie's three consecutive no-hitters. The Phillies drafted Grime in the eighth round, and he played only two years, one at Pulaski and the next at Class A Spartanburg. At Spartanburg, with only thirty-three innings pitched, he was named the team's Fireman of the Year, and the team won the South Atlantic League title.

"But after that year," Tony said, "you never went back. And I never found out why."

"Well, I thought, you know, I had the arm problem and—"

"I didn't know you had arm problems!"

"Yeah, and I had a rough time with, oh, What's-his-name. Howie. Howie Bedell. I had a rough time with Howie."

"He was something else."

"I was striking out a batter an inning, with an ERA of about 3.00, but they never used me. Howie'd bring other lefties in off the street and put 'em in the game. They'd have me up throwin', using my arm up in the bullpen, and I'd never get in the game. I'd throw three innings and then they'd just sit me down. It got to the point where my arm was struggling: after three innings it'd just go dead, limp, sore. But no one seemed to care."

Tony told the story of Bedell's firing, which Grime hadn't heard and which seemed to disappoint him not at all. Then he shouted to his boys that they had to go eat. "You know, Jordan's starting out this year in seven-year-old Little League. He has some natural ability."

"I know," Tony said. "I've been watching him."

Giggling and filthy, the boys ran over to their father.

"What's that on your face?"

Jordan laughed. "Snot!"

Eddie said he'd come by and watch the game with us, then loaded his kids back into the car.

"Wait," I said. "Did your parents own a Holiday Rambler?"

"A what?"

"A Holiday Rambler. A travel trailer."

"Yeah. I think so."

Eureka.

My parents owned an RV dealership and sponsored an owners' group called—cleverly enough—the Holiday Ramblers, which took weekend trips to state campgrounds through Ohio, Indiana and Michigan. Most of the Ramblers were senior citizens, and because there were rarely any kids around, I hated these trips. But one autumn weekend fifteen years ago, at Harrison Lake State Park, twelve miles due north up Ohio 66 from Archbold, I had played catch with this big kid who let me keep the baseball when we were done. I still have the ball. It's scuffed and grass stained and on its horsehide it says "Phillies."

"I think we played catch once, you and me, up at Harrison Lake. You gave me a ball."

Eddie Grime smiled wanly. "Did I?"

"Yeah. It had to be you. Your hair was longer then."

"So was everybody's. Except maybe Tony's. I don't think about his hair at all. Just the hat."

"I took *The Sporting News* then," I said. "You told me you'd be playing at Spartanburg that next year and every week I looked for your name in the South Atlantic League stats."

"I was never in 'em," he said, uncomfortable. "I never had enough innings."

"Yeah. Well. Um." I felt every inch the moony-eyed twerp.

He hadn't remembered me, of course; I had hardly remembered him. But that moment was as satisfying as it was awkward. Could you have imagined a shaggy-haired lefty and a starstruck ten-year-old running into each other fifteen years later, twelve miles south, under these circumstances? I said the only thing there was to say: "Thanks for the ball, Eddie."

He grinned. "My pleasure. You know, I kept a lot of that stuff: bats, balls, anything that says 'Phillies' on it, and I'll give 'em to Jordan and Philip when they're old enough to appreciate 'em."

Throughout all this Tony seemed impatient. Instead of listening to my reconstruction of personal history, he watched Jordan and Philip playing in the backseat. As Eddie put the car in gear, Tony placed his hand on Eddie Grime's once-fearsome left arm. "During the game tonight," Tony whispered, "remind me to tell you about the wall."

13

Next Year's Model

In July my wife, Laura, came home clutching a white plastic disk with a small piece of gauze in the middle. "It's blue," she said in a thin voice, near tears. She showed me the blue " + " on the gauze.

"Yeah?" I was the one who'd thought she was pregnant. Ever one to protect herself from high hopes, she'd been skeptical. But she was so emotional, I couldn't distinguish elation from disappointment. "What's blue mean?"

Then she hugged me, and that settled that.

When I told Tony—a couple days later, riding in his Caprice to Michigan—he punched my shoulder, beaming. "Hey, you're gonna be a papa!" He chuckled. "Of course I know you'll build a wall."

I told him we lived on the third floor, but as soon as we could afford our own little piece of suburban turf, yep, I sure would.

Tony punched my shoulder again. He was positively giddy. "I know you'll do it. I know you will because you believe in it."

We stopped in Toledo for a quick lunch at Miller's Restaurant before a few innings of the Great Lakes Collegiate League game at the University of Toledo. The Toledo Turnpike Inn was closed, soon to be bulldozed and replaced by a Toys 'R' Us. Tony's excuse for his hurry today was that normally we'd have stayed the night in Toledo, but now we had to get to the game and on to Detroit before rush hour. "I'll have to find a new home in Toledo," Tony said, looking at the vacant motel and shaking his head. "That's always hard."

"What's hard? Finding a new motel in Toledo or just finding a new motel?"

"Both, I guess. The people there were good to me. They were friends. They were like family. They knew me by name. Hey, speaking of names, do you and the missus have any picked out?"

"Not really." Laura and I had decided to ward off this conversation by saying, yes, we had settled on Gomer Cletus for a boy; Gomerina Cletusa if it's a girl. But I spared Tony this.

"Well, have I got a name for you."

"What's that?"

"You tell your missus you've got a name all picked out: 'Anthony Reno.' "

"Your middle name's 'Reno'?"

"One time, a waitress saw that on a credit card or something, and she says, loud enough for everyone in the place to hear, 'You missed your calling, Mister. "Anthony Reno Lucadello." With a name like that, you ought to be playing a guitar in Las Vegas.' "

The tiny, seventy-five-year-old ex-shortstop sipped his soup and smiled. He leaned across the formica table and said, "I just know you'll build that wall."

Tony set up his lawn chair under a small tree in right field, the better to make a quick getaway. Four or five other scouts were there, seated behind home, and during the course of the game, they came one by one to say hello or to use the field's lone portajohn, a few yards away from us.

Tony exchanged pleasantries with his colleagues, but his mind was on the game. He'd found himself a prospect behind the plate, a six-two, 185-pounder named Scott George. "For his age, he has the most talent I've ever seen," Tony told me.

"Ever?"

"Ever. He has the size, he has the speed, he has that quick mind on the field. For every play so far, he's positioned himself as well as you can. I truly believe he could go right to double A. Maybe triple A."

"That's a heck of a leap," I said. "From a college league to triple A."

"Well, of course it is. But you've seen him now for three innings. You tell me. You've seen a lot of minor league games this summer. Did you see any umpires better than this kid?"

Scouting umpires was not Tony's job of course, and the Phillies had little to gain, at least directly, from the prospect Tony found that day. But though Tony may be the Phillies' most loyal employee, he has a higher calling, and he bypasses nothing that might help save the game. That night, in a suburban Detroit Knights Inn, Tony wrote a letter to Dr. Bobby Brown, recommending that Scott George be signed to a professional contract.

Bob Kowaleski, who covers Michigan, especially Detroit, for Tony, had spent the past two months looking for '89's. He thought he'd found enough of them to give Tony a three-day guided tour of Michigan's best prospects. When Tony traveled with his part-time scouts in the cities, he had them drive. "This trip could easily have taken up a week of Tony's time," Bob told me, driving us to a Connie Mack game between Roseville and G. W. Industries. "But Tony's trained me. I study the schedules and make phone calls. Rather than taking a look at kid A on Monday and kid B on Tuesday and kid C on Wednesday, why can't we see kid A for three or four innings on Monday and kid C for three or innings? And then on Tuesday we'll go see kid B, and if something else pops up, some kid we heard about on Monday and Tuesday, we won't see kid C again on Wednesday. We'll go see a couple kids we didn't know about: kid D for a few innings and kid E for three or four."

In the backseat, Tony nodded, slowly and with obvious approval. He'd insisted that I ride up front with Bob—at six-six, five inches taller than me—where we'd have enough legroom.

Though you could see a blade or two of grass if you used your imagination, the field at Mt. Clemens Clintondale High School looked like a cinder track. We sat on the cool cement of a sidewalk near the brick school while Bob gave Tony exhaustive biographies of the three players he considered worthwhile.

Behind Bob's tinted glasses remain fleeting traces of what must have been, in its day, a wondrous scowl of a game face. Bob Kowaleski is the highest paid and most ambitious of Tony's part-timers, although his salary is less than the price of any American-made car and his ambition is merely to become a full-time scout when he retires from his job as an industrial arts teacher.

Twenty-five years earlier, Tony Lucadello came to Kalamazoo to scout Joe Sparma, an Ohio State pitcher who'd go on to play eight years in the majors, mostly for the Tigers. Tony stood near the home Western Michigan dugout, away from the horde of scouts. In both ends of that day's doubleheader, the Western Michigan coach had Kowaleski, then a gangly sophomore, warming up from the second to the fifth innings, then sat him down and brought in his short man instead. Disconsolate about using all his best stuff in the pen and never having the chance to pitch in a game so heavily scouted, Kowaleski's encouragement that day came from the little, hatted man in the coat and tie who gave the young pitcher a business card.

A few months later, after a hotel room Kowaleski had signed for became the scene of debauchery and fisticuffs, Western Michigan placed him on social probation. Translation: no baseball. Bob packed his things, got in his car and drove south. First stop: Fostoria, Ohio, to beg the scout to sign him. Tony wasn't home. Bob made the rounds of a few other scouts' homes and eventually inked a pact with the Orioles.

Kowaleski's pro career fizzled a couple years later, so he finished his degree, got a teaching job and began coaching. His teams were good, and before long he was working as a bird-dog scout for Tony Lucadello. When Tony's part-time scout for Michigan retired, Kowaleski took over. Under the tutelage of the old scout, Kowaleski improved and in 1979 quit coaching to devote more time to the Phillies.

"Tony, Valisevic's not here," Bob said during infield. Valisevic, a shortstop, was the main player he wanted Tony to see.

"Good," Tony said. "That shortstop they have's a stiff."

After it was plain both teams stank and that the marginal prospects remaining were out of shape, Kowaleski stopped by the dugouts to chat with the coaches. When he had finished, he motioned to us with his head, and we snuck away.

"Sorry about that, Tony."

Tony shrugged. "Talent is where you find it."

"Well, maybe I found it," Kowaleski said. "I found out what team Valisevic's playing for. And that team has another good kid."

"Good. When will we see them play?"

"Now. I found out they're playing right now, just up the road."

"Good for you."

We drove east toward Lake St. Clair, where there was

another Connie Mack game, this one between Mt. Clemens and St. Clair Shores. Valisevic and the other prospect, a center fielder, played for Mt. Clemens. But while the two had been impressive during their high school seasons, they had jobs and other distractions in the summer, and baseball was clearly a lark—as it was for the kids on both teams. They joked in the field, jogged after grounders, tried to make easy plays look flashy, approached each at-bat as a turn in a backyard home-run–derby contest, each time on base as an occasion for pointless, reckless steals.

Tony, ever the iconoclast, rarely sits with any scouts for a whole game, even his own employees. Kowaleski, sheepish that players he'd built up now seemed anything but prospects, wandered up and down the third-base line, hoping to glimpse the talent that had so excited him in the spring. Tony, meanwhile, sat in the bleachers, his mind made up about these lackadaisical Fancy Dans, his eyes drifting a few hundred yards away toward the Koufax League game on the adjoining field, where fourteen- and fifteen-year-olds ran out grounders and slid feet-first and chanted at the hitters and at least had a chance of being the kind of young men Tony hoped would save the game of baseball.

While Tony's acolytes are well trained, they aren't clones of the master. None, for instance, wears a necktie to the ballpark. Before games, they look for loose change, but none of them gives his yearly take each September fifteenth to the first church he sees. They all eschew the stopwatches and radar guns, but none with the passion of their mentor; some, in fact, wonder aloud what would happen if they put the receipts for those gizmos on their expense account. And none, least of all Bob Kowaleski, follow Tony's monastic rigidity of diet. When Tony and I traveled alone, I always felt bad ordering things other than salads and fruit. When I did, Tony'd say,

"Sure looks good," and then wave me off when I offered him some. But Bob Kowaleski scouts restaurants with the same zeal he scouts shortstops, and he and I ate big helpings of rich food. Tony seemed to take vicarious joy in his proximity to delicacies he'd never order for himself.

The next day at dinner, which we ate at four in deference to Tony, I asked Kowaleski if he really thought the skills of players today had eroded or whether at least some of that perception was the result of the Everything Was Better in the Good Old Days fallacy.

"No way," he said between bites of mako shark. "They've absolutely gotten worse. The kids out there are better athletes but worse players. You know, I talk to a lot of other scouts, younger scouts, and a lot of 'em don't like Tony. You know, they think he's over the hill." He laughed. "Of course, a lot of these same guys have been burned by him on a player and they're bitter. Anyway, they might say talent levels stay about the same, but look at the facts. When I first started scouting, just twenty years ago, kids filled their summer with baseball, then maybe golf or tennis, then going to the beach. Now you have summer football and basketball camps. Around here, summer basketball leagues play sixty-game schedules. In football and basketball, kids are doing more work than they were twenty years ago. In baseball, less. In football and basketball, there's never been more talent. In baseball, there's never been less."

Tony nodded in agreement. "You're right, Bob. That's why the wall's our only hope." He pushed us to order dessert. We hadn't intended to, but the cheesecake on the dessert cart called to us in a thick and sultry voice.

"Tony's always doing things that will improve this game of baseball," Bob said, "and that's shaped my attitude. Now I look for ways of helping coaches, passing out booklets, suggesting this, suggesting that. It seems like charity, maybe, but it pays off. Like for Tony, it pays off directly when he builds a relationship that helps him find a ball player. But he touches so many people in this game. Tony's a legend in little towns all over the state of Michigan, places I'd go where I'd never heard of the *town*, yet everyone at the ballpark had heard of Tony."

Michigan's always been a good territory, Tony and Bob said, considering the havoc the weather there wreaks on the baseball season. But now most of the good players come from the Detroit suburbs and medium-sized towns like Jackson and St. Joseph in the southern third of the state. "North of Midland, it's just resort towns and woods. I went to an all-star game upstate once, and the players were wearing blue jeans! It's a wasteland. I can't remember the last player to go to the bigs from the Upper Peninsula, if there's ever been one."

Tony smiled, watching us finish our cheesecake. "The last one was a pitcher, name of John Goetz, from Goetzville, Michigan."

"Never heard of him," Bob said.

"Oh. Well, I signed him."

"Was he any good?" I asked.

"He made it to the major leagues," Tony said, offended. "How good is that?"

A few weeks later, I looked up John Goetz in my *Baseball Encyclopedia*. He was on page 1833. He pitched six innings for the Cubs over four games in 1960. In those six innings, he gave up 10 hits and his ERA was 12.79. But he did come from the Upper Peninsula and he did pitch in the big leagues.

On the day of the major league all-star game—in which the last-place Phillies were represented by the minimum one player—Tony was out looking for future all-stars. In the remote Detroit suburb of Milford, on a parched field half a mile from the nearest restroom, Westland was playing Huron Valley. Bob Kowaleski projected Huron's star, Jeff Irish, as the top prep catcher in the state. Last year Irish led the Milford Mickey Mantle team to the national championship. His signability was poor, though, because he was a 3.9 student.

As usual, there were more people in the dugouts than the stands. Tony sat in the aluminum bleachers, clipping his fingernails. A casual observer might have thought him a dapper old man out to kill a July evening. If Tony had charts and rosters on clipboards and a stopwatch in his hand, every parent there would know he was a scout, and most of them would eventually come around to ask his opinion of their sons. Boredom was Tony's poker face; often he appeared to doze through innings, only to reveal in the car, as we drove away from the ballpark, that he'd seen something about a player no one else had.

Bob Kowaleski and I left Tony in the bleachers and wandered around behind the backstop. Bob sought out Irish's dad and—a well-trained Lucadello understudy—chatted him up. I wouldn't even give odds on Jeff signing out of high school. He's going to college, either at Michigan or—bless him— Miami. My Miami. I knew Tony preferred his prospects avoid Michigan. The Evil Empire has a tendency to swallow players up, signing more than can possibly see action. I spent most of the game selling Mr. Irish on my alma mater. I stopped just short of singing the fight song.

Jeff Irish impressed the hell out of me. Behind the plate he had quick hands and a quick release. He was a leader on the field, yelling instructions to the infielders and playing with enthusiasm. His arm seemed strong and sure; runners thought so, too, and didn't test him. At the plate, he was patient and had the cocked bat and level swing reminiscent of such Charlie Lau disciples as George Brett and Pete Rose. Dead center field was a 420-foot poke into a stand of jackpines, but Irish hit a climbing line drive that hit the outfield fence on three bounces, a stand-up triple.

In the fourth inning, Tony began taking a meandering

route back to the parking lot. I figured he'd made his mind up and wanted to go before any of the parents picked up on his enthusiasm for Irish. As we drove away, Tony had me give my scouting report first, and I did, dissecting what impressed me about Irish's hands and arm and swing. When I finished, Bob Kowaleski laughed and said I'd been around Tony too long. Maybe I might want to give up writing and become another of Tony's bird-dogs. I felt proud and manly.

Tony withheld judgment. Bob Kowaleski amplified my praise of Irish's hands and arm and swing. Finally, Tony could take it no longer and interrupted us.

"Everything you two said is right," he said. "But you're leaving out the most important thing."

Bob and I looked at each other, two hulking students about to shrink in their seats and weather their tiny professor's upbraiding. I turned around to look at him. "The, um, most important thing?"

"Yes! Eighty-seven percent of baseball is played below the waist! Right? Well, hands and arm and swing, those things are important, yes, but they're above the waist. That kid don't position his feet right on his throw to second, and at a higher level, base runners'll eat him for breakfast. He don't have as smooth a swing as you think, either, not if you watch his feet. He lunges into the pitch, with way too long a stride. The pitcher he faced today I could hit. A better pitcher'll jam him with the inside stuff. And while he does have a good, live body, the kid's bottom heavy. Most catchers are, but not at his age, and I worry about that."

Bob feebly defended the kid, and Tony agreed that Irish's skills were fairly advanced for a seventeen-year-old and that he was indeed a prospect, though not a blue-chip one. Tony thought it best that Irish go to college, where perhaps he'd develop. "There *was* a player there that you better keep your eyes on, Bob."

"The center fielder?" he guessed.

"Well, he's all right. But no."

"That first baseman on the other team?" I guessed. The kid had hit a ball into the jackpines.

"Him?" Tony said, horrified. "No."

We made a couple more guesses before settling on the Huron Valley shortstop.

"I *like* him," Tony said. "He's just a sophomore. He's a '91, for heavens sake, playing with kids two years older. And playing shortstop! Now, he's less advanced, but I project that he'll be the best kid of anyone out there."

By the time we got back to the motel, Bob and I agreed about the shortstop's awe-inspiring tools, with such enthusiasm that Tony had to calm us down and reiterate that the kid was raw and time will tell.

We turned on the TV and watched the first few innings of the All-Star Game together. By nine Tony looked sleepy, and so Bob left and I went to my room. Back in my garish purple and scarlet quarters, I sipped a warm beer and—in my underwear, atop the purple bedspread—watched the singularly dull game. As part of its television contract, Major League Baseball gets a few free commercials during every broadcast—don't drink at the ballpark and drive home; baseball fever, catch it; palaver like that. Late in the game came a commercial I'd never seen before. It was a thirty-second spot for *A Coaching Clinic*, Tony's videotape. Startled, I spilled beer on the bed, but stayed glued to the screen, hoping for a glimpse of Tony Lucadello on national TV. Though the spot featured excerpts from the video, Tony apparently wound up on the cutting-room floor. Still, there it was, for millions to see, an actual commercial touting the benefits of throwing a baseball off a wall.

When the spot finished, I pulled on a pair of pants and went next door to see how excited Tony was by this sudden, if brief, national exposure. I expected Tony to be giddy. He wasn't. His room was dark. He was asleep.

* * *

About a hundred college baseball players, in motley uniforms sporting the logos of car dealers, plumbing supply shops and banks, played catch in the dewy grass and white morning sunshine of Tiger Stadium, warming up for the Adray League All-Star Game Tournament. The Great Lakes Collegiate League has no teams in Michigan, the Great Lakes State, because of the might of the Adray League, which has teams in all the big southeastern Michigan cities. Like any all-star game of a decent league, this tournament drew more scouts than players. The league wanted its players to be seen, of course, so it had finagled the use of Tiger Stadium on an off day and seated spectators in the upper deck, leaving the good, behind-the-plate seats to the clicking stopwatches and clubby buzz of the scouts.

In years past, Tony had found scores of good players in this league, but what he'd seen of the Adray regular-season games had left him cold. The all-star game proved no better. The only player Tony saw that he liked was a '90 that he already knew about: an outfielder from Indiana University. Though we stayed for the first two games and a couple of innings of the third, Tony saw no one worth a report to the home office.

Bob Kowaleski was down. For weeks, he'd built up this trip to Tony, and now nothing was going right. Two of the Adray League players he had hoped to show Tony missed the game due to injuries. Of the others Bob liked, none played worth a damn. "There's two more players we're going to see today," he said. "Maybe our luck'll change when we get out of here."

Tony was disappointed he'd gone to bed before the commercial aired and kept asking me to describe it to him, which I did at least six times. "I gave up on that game after that one pitch," he said, referring to Bob Knepper's third-inning wild pitch. "You see what I mean about our game? Even in the All-Star Game you see second-division major league ball players."

"Oh, now, c'mon, Tony." I couldn't let this drop. "I mean, even Christy Mathewson uncorked a wild pitch now and then."

He looked at me, the corners of his mouth drawn tight, ready to argue, but then he laughed and sat back in his seat. "No matter what I say, it's guys like you who're going to save our game, because you'll put up with it. Maybe that's okay, I don't know. But it's just beyond my taste."

All morning, other scouts stopped Tony to tell him they'd seen the commercial. Tony would look a little embarrassed and say, "Well, I hope it helps. I hope it gets the kids to practice again." And he and the other scouts would nod, and then they'd look out at the field, and then they'd just shake their heads.

Not long before we were to leave, the Michigan State University coach came by to say hello. They chatted for a while about former Spartan Kirk Gibson, on his way that summer to an MVP season with the Los Angeles Dodgers, and about current MSU slugger Dan Masteller, playing in the Great Lakes League and high on Tony's list. The coach, shy and soft-spoken, had approached Tony as a fan would a big-leaguer. Before I knew it, he had coaxed Tony into giving an impromptu clinic on all his pet ideas. The wall. The plastic golf balls. The videotape. Choke up on the bat. Eighty-seven percent of baseball is played below the waist. The biggest mistake most pitchers make is keeping their front leg so stiff they can't bend their back or their trail leg properly. "I have a new theory, too," Tony said. "Goggles."

"Goggles?" said the coach, beaming and trying to take in the flood of information.

"I've never signed a position ballplayer who wore glasses or even contacts, because they get fooled on that low inside pitch. They can't see it right. But I've been watching this Chris

Sabo kid this year, and in the All-Star Game last night." Tony had passed on Sabo when he'd played for the University of Michigan, largely because he figured the eyeglasses would catch up to the young third baseman. Now, with a new pair of prescription goggles, Sabo was on his way to a Rookie of the Year season with my beloved Cincinnati Reds. "Goggles wrap all the way down to your cheek, see. Players can focus on that low pitch. You watch and see if this isn't the coming thing. It ought to be the coming thing, at least if we can get the word out." He looked at the coach. "You'll help me get the word out, won't you?"

"You bet I will," he said. "You know, Tony, I learn more talking to you for ten minutes than I could learn in a month of seminars. You've forgotten more baseball than we'll ever know."

As an unrelenting stream of traffic growled up I-75 nearby, Bob and Tony and I looked for shelter on a hot wind-whipped field in Auburn Hills. Bob was excited because here, in our fourth game of the day, was a six-three right-handed pitcher he was sure was a prospect.

Alas, no.

I stayed with Tony atop a steep stand of third-base bleachers while Bob walked to the left-field line to watch the kid warm up. Tony tapped me on the shoulder. "Now will you look at that," he said, disgusted. "See how he strides so far out that he can't go over the top with his left knee? He strides so far that he can't bend that left knee." He shook his head. "Bad mechanics."

The pitcher struck out the side in the first inning. That sounds great, but the batters swung at pitches outside the strike zone, and in the same inning, he gave up a single, a balk, a warning-track sacrifice fly, a double, and a home run to straightaway center. After another sorry inning, Tony signaled to Bob. "I've seen him better," Bob apologized.

Tony waved him off. "The kid has bad mechanics."

Bob had to accept that, but he still tried to defend his prospect. "I talked to the coach," he said. "The kid just got back today from a week at football camp. His arm's tired, Tony. He's a quarterback. They had him throwing two hundred passes a day up there."

Tony shrugged. "The heck with him. Let him play football."

We stopped for dinner. Bob hit the pay phone, anxious to call the coach of the day's last prospect, Brent Hayward, an outfielder for the Chief Pontiac American Legion team. "Sometimes he pitches the kid. I want to make sure he's playing outfield tonight. Otherwise, we'll just chalk up today as one of those days."

"That's okay, Bob," Tony said. "I've had years filled with one of those days."

But the coach told Bob that Hayward would indeed start in center field, so after Tony finished his salad and Bob and I polished off our pasta, we hit the road for our fifth ball game of the day.

When we arrived, Brent Hayward was loosening up in the bullpen. The last-minute change made Bob Kowaleski mad enough to barbecue—perhaps even fricassee—the Chief Pontiac coach. Tony tried to placate his protégé. "We'll see just a couple innings," Tony said. "I can see him bat once, maybe twice, and then we'll go."

The batteries on my tape recorder had died and I was out of film. Eager to escape the day's malaise, Bob volunteered to take me for a supply run. "Tony can stay here. I've seen Hayward enough to know I like him, and with him playing out of position and all . . ."

The nearest 7-Eleven wasn't as near as you'd think, given how deep in suburbia we were. A couple of supermarkets were closed, and we got lost twice.

When we got back, almost an hour later, Tony was leaning on the backstop, face resolute, a scrap of paper palmed in his left hand. When we asked how the game was going, he shushed us and scribbled more notes on the paper. He moved around the perimeter of the field, hitting all eight of his favored scouting positions with the efficiency and grace of a savvy actor hitting his marks. There were no other scouts present, but Tony still feared he'd attract attention, so he said almost nothing to us. I asked how Hayward was doing, but it took Tony an inning to answer. "He has a no-hitter going. He's striking out every other hitter, and the pitches are in the strike zone."

Brent Hayward had the lean, limber body Tony looked for, and he bent that front knee as much and as expertly as many a big-league hurler.

"He comes up third in the next inning," Tony said, almost salivating. "After he bats, we go. I don't want everyone to be onto me."

The first batter walked. The second singled. Bob Kowaleski whispered to me that it'd be just his luck that Hayward would get an intentional walk, but he didn't. He was a patient hitter with a quick and compact swing, with that trace of controllable uppercut common to natural power hitters.

"What'd he do the first time up," I asked Tony.

He showed me the scrap of paper on which he'd diagrammed the flat trajectory the ball had taken on its way out of the park.

The opposing pitcher seemed to want to pitch around Hayward, but Hayward kept fouling off bad pitches. Finally, in an at-bat that must have lasted ten minutes, he pulled an inside fastball that leapt off the ping of his aluminum bat and left the park, screaming, toward a clutch of parked cars whose owners had assumed them safe. The ball ripped through a windshield and at the dull explosion of shattered safety glass, the crowd's cheers changed into a uniform "Aww" of sympathy for the car's owner.

Before the cheers dimmed, we were on our way. Tony had seen all he needed to see. Brent Hayward was the top kid in his territory.

14

The Fourth-Biggest Thrill

In late August, even the casual fan's attention turns to baseball, as major league pennant races heat up and optimistic teams in a dozen cities print playoff tickets. But for scouts, August is a month of tournaments and lulls. Amateur baseball seasons end early in the month and settle their playoffs a week or two later. After that, scouts don't see many players until mid-September, when the colleges begin playing fall baseball.

Some area scouts also cover the minor and major league teams in their territories, but even the minor leagues wind up their seasons in August. Earlier in his career, Tony, too, had been given such scouting assignments, and he'd been forced to make a few dozen visits each year to see the Reds and Tigers, the Toledo Mudhens and the Louisville Redbirds, and the Indians of both Cleveland and Indianapolis. For most scouts, these trips are perks, a chance to sit right behind the plate at big league games, maybe even recommend a trade that might bring the team a pennant. But Tony hated them. To him, such scouting was unproductive drudgery. He had ball players to see who weren't signed yet. Scouting professional teams just interfered with the way he wanted to do his job.

Eventually the Phillies relieved Tony of this chore, and it had been years since he'd been to Ned Skeldon Stadium, the converted harness-racing track where the Toledo Mudhens play. But today was an obligation Tony couldn't dodge. We arrived an hour before batting practice, the only people in the ballpark other than concessionaires, groundskeepers and a few overeager Mudhens and Columbus Clippers.

The Ohio Baseball Hall of Fame sits in an aluminum barn tucked underneath the stadium. To kill some time, we strolled through the museum's exhibits, all housed in a room about the size of a junior high cafeteria.

"Well, will you look at this here?" Tony pointed to the forty-three plaques just inside the hall. "There's Jesse Haines. He's in this hall of fame, too. Good for him. I sure am glad we got to pay our respects to him, aren't you?"

He stood before the plaques in a newish navy suit and the requisite center-dent straw hat, hands in his pockets, shaking his head and scanning the names: Bob Feller. Lefty Grove. Waite Hoyt. Ted Kluzewski. Nap Lajoie. Kenesaw Landis. Satchel Paige. Frank Robinson. Red Ruffing. Joe and Luke Sewell. Tris Speaker. Casey Stengel. Early Wynn. Cy Young. Even Nick "Tomato Face" Cullop.

"Amazing," he whispered. "All these accomplishments. Amazing."

Most of those enshrined were either born in Ohio or played most of their careers for the Reds or Indians, but the criteria also allows for the admittance of those who played for or managed Ohio minor league teams and of those who "have substantial ties to the Buckeye State." In some cases, this seems to have been interpreted to allow the induction of those who've made a connecting flight in Cleveland or been weighed by a scale made in Toledo.

It's actually a good hall, at least for the hard-core fan, with special sections for mementos of the Indians and Reds, including seats from Cincinnati's late, lamented Crosley Field. Special sections are devoted to such legitimate favorite sons as Frank Robinson, Cy Young and Bill Wambsganss, who is represented by the very ball with which he made the only unassisted triple play in World Series history. A random collection of old uniforms and sweat-grimed caps are included just for fun apparently, since only a few had any Ohio ties whatsoever.

"Mike will be here someday," Tony whispered. "He'll have his whole wall. He's hit more home runs than anyone ever born in this state."

We walked back up to the empty grandstand. When I was a kid, the local radio station in Bryan, Ohio, would often intersperse its cash grain prices and recipe call-in shows with little giveaways, and I'd been to this stadium several times on tickets won by identifying county seats or local golf heroes. But that was one stadium renovation ago; Tony sat with me and pointed out where the old barns used to be and what the place had looked like when part of the horse-racing oval was converted to a warning track.

"This is a beautiful place now," he said. "I haven't been here since they added that skybox thing and all those extra seats. This used to be one of the real odd ballparks, at least for professional ball."

"What was the strangest park you ever saw?"

He thought a minute. "I guess in Elmo, Indiana." Several Augusts ago, Tony was sent to Elmo, a burg that didn't appear on his Esso road map, to scout an infielder recommended to the Phillies office by an ex–minor leaguer. "I had a heck of a time finding Elmo, Indiana. I had a hunch about where it was. When I thought I was close, I pulled into this small store connected to a home, and I went in and asked the man behind the counter. I was close, he said, so I asked him is there a baseball game going on today and he said, oh yes, and I asked him if they had this certain player, and he said, oh yes. It's kind of confusing though, he said, on account of to get there you have to drive through this thick-wooded area, but his son, about twelve years old, wanted to go to the game, and the boy could show me how to get there."

Without the boy, Tony said, he'd have never found the park. The road—a path, really—wound through the woods for about half a mile and stopped in the small clearing that was the ballpark. Across the clearing, boards were nailed to the tree trunks at the edge of the thick woods to form a ramshackle outfield fence. "The strange thing about this field was they had high-tension wires running right through left field to center."

The infielder Tony'd come to see had played in his final baseball game of the season the previous Sunday; this game was an all-star softball game. But Tony'd gone to a lot of trouble to get there, so he stayed, trying to assess the kid's basic tools.

"The oddest thing about the game," Tony said, "was the umpire, a tall, skinny guy, just straight as an arrow, and he had those red shin guards on, and the long belly protector and the face mask and all that bit. He was the only one calling the balls and the strikes and the men on bases. He stood there straight up, without bending over, making all his calls with hand signals. He never spoke to nobody."

In the proverbial bottom of the ninth, with the proverbial two outs, the score proverbially tied 2–2, the proverbial star of the game stepped to the plate and whacked hell out the proverbial first pitch, hitting the proverbial long, rising fly ball.

"That fat ball left his bat just like a golf ball," Tony said. "But it struck those high-tension wires, and they cut the ball in half. Half stayed in the playing field and the other half went sailing into the woods."

The left fielder threw half the ball to second, but the batter beat the tag. The umpire just stood behind the plate, ramrod stiff, and pointed the runner to third. The kid jogged to third.

Then the ump pointed at the plate, and the kid shrugged his shoulders and ran home.

The crowd, forty people or so, confused and a little intimidated by the skinny cipher behind the plate, sat still, and the ump turned around and began paging through a rule book. I'm the umpire-in-chief of this game, he says, and I have a rule here that states if that ball hits those high-tension wires and goes over the fence it's a home run. But if it drops in the playing field, he has to run for what he can get. You folks have just witnessed an act of God. The ump pocketed the rule book. Acts of God, he says, are entirely different from the rules of baseball. But I'm in charge here so it's my job to interpret acts of God. I'm giving Elmo half a run, and they win, two and a half to two.

"Well," Tony said, watching the Mudhens warm up. "Ask me the question."

I knew what he meant, but I toyed with him. "So was that the right call?"

"No. There's no such thing as half a run. I don't know any reason acts of God can't work together with the rules of baseball, for heaven's sake." He folded his arms and studied the lower half of the player in the batting cage. "That's not the question."

I humored him. "Okay. Is that a true story, Tony?"

He grinned and looked at me. "Do you think it's humanly possible," he said, voice hushed, index finger punching the air, "for me to tell a story like that if I hadn't seen it with my own eyes?"

"Maybe."

"*Maybe?*" he scoffed. "Yes or no. You've been with me for a year now. Yes or no."

I realized then that his question was not rhetorical, and I realized, too, what the answer was. Tony embodies the rootsy, midwestern, baggy-pants charm that attracted me to baseball in the first place. From age nine to thirteen, I read *nothing* but sports books, mostly baseball books, canned as-told-to's, serious histories, life-is-a-ballpark novels. The first subscription in my name was *The Sporting News*, a birthday present from my Grandpa Bob. I whined until my parents finally took me to the Hall of Fame in Cooperstown, where I lingered over every bust, trying to commit to memory the features of Wahoo Sam Crawford or Cool Papa Bell. That desire for knowledge spilled over eventually into areas other than baseball, but it was baseball that gave dimension to the notion that there was a vast cultural history out there, compiled by real people—breathing, praying, farting, sleepy, hungry, happy, curmudgeonly, gracious three-dimensional people, who climbed trees and argued with their sisters and practiced their pianos (or their relay throws from the outfield) and yearned to leave something of themselves in this world.

The sport's empirical data, averages and totals and new statistics dreamt up every minute, gave me the illusion that the world was knowable, the truth definite. Yet eventually the fallibility of the numbers allowed the frightening suspicion that the world may be unfathomable, the truth malleable.

Tony Lucadello has spent his life mastering one small thing, the appraisal of young baseball players. He's as gifted and as devoted as anyone in his profession could be. Yet he's still wrong about a few players every year. Even when he's right, life and circumstances often intervene and he'll have nothing to show for it. He was once a young man idolizing men who got paid to play a game. Cobb. Young. Ruth. Mathewson. Johnson. He dreamt of joining them, and as it was for most of us, it was only a dream. But he found his calling and not only helped add at least one more name to the pantheon—Schmidt—but also, in fact, became a legend of the game as venerable as any of those people. The little old man in the coat and the tie and the center-dent hat. The old scout. Those trained eyes, honed on half-buried nickels and nascent shortstops, do most definitely see things others do not. All beginning novelists learn there are things in life more truthful than the facts. Whether Tony's stories are factual is not the question. The question is this: did he see what he's told you with his own eyes? Is it a tall tale or is it something he's seen with his own eyes: the truth?

"Nah," I said. "It's not humanly possible to have made that story up."

He nodded, mulling over my answer as if it was the first time he'd heard it. "Well, you gotta admit, anyway, that every story I tell is a story you've never heard before, unless you heard it from someone who heard it from me. You see, things that are mystifying and kinda strange to believe and all that bit, they had to happen, you had to see it, or you couldn't tell it. If it would have happened to somebody else, they would have told it. But it didn't happen to them, so they never told it. These things happen to me, so I'm the one who tells the stories."

By that time, batting practice was well underway, and a group of officials in tomato-red sportcoats had finally found Tony Lucadello. C'mon, they said. It's time to go upstairs now. It's time to induct you into the Ohio Baseball Hall of Fame.

Tony's nominating letters had come from Dr. Bobby Brown and the Orioles general manager, Roland Hemond, among others. All cited Tony's scouting achievements, which, as far as anyone knows, are unmatched, but stressed Tony's character as an even more important reason for induction. Brown wrote that Tony "has spent countless hours with the children and young adults of Ohio teaching them the fundamentals of baseball [and] has demonstrated repeatedly the necessity of maintaining integrity, good character, fair play and understanding of your fellow man." Hemond called Tony "one of the great gentlemen of Baseball." The University of

Toledo coach simply wrote that "when baseball is remembered in Ohio, somewhere Tony had something to do with it."

The hall had never inducted a scout before, had never considered the possibility. When Tony's disciple Bruce Edwards began to push for Tony's admittance, the board of selectors wasn't encouraging. They didn't know what the criteria for scouts should be. They worried that scouts, hardly famous people, would water down the concentration of fame in their hall. Then the letters came in. After a few calls, board members realized that if other scouts had to match Tony's achievements to be admitted, the hall wouldn't be admitting another scout anytime soon.

Actually, Tony probably has a better chance of being inducted into the real Hall of Fame than anyone else honored that day in Toledo. The most notable were two ex–Cleveland Indians, slugger Hal Trosky, their first baseman during the thirties, and second baseman Bobby Avila, who won the American League batting crown in 1954, the year the Tribe won a record 111 games, its last pennant season.

A reception was held for the inductees up in the stadium's skybox—The Diamond Club—with an open bar and free food. The place was packed, and it was the ex-players, no matter how obscure, who received the most attention. Even a Toledo sportscaster attracted more handshakes and backslaps than Tony Lucadello. Tony, Bruce Edwards, his wife and I sat at a table to one side. Unnoticed, Tony drank apple juice, his hat on the table.

"I hope we can get this over with," he said. "All this fuss. I'm honored, of course, but I'm a behind-the-scenes man. All this attention, you can have." He was clearly a happy scout, though, and we sipped our drinks and looked down on the field, where Cooperstown and Toledo Hall of Famer Bob Feller, seventy, put on a show, throwing slow, deceptive curves to baffled teens plucked from the crowd.

Tony's wife, Virginia, his daughter, Toni, and granddaughter, Laney, arrived well before game time, joining us at the table with a friend of Toni's, a woman who worked for the Fostoria newspaper. She took Tony to a quiet corner of the Diamond Club for a brief, by-the-numbers interview ("Who's the best player you ever signed?" "What do you look for in a ball player?").

"Isn't this exciting?" Virginia said. "Tony's awful excited, too, but he doesn't want to let on. It's nice for someone like him, someone who's not a Mike Schmidt or a Bob Feller, getting this kind of recognition."

Tony finished his interview and returned to the table. The men in the tomato-red sport jackets were rounding up the inductees and heading them down to the field when one handed Tony a telegram. "Congratulations on your being inducted into the Ohio Hall of Fame. May your next stop be Cooperstown. Best Wishes, Bill Giles, Lee Thomas, Jim Baumer and Jack Pastore."

Tony read the telegram from his bosses, once silently, once aloud. He swallowed hard, donned his hat, handed the telegram to his wife and headed down the stairs, toward the microphone at home plate.

Sitting in the stands behind the plate were two of Tony's closest friends in scouting, Whitey Hafner and Carl Loewenstine, who'd come to work the game and been surprised to see their friend on the program. Tony had found out about the honor a few weeks before but hadn't told any more people than he had to. Though Whitey and Carl razzed him a bit as the inductees filed past—"They ought to bronze one of those hats, Tony"—they were awed and giddy to see one from their obscure fraternity so honored, especially the one who ought to be so honored.

The crowd of a few thousand seemed underwhelmed by the inductees but applauded politely at the appropriate cues, like Bobby Avila's comment, "Even when I went 3 for 3, or 4 for 4, I believe today is 5 for 5."

The seven new members of the hall stood in a tight semicircle in front of the pitching mound, each flanked by one of the men in red. One by one, the sportcoats stepped to the mike and ticked off the achievements of an inductee, and one by one, the inductees received a big brass plaque and stepped to the mike for an acceptance speech. As he waited his turn, Tony, by far the smallest man on the field, shifted his weight and kept taking off his glasses and wiping his eyes with a handkerchief. He wore the striped blue tie I'd given him last Christmas and a smart blue suit far more tailored than his everyday jackets. He applauded the other inductees, but his eyes roamed the ballpark, as if he were cataloging the nearest exits, scouting the fastest route to his car.

Five men had been inducted by the time the tomato-red sportcoat with Tony finally got his turn. "Ladies and gentlemen, I can't tell you what a pleasure and an honor it is for me to induct the first major league scout in the Ohio Baseball Hall of Fame." He was a barrel-chested man, a hearty, back-slapper type with hair the color of his sportcoat. He yelled his speech, but included many pregnant pauses, waiting for the echo like a man who's seen *Pride of the Yankees* a dozen times too many. He lived in Philadelphia and was inflated by the chance to honor the man who signed Mike Schmidt. The effusive quotes from coaches and officials in the Phillies organization seemed a bit hypocritical, given how little faith they'd shown in Tony's judgment recently. The sportcoat ended the litany with a quote from Mike Schmidt, "That gentleman is the reason I'm wearing a Phillie uniform today."

"Ladies and gentlemen," the sportcoat concluded, "I present to you a legend in the City of Philadelphia. A gentleman and a great man: Mister Tony Lucadello."

Tony stepped forward. The sportcoat handed Tony a huge plaque, almost as wide and long as Tony's upper torso. Here was his chance, in front of thousands of baseball fans, to preach chapter and verse from the baseball gospel according to Lucadello. He stood still, waiting for the applause to wane, but the fans, buoyed by the rabble-rousing introduction and charmed by the sight of the dapper little guy in the hat, kept cheering. The microphone was a little too high for him, and he stepped closer. We waited for Tony to say what baseball had meant to him, to spin one good Lucadello yarn, perhaps the one about Philip Wrigley saying, "Young man, you were born to be a scout." The applause faded and Tony waved his acknowledgment. He raised his head to the mike. "Thank you." His voice cracked, and he added, softly, "Everyone."

Clutching his plaque, he turned and rejoined the other happy plaque-clutching, white-haired men behind him.

The officials ushered their wards back to the hall for a group picture. A TV crew from Toledo's CBS affiliate intercepted Tony. By then, the old scout had regained his composure. Away from the roar of the crowd, he gave a vintage Tony interview. "Eighty-seven percent of baseball is played below the waist," he said, off and rolling. "And I scout down there to look for body control. If a player has body control, if he knows how to place his feet, then I know I got something. But it starts there. The upper part of the body will follow because it's the lower part that guides the upper part."

The camera crew, rapt, let Tony run through a handful of his pet ideas. He was the only Hall of Famer whose footage made the eleven-o'clock news.

The photo was staged in front of the wall plaques in the Ohio Hall of Fame. Tony stood in the back, far right, beaming, but glad to be just a little bit out of the way now.

* * *

Back up in the Diamond Club, Tony spent the first few innings of the game signing autographs and answering questions. Now that he'd been out there on the field, everyone knew who he was, and even little kids were coming up and asking who was the best player he'd ever scouted. "Mike. No question," he said, again and again. "Mike and Ernie Banks might have been about equal, but I don't count Ernie Banks. Ernie Banks was already playing pro ball in the Negro Leagues. He claims that I signed him, but all I really did was recommend that the Cubs buy his contract."

The Diamond Club was packed, and Tony's wife and family eventually tired of the attention and left. Tony's hand ached and his face was tired from smiling for photos, but he didn't want to offend anyone, so he sat at his table until the game was half over, obliging any request.

"Whattaya think they'd think," he whispered to me in the sixth, "if we snuck out?"

I shrugged. "One of the other inductees already left."

Tony brightened. "Really! Oh, well, c'mon then. Let's get out of here." He scooped up the box of memorabilia the hall's president had given him, handed the plaque to me to carry, and we headed out the back door. He wanted to go home, but the pull of the game proved too much. He couldn't remember the last ball game he'd been to that he didn't scout. He spotted a couple of empty box seats near Whitey and Carl. While they congratulated him and fondled the plaque, Tony trained his eyes on the game. After an inning we left.

"I liked that third baseman for Columbus," he said on our way to the car.

"He didn't have a good game," I said. "Two errors and every time I saw him at bat he whiffed."

"Well, there you go, being a performance scout. Haven't I taught you how to project? How old did you say he was?"

"Twenty."

"You see. He's just a little over his head in triple A. If the

Yankees don't rush him too much, he'll be a good one. What'd you say his name was?"

Tony had no idea who the third baseman was, but I did: Hensley "Bam Bam" Muelens. Though he'd done nothing that day to distinguish himself, and looked like hell to me, he was the highest-rated minor league prospect in all of baseball, according to *Baseball America*.

The old scout tossed me the keys. "Good catch. You drive, okay? I'm tired. All that attention. It's nice, but . . ." He thought that over. "Well, it is nice."

I pointed the Caprice south toward Fostoria, where Tony would spend a rare summer night in his own bed. "You were pretty choked up out there," I said.

"Well. Yeah."

"So was I."

"It was quite an honor, you know, for someone like me, someone who's not known."

"Would you say this was your biggest thrill?"

He set his straw hat gently on the seat between us. "To be honest, I'd've rather signed a player."

I laughed. "Signed just any player?"

"Yes, to be honest about it. That's a bigger thrill than this."

"Has anything been a bigger thrill?"

He thought this over. "When Mike invited me to take part in the celebration for his five hundredth home run, that was a big, big, thing. No scout in the history of baseball's been honored like that."

I missed a turn, but Tony directed me back on the right road.

"My biggest thrill of all happened to me forty-nine times," he said, "when a player I signed gets that first game up in the big leagues."

We drove in silence for several miles, and I thought he

must be asleep. On the edge of Fostoria, he reached over, put on his hat and tapped me on the knee. "The only thing that could top that," he whispered, "would be if people really got the message about that wall."

15

Milestone

The rain came down medium fast, in fat, relentless drops, and the ball players in Old Orchard Beach, Maine, left their apartments doubting the game would be played. This would be the last home stand of the last year for a AAA club in Old Orchard Beach. Given the attendance figures, this was fine with everyone. It was certainly fine with the players, who called the place Mosquito University. Scott Service got a ride from his girl friend to the ballpark, imaginatively christened The Ballpark. He kissed her good-bye. As she was driving away, a group of players coming from the locker room told him the game had been called. "You better catch your ride home," they said.

Scott ran after her and she stopped. He was about to get in when one of the Maine Phillies' coaches called to him. Skipper wants to see you, Scott. His girl friend waited in the car, engine idling, while he jogged into the clubhouse for a few words with manager George Culver.

It's probably about my start tomorrow, Scott thought, how the rainout will juggle the rotation. Or maybe it's about that sore arm I had a few weeks ago. Geez, I hope it's not that. Or maybe it's about . . . He didn't dare think it.

"Close the door," Culver said, seated in his office. Scott's hands were trembling. He'd started the season in AA, and he had little right to expect that this conference was about what he hoped it was about. But he *had* won his last five starts. It *was* a possibility.

"I just got the call," Culver said, sitting back in his chair and eyeing the twenty-one-year-old pitcher. "You're going up. You report Friday."

Scott could hardly breathe, but he nodded, smiled a little and said, softly, "Great. That's good."

Culver gave him some standard advice. "Just throw strikes and get ahead of the hitters. Just go up there and be Scott Service."

Scott climbed into his girl friend's car, his face long. "You remember those arm problems I was having?" he said. "Well, they're sending me away."

"Away?" She was panicked.

He laughed. "Well, yeah. Away to Philadelphia."

A few days later, Scott drove to Philadelphia with team-mate Alex Madrid, both six-five pitchers folded into Madrid's Ford Escort. Windows open and the wind whipping through, they laughed and reminisced about the minor leagues as if they would never eke through another day on a minor league per diem, never see another minor league inning.

They reported to Veterans Stadium. Scott walked out onto the surface of the tiered and carpeted giant samovar and just shook his head. Good-bye, Mosquito University. And good riddance. Hello, dreams come true.

The first Phillie Scott saw in the locker room was fellow Lucadello prospect Michael Jack Schmidt. Scott introduced himself, and Schmidt warmly shook his hand. Scott was born about the time Tony Lucadello first began scouting the skinny, free-swinging Dayton shortstop who became the best all-around third baseman in the history of the game of baseball.

Now Schmidt and Service were coworkers. Back in 1972, Schmidt had been Tony's thirty-ninth big-leaguer, followed by Larry Cox and Jim Essian in '73, Tom Underwood in '74, Dyar Miller in '75, Bill Nahorodny and Fred Andrews in '76, Barry Bonnell in '77, Todd Cruz in '78, Scott Munninghoff in '80 and Len Matuszek in '81. Now, after a seven-year interregnum came Scott Service, the fiftieth.

The Phillies and the Cubs, each several thousands of games behind the division-leading Mets, played a Labor Day doubleheader at Wrigley Field. The wind was blowing in. It happens. Not often, but it happens. Still, by the sixth inning, the Cubs led 10–3, putting together rallies with strings of singles and the extraordinary charity of the walk-prone Phillies pitchers. On the mound was Alex Madrid, who, in the fourth, had become the Phils' fourth pitcher. Madrid struggled, and in the top of the sixth, the call came to the bullpen. Get Service up.

Just be Scott Service, he thought, warming up. *Just stay ahead of those batters.* He tried not to think of anything else, not the beauty of Wrigley Field, not the biggest crowd of his life, not the national viewing audience on the Cubs' WGN superstation. *Just throw strikes.*

Ahead in the count to the first batter, Shawon Dunston, the Cubs' free-swinging shortstop, Scott got too clever, trying to aim a sinker that didn't break, and gave up a sharp single to left. *No big deal*, he thought. *Here comes the pitcher.* He tried to jam Rick Sutcliffe, actually quite a good hitter, on an inside fastball, and Sutcliffe slashed a line drive that looked like a sure single to right. But Phillies second baseman Juan Samuel speared the ball and tossed it to first, doubling up Dunston.

Settle down now. No damage at all. Just throw strikes. And he did, getting Doug Dascenzo on a routine grounder to second.

In between innings, Scott sat on the bench, second-guessing that pitch to Dunston. *Don't think about it anymore. I'm a starter. Once I settle down, I'm as tough as anyone.* He tried not to think about the fearsome trip he'd face in the seventh: Ryne Sandberg, Mark Grace and Rafael Palmeiro.

As Scott headed to the mound for his warm-up tosses, Harry Caray led the crowd in 'Take Me Out to the Ballgame.' *I'm here,* Scott thought. *I always knew I belonged right here.*

He threw Sandberg, the game's best active second baseman, a fastball for a strike, a curve that just missed and a fastball that Sandberg fouled off. Ahead 1 and 2, Scott ignored the scouting report on Sandberg—*Don't throw him breaking stuff when you're ahead*—froze him with a wicked roundhouse curve. Sandberg, who rarely strikes out and who'd obviously been looking for a fastball, walked away shaking his head.

One down.

Deep breath.

Scott got Grace out on a bouncer to first and then faced the Cubs' all-star left fielder, Rafael Palmeiro, who strikes out as infrequently as Wade Boggs—less than 6 percent of the time. But Scott was in a groove now. Fastball: strike. Nibble with the sinker: ball. Fastball: checked-swing near miss; ball. Fastball, fouled off. Count, 2 and 2. *It worked with Sandberg. What the hell.* And in came a backdoor breaking ball for a called strike three.

Having handcuffed three of the league's best hitters, Scott Service jogged to the dugout, trying to put on his best blasé game face. But the pull was too strong and he was grinning, already thinking about the phone calls he'd make after the game, the first to his dad, the second to Tony Lucadello.

No, Virginia Lucadello said when Scott called, Tony's not here. He's over in Kokomo, Indiana. She gave him the number of the motel, but Tony was out at a ball game. There was this free-agent third baseman, you see, that he was about to sign. A sleeper. Quite a story behind him. And then there were those players in his files, those seventy-seven prospects eligible for the draft in 1989, those seventy eligible in 1990. He had to see them, too. The Phillies would, for a change, have a high draft next year. His draft list was due in Philadelphia in eight months. On the back of a ten-year-old notepad, he already had sketched the list, as he saw it now. But you never know. There's always another ball game to see, and if you do your homework, if you project the kid's tools, if maybe the other scouts don't learn how much you like your top kids and if the cross-checkers like your ball players and if you don't get fired in the team's front-office shake-up—don't laugh, they might think I've had it; we'll just see, okay?—why then, you never know. You might just get that second fifty.

As it turned out, the Phillies' new regime made a series of cost-cutting moves—several, inexplicably, to their player-development system. They sent all their scouts, Tony included, a letter telling them to cut down on their meal money and their motel expenses. Tony read it again and again, wondering why they would send such a letter to him. When did he ever waste a dime of the team's money?

A few weeks later the new brass forced Tony to fire two of his part-time scouts: Pete Mihalic in the Cleveland area and Bob Kowaleski in Michigan. Mihalic, actually, was almost eighty and set to retire, but the team wouldn't allow Tony to replace him. Kowaleski, however, was fired partially because he was such a dedicated scout: he attended more games than any of Tony's part-timers and, consequently, ran up a larger tab on his expense account. Over Tony's strenuous objections, the Phillies decided to rely on the Scouting Bureau to cover Michigan.

The team had the lowest-rated farm system in baseball and still chose to penalize a scout who had found its few decent prospects, whose network of part-timers and friends had helped scoop up—cheaply, in low rounds—players like Mark Cobb and Tom Marsh and Tim Dell, players like Scott Service, an undrafted free agent signed for just five thousand dollars, who reached the majors in three years. Good plan, fellows. Enjoy your stay in the cellar.

It was September 15, 1988. Tony Lucadello, on his way to see a catcher, drove south toward Minster, Ohio, a town of about three thousand, where the catcher lived and where Tony had arranged that day's tryout. All his career, Tony has used the fifteenth to mark the end of his year. And this had been a bad year, one of the worst. Oh, sure, he signed a lot of ball players, six in the draft and three free agents. And of course he got his fiftieth big-league ball player. And yes, the word about the wall seemed to be getting out. Still, it was a bad year. His best year had come in 1972, when he'd found almost twenty-seven dollars. This year, though, the change he'd found totaled only a little over five dollars.

He spotted a church just inside the Minster city limits, the first he'd seen that day. He pulled into the parking lot without checking the church's name or denomination and grabbed the glass jar of coins. He knocked on the front door. No one answered. The door was open.

"Hello?" he called. "Is anyone home?" His words echoed off its cement floor. He set the jar just inside and pulled the door closed. On his way back to the car, he kept his head bowed.

But he didn't find any coins, not one, in the church's gravel parking lot.

He got in the car to begin his forty-seventh and last year as a major league baseball scout. He looked at the odometer.

Almost forty thousand miles this year. Coming up on two and a half million, career: the equivalent at his latitude of 128 trips around the earth. He set his narrow-brimmed hat on the seat beside him and tuned in some big-band music on the radio.

Then he drove away.

16

Epilogue:
Edison's Drugstore

Tony had talked about retirement for years, and the Phillies now seemed to encourage it. Publicly, they said he had a job for life, but the club's decision to drop two part-time scouts crushed him. Tony was loyal to those men, and without them he couldn't cover his territory as well as his own standards required. That winter, as he drove from town to town, working out his minor-league players, Tony would pull the car over and jot down ideas for a letter of resignation on the same scratch pad he used for calculating mileage. Before he could send the letter, the Phillies assured him they wanted him to stay and offered him a thousand-dollar raise.

Tony was rarely offered raises, but he didn't accept right away. Tony insisted Hugh Higdon, his part-timer in Cincinnati, get one, too. "Hugh saw three hundred ball games this year," Tony said, "and he spent almost every day working out various sleepers. He only makes fifteen hundred dollars. Can you give him a thousand-dollar raise, too?"

"Sorry," the Phils said. "We're cutting down on part-timers."

"Well," Tony said, "how about if you give Hugh half my raise?"

The Phillies agreed.

Tony kept talking about retirement, but old friends from better times convinced him to stay. As he had each of his years with the club, Tony signed his contract—this one, at twenty-seven thousand dollars, the fattest of his career—and mailed it back the very day it arrived.

Tony was sure the weather got worse every year. "Is that just old age talking," he asked me.

"No," I assured him, "it's not just old age." Time magazine had recently run a cover story on that very topic.

Tony had called to congratulate me on the birth of my son. I'd repeated my oath to build a wall, and we'd moved on to the weather. Tony was having a rough time seeing all the kids he wanted to see.

"Remember Hayward?" he said.

"Yeah. Up in Detroit. Your top kid."

"No more. He's still got the tools, but he's not hitting. I'm going to cut him down on my list if I can't see improvement. I believe it's due to the fact of bad work habits, but it might just be that the boy doesn't play well in the snow and the mud. I was up there three days before they got a game in, and that one was stopped in the second inning. It's April, for heaven's sake, and yet this big snowstorm rolls in."

Tony complained that the Phillies had changed the expense forms and installed a voice-mailbox system he didn't understand. The phone system required touch-tone phones, and since most places he stayed had rotary-dial phones, Tony was worried he'd have to change his motels. "Of course, new people come in, and they want to change everything. I've seen it before. Maybe I ought to retire. You were with me a year. Is the old man slipping?"

"Not a chance," I said, for what must have been the hundredth time. But scouting had come so naturally to Tony Lucadello that he distrusted his success. He needed to be reassured, like a gorgeous woman who's unable to believe the mirror, who needs to *hear* that she's beautiful.

That was the last time I talked to Tony.

Tony woke up at about six, at home, on a windswept and rainy Monday that didn't seem to promise a ball game for a hundred miles in any direction. Still, dressed in a shirt and tie, Tony sat in the kitchen, eating a bowl of cereal and the last bran muffin and watching the rain soak his backyard.

Although it was only May eighth, Tony decided to mail his final draft list. The 1989 draft would begin June fifth, and the Phillies needed his list a couple weeks before that. In the past Tony had express-mailed the list on the last possible day, giving himself every chance to find one more prospect.

He sat in his tiny study and filled out the form in his small and painstaking block letters. Only ten kids made the list this year: one from Indiana, two from Michigan, seven from Ohio. There just *had* to be another sleeper out there, even if there probably never would be another Mike Schmidt. Tony had done the best he could, what with the weather this year and without his full staff of part-timers. In the past, he had made carbon copies or stopped to use the copier at the library. Not this year. He slipped the three originals into an envelope and sealed it.

Tony and Virginia spent the morning watching quiz shows. Around noon the sun came out, and Tony began to talk about games he ought to see. Fostoria's St. Wendelin High School was at home, but that game had already been called. "I believe I might go over to New Reigel," Tony said. "We'll see if they can play."

"It's still chilly out," Virginia said. "You be sure and take a sweater." She had an appointment at the beauty shop. As she left, Tony asked if she could stop on the way home and pick up fruit, soup and bran muffins.

Soon after she left, Tony got in his car and drove downtown. He dropped the list in an iron street-corner mailbox and stopped at the hardware store. "I'm scouting a ball player up in a bad section of Detroit," he told the clerk behind the gun counter. Tony showed the clerk the .32-caliber revolver that he'd taken from his wife's dresser drawer. He'd bought the gun for her a few years back, thinking she'd want it to protect herself during his long absences. But the presence of a loaded gun in the house scared Virginia; she figured it was as likely to be used against her as for her, so she hid the bullets and the gun in separate places. That morning, all Tony could find was the gun. "Don't tell my wife about this," Tony said, paying for the bullets. "I don't want her to worry."

The clerk knew Tony and had, years ago, dated his daughter. While the clerk loaded the gun for Tony, they talked baseball, laughing and nostalgic, like hundreds of other men paired off in hardware stores across the Midwest.

Tony drove down Union Street, which crosses several sets of weather-buckled railroad tracks, runs past a trailer park and, at the south edge of Fostoria, dead-ends into Meadowlark Park. The town's blue water tower hovered in the distance. The park was wet, tidy and deserted. Meadowlark Park has three ball fields ringing a parking lot not much larger than the nearby tennis court. Field 2 and Field 3, the best maintained, are softball fields. Demand for field time threatens to crowd baseball off Field 1, where St. Wendelin High School plays home games on a dirt infield at the edge of a woods. Scattered between the fields are clumps of slides and swings and merry-go-rounds. In a corner of the park is an unfinished baseball wall.

Tony locked his glasses and keys inside the car. Near the third-base line of Field 1, he faced the sandlot infield, put the gun in his mouth and pulled the trigger. Tony fell to the ground and lay still, a few hundred yards of mud and weeds from the thicketed field where there'd once been a ballpark, where the Fostoria Redbirds once played D baseball. At the corner of that field stood a For Sale sign.

The St. Wendelin coach had, unbeknownst to Tony, scheduled a practice that afternoon in lieu of the rained-out game. First to Meadowlark Park was Jason Myers, the resolute pitcher with a wall in his backyard, the second prospect Tony and I had seen together, now St. Wendelin's most valuable player. He spotted Tony's car, then the body in the grass. For a thick and surreal moment he thought the scout was trying to get a suntan. Then Jason saw the scout's hat several yards away, and it clicked. *Something's wrong.* Jason ran toward the car, saw the blood but not the gun. Tony was choking and Jason turned him over. Other players now stood nearby. Jason was a hunter and fisherman, and the blood didn't freeze him as it did his teammates. He jumped in the car, tore off, got an ambulance, got Virginia Lucadello.

Virginia thought Tony must have been shot by a stray bullet, and the truth took a while to sink in.

Jason Myers went with her to the hospital. He stood beside her, quiet and strong, a hand on her shoulder.

There was no exit wound. Tony's heart had stopped, but on the helicopter ride to Toledo, he was revived. Still, there was no chance, the neurosurgeon said, that Tony'd ever be right.

Tony had first seen Virginia at Fostoria's old Civic Theater, a nineteen-year-old actress playing Mae West, dressed in a gold lamé gown, laden with real diamonds on loan from the local jeweler. Tony leaned to the second baseman in the seat next to him and said, "Pete, that's the girl I'm gonna marry."

She worked at Edison's Drugstore, next to Pop Morgan's

Pool Hall, a ball players' haunt. Each day, Tony came into Edison's and bought a three-cent stamp from the pretty girl behind the counter. He made forty bucks a month; stamps were all he could afford.

"Some girl sure is lucky," Virginia said, "getting a letter from you every day."

"I don't have a girl," Tony said. "The letters are for my sister."

A few days later, Tony stopped in the doorway on his way out. "Hey, if I make it to the big leagues, do you think you'd give me a date?"

Virginia smiled. She wasn't even a baseball fan—yet. "Aw, you don't have to wait *that* long." On their first date, they went to the city swimming pool. Swimming was taboo for ball players on game days, and the Redbirds' manager fined Tony ten dollars, a week's pay.

The following winter, Virginia took a train to Chicago to meet Tony's parents. One night, they went to the Trianon Ballroom to see the Ted Weems Orchestra, which was breaking in a kid singer named Perry Como. Tony requested a song and asked Virginia to come with him to one of the velvet-curtained balconies. Como sang "It's a Sin to Tell a Lie," their song. Tony dropped to one knee and proposed. The ring was modest, but to Virginia it looked as big as the moon.

They were married two years later and began their honeymoon at a ballpark in Norwalk, Ohio, where Tony made five dollars for playing in a semipro game. After the game, they had twenty-five dollars to their names. They felt rich, good-looking and immortal.

We had high hopes, Virginia thought, and most of them came true. Inside, she still felt like the girl in the gold lamé gown.

The neurologist disconnected the respirator, and Tony Lucadello died.

* * *

For weeks, the old black rotary-dial wall telephone rang day and night, and Virginia sat at the kitchen table, filling ashtrays and talking to the people who'd known her husband. She'd hang up, and before her fingers left the receiver, the phone would ring again.

Tony Lucadello had his hands in a lot of lives, more than anyone knew. A player Tony'd signed in the early 1960s told Virginia that after he'd been cut and drafted into Vietnam, Tony wrote him two letters every week, without fail. My father was dead, the man said, and Tony's letters were what got me through.

Virginia had to suffer calls from reporters who said they'd heard that the Phillies had fired Tony. Others said they'd heard Tony left a note. Several newspapers reported the rumors as fact. In searching Tony's car, the state police had found the notes for Tony's unsent letter of resignation; some dime-store psychologists interpreted that as a suicide note. In addition, Tony—the inveterate list-maker, the man who felt late unless he got to a ballpark two hours before batting practice—had arranged his funeral plans years ago. Included in those plans was the following list:

In Case of My Death: Funeral Arrangements + Etc.
1st Harold's Funeral Home.
2nd Private—closed coffin.
3rd Cremated as soon as possible.
4th Cheapest coffin and cost. Reason: waste of money.
5th No flowers.
6th Phone my office. *No one* is to attend. Remember me the way I was.
7th Phone my sisters + brother + relations. *Not to attend.* Reasons: it would be too hard on them and costly. Just remember me how I was.

8th   Everyone be *happy* + not sad over me. I had a good
long life. So enjoy yours. I love you all.

Love me,
Tony Lucadello

On Memorial Day, in the middle of a road trip, Mike
Schmidt retired. He was only batting .203, with a respectable
6 homers and 28 runs batted in. But he'd had slower starts at
the plate. What was eating Schmidt was how his fielding had
declined. He could have wrangled a trade to the American
League and fattened up his home run total as a designated
hitter. But he prided himself on being an all-around player,
and so that was that. No more baseball. No final carnival tour
of the league. Of all the players Tony Lucadello signed, he was
proudest of Mike Schmidt—not only for being the best third
baseman in baseball history but, more so, for living up to the
scout's standards of character. Three weeks after Tony died,
Schmidt called a press conference in San Diego, sat in front of
his locker and announced his retirement. When Schmidt
began talking about his beginnings in pro ball, about signing
and leaving Dayton, Ohio, with two bad knees and the dream
of becoming a major league ball player, he began to sob.

The Phillies didn't draft anyone off Tony's final list, even
though several players were still available long after the round
where Tony had projected them. Tony had one sleeper, a
paunchy left-handed pitcher named Scott Young who'd been
in hiding for months, throwing off walls and waiting for a
chance. The Phillies scouting director told me they had Young
projected for the thirty-sixth round, where the bonus they
wanted to pay would be only a thousand dollars. They placed
him on their "Would Not Sign" list. Tony had Young down for
fifteen thousand, though the report on him clearly indicated

that he would indeed sign; the higher bonus was just Tony's attempt to keep the Phillies from yet again overlooking one of his players in whom they didn't have much money invested.

A scout from the Atlanta Braves heard that Scott Young was Tony's sleeper. Though he'd never seen the boy play, the scout signed him as a free agent for a thousand dollars.

The day after Tony's memorial service, five weeks after he died, Matt Stone and I drove down the wet streets of Wayne, Ohio, to see if the field was playable. We passed the town's entrance sign, which touted Wayne as the home of Monica Stone, Matt's sister, 1988 state champion in the two-hundred-meter run, then past the sign painted on an abandoned building downtown: Welcome to Wayne—Population 948 Nice People and One Sorehead. His hometown, Matt told me, holds a Sorehead of the Year contest. People campaign for it, and the town votes on a winner.

Matt had been at the memorial, but I hadn't recognized him. He'd filled out and grown six inches since the fall day when I'd seen him throw baseballs off a wall in his backyard. By the time someone told me Matt was there, he'd left. He and his cousin Todd Adkins ducked out and went for some batting practice. In addition to the wall, the Stones' backyard now featured a rope batting cage. Todd had been signed by Tony and had played four years in the minors. Now he was in college nearby, and whenever he could, he worked out with Matt.

Tom Thompson Field looked like watery oatmeal. "Rain-out for sure," Matt said. "That sand drains pretty fast, but it'll be a while before we can play on this."

We sat on the wet blue aluminum bleachers. Beyond the outfield fence, workmen on the tailgate of a green pickup pointed toward the field and shook their heads.

"I know he's gone, but—" Matt shrugged. "It just seems

like he's away on a trip." Matt, a freshman, played high school ball that spring and endured his first long batting slump since before he met Tony Lucadello. "When I got in a slump, he always knew what to tell me, and once I did it, I'd be okay."

Kids at school had teased Matt ever since his father built the wall. *You think you're so big,* they'd say, *just because you have a scout watching you.* When they heard Tony died, they taunted Matt: *Too bad, now you'll never make it.*

Matt looked toward the puddle that covered his whole territory at shortstop. He drummed his fingers on the bleachers. "Tony told me that if I was good enough, he'd sign me, and I wanted him to sign me *bad.* That was my goal. Lately he knew he wasn't going to be scouting that long, so he'd tell me things to do that would impress other scouts. You know, step back some to make the throws longer and show 'em my arm. Keep my grades up. Have a firm handshake. Big things. Little things."

We drove back to Matt's house, and he showed me a bat Tony had given him only weeks before. A metal plate on the bat commemorated the Phillies' 1980 World Series victory over Kansas City—the only world championship of Tony's career.

In the backyard, patches of gray cinder block showed through the peeling paint on the Tony Lucadello wall. "The first sunny stretch we get," Matt said, nodding. "My parents and I talked about fixing it up all winter."

I told Matt I was sure Tony would have seen the battered wall the way writers view dog-eared and well-thumbed copies of their books.

Matt looked at his feet. "When it first happened, I didn't want to do anything. My first instinct was, I'm never gonna make it now, 'cause he won't be around to show me anything. Then I thought about it, and I thought, You know, Todd's around, and Tony told him everything. And Tony told me a lot. Tony taught me a *lot*. But Todd was in the minor leagues, and I figured that maybe that's something I can hang on to."

We shook hands good-bye. His fingers curled around my palm and pressed hard into the bones on the back of my hand. "Now I just want to prove to everybody that I can play pro ball." He took a deep breath. "That Tony was right about me."

Late that summer, the City of Fostoria renamed Meadowlark Park's Field 1 "Lucadello Field." The city asked Virginia what Tony would have wanted on the plaque. "Don't make a big fuss," she said. She told them how the sign should read and the city obeyed her request to the letter:

Tony Lucadello
Phillies Scout
Baseball's Friend

Appendix

Signed for the Chicago Cubs

(player, position, major league debut)

John Lucadello, 2b, 1938
Hank Edwards, of, 1941
Ed Hanyzewski, rhp, 1942
Russ Kerns, c, 1945
Bob Rush, rhp, 1948
Wayne Terwilliger, 2b, 1949
Harry Chiti, c, 1950
Bob Kelly, rhp, 1951
Fuzzy Richards, 1b, 1951
Don Elston, rhp, 1953
Duke Simpson, rhp, 1953
Jim Brosnan, rhp, 1954
Bob Speake, of, 1955
Bob Anderson, rhp, 1957
Dick Drott, rhp, 1957
Eddie Haas, of, 1957
Gordon Massa, c, 1957
Gene Fodge, rhp, 1958
Dick Johnson, of, 1958
Don Eaddy, 3b, 1959

Ed Donnelly, rhp, 1959
John Goetz, rhp, 1960
Lou Johnson, of, 1960

Signed for the Philadelphia Phillies
(player, position, major league debut)
George Williams, 2b, 1961
John Herrnstein, 1b-of, 1962
Alex Johnson, of, 1964
Grant Jackson, lhp, 1965
Fergie Jenkins, rhp, 1965
Bill Sorrell, 3b-of, 1965
Terry Harmon, 2b-ss, 1967
Clarence Jones, 1b-of, 1967
Mike Marshall, rhp, 1967
John Upham, lhp-of, 1967
Larry Hisle, of, 1968
Robert Richmond, rhp, 1968
Steve Arlin, rhp, 1969
Toby Harrah, ss, 1969
Dave Roberts, lhp, 1969
Mike Schmidt, 3b, 1972
Larry Cox, c, 1973
Jim Essian, c, 1973
Tom Underwood, lhp, 1974
Dyar Miller, rhp, 1975
Bill Nahorodny, c, 1976
Fred Andrews, 2b, 1976
Barry Bonnell, of, 1977
Todd Cruz, ss, 1978
Scott Munninghoff, rhp, 1980
Len Matuszek, 1b, 1981
Scott Service, rhp, 1988

Mark Winegardner was born and raised in Bryan, Ohio. A graduate of Miami University, he teaches fiction writing at John Carroll University in Cleveland, where he lives with his wife, Laura, and their son, Samuel. He is the author of the travel book *Elvis Presley Boulevard* and is now at work on a novel.